ASPECTS OF
BRITISH ECONOMIC HISTORY
1918–1925

ASPECTS OF
BRITISH ECONOMIC HISTORY
1918−1925

BY

A. C. PIGOU, M.A.

EMERITUS PROFESSOR OF POLITICAL ECONOMY
IN THE UNIVERSITY OF CAMBRIDGE

AUTHOR OF "THE ECONOMICS OF WELFARE", ETC.

LONDON
MACMILLAN & CO. LTD
1947

COPYRIGHT

PRINTED IN GREAT BRITAIN

PREFACE

THE period covered by this study extends from the Armistice in November 1918 to the restoration of the Gold Standard in Great Britain in April 1925. The object of the study is to set out and, so far as may be, to explain the facts of the immediate post-war period, not primarily for their own sake, but in the hope that knowledge about them may provide some guidance for current post-war policy. This object has in part dictated the comparative fullness with which different topics are treated. It is not, of course, to be supposed that the economic effects of the war of 1914–18 had exhausted themselves by 1925. On the contrary, the aftermath of that war continued up to, and beyond, the outbreak of the more recent catastrophe. But an end-point for our study must be chosen somewhere, and the plateau of relative stability that had been reached by then affords a convenient stopping place.

The work was done in 1941–2 at the request of the Government for use in the Departments concerned with the problems likely to arise when war should end, and I was, therefore, allowed access to some unpublished material in the possession of Government Departments. The Director of Statistics in the Ministry of Labour helped me greatly by unearthing and allowing me to use the very important Z8 employment returns that were compiled down to November 1920. Mr. Baster of the Reconstruction Secretariat was very patient in answering questions and obtaining information for me ; and Miss Callard, his secretary, did an immense amount of work in checking up details and correcting slips. I have also to thank the Ministry of Labour, the War Office, the Admiralty and the Bank of England for allowing me to print the statistics supplied by them and set out under the appropriate headings in Sections I and IV of the Appendix. No official, of course, has any responsibility for anything that I have written.

In Part IV, Chapter I, on the Rise and Fall of Industrial Controls, and also in a portion of Part II, Chapter II, I have made extensive use of a memorandum prepared in connection with this work by Mr. M. Dobb of Pembroke College, Cambridge ; he is really the author of the factual parts of the chapter on Controls. A portion of Chapter II of Part III on Ship-building, and the whole of Chapter IV on Cotton Exports, are based on a memorandum by Mr. W. J. Corlett ; and the account of the Iron and Steel Subsidies in Part IV, Chapter II, on one by Mr. D. Burn. On the statistical side I had valuable help from Mr. Rothbarth, Assistant to the Cambridge University Lecturer in Statistics, who was afterwards killed in action in Belgium.

This volume is not a work of scholarship. While parts of it have involved a good deal of labour and some thought, other parts are little more than précis-writing from secondary authorities. Time and the materials available did not permit of anything better. It was obviously out of the question to survey the fortunes of all the main industries of the country ; so that the discussions in Part III, Chapters II–IV are merely illustrative. The Chancellor of the Exchequer now allows what I wrote to be published. In availing myself of that permission I ask the indulgence of readers for this intrusion by an economist into the domain of Economic History. In war-time many of us had to do the best we could in jobs for which we were ill equipped.

A. C. P.

King's College,
Cambridge, *May* 1946

CONTENTS

PART I

INTRODUCTORY

PART II

EMPLOYMENT

PART III

PRODUCTION

PART IV

GOVERNMENT INTERVENTION IN INDUSTRY

PART V

THE MONETARY FACTOR

PART I

INTRODUCTORY

CHAPTER I

AN OUTLINE MAP

THE history of that post-war period is so closely intertwined with, and so much disturbed by, monetary happenings that the real situation which underlay and dominated everything else is not always clearly envisaged. The bones of this skeleton must be displayed in full light without their trappings of flesh. Only so will it be possible to understand the many and subtle ways in which these trappings reacted on the development of the skeleton itself. To that end I have set out in this preliminary chapter a brief account, not of what was, but of what, had the trappings been absent, might have been.

In the later stages of the war the people of this country were putting out an enormous military effort and, to support it, an enormous economic effort in the manufacture of weapons. The proportion of the population engaged in work of one sort or another and the intensity of their work were substantially larger than in normal times. When the war stopped, therefore, two things were sure to happen. First, the community as a whole would not wish to do so much work, military and civilian together, as they had been doing during the war ; and, secondly, they would wish to transfer the direction of a great part of the work they continued to do away from military activity and munition-making to services proper to peace-time. Thus a good number of war workers, particularly women who

1

had entered industry " for the duration ", might be expected to pass out of wage-earning employment altogether. But there was bound also to be an enormous transfer from one kind of employment to another.

As a result of the nation-wide absorption, while the war lasted, in war effort, at the close of it the plant of the railways and of many firms engaged in industry was seriously depreciated ; normal renewals and repairs had not been carried out. Among ships, over and above this, there had been heavy destruction by enemy action. Moreover, in warehouses and shops the stocks of many kinds of consumable goods had been allowed to run down ; while the distributing trades and the hotel and restaurant trades were very short of hands. Finally, among private individuals houses had fallen out of repair, and furniture, clothes, boots and so on — not to speak of carriages and, among the rich, motor cars — were in need of rejuvenation and renewal. Consequently, there were plenty of directions in which persons set free from war work might expect to find their services urgently needed. A large number of them could simply step back into jobs of the same kind, if not the same job, as they held before the war, and all would be well. The *immediate* problem of transfer, though enormous in scale, was thus not in its nature difficult. There was no reason why the transfers required should not be carried through smoothly and fairly quickly.

Replacements, repairs and renewals after such a catastrophe entail an immense amount of work. But this work is, so to speak, once-for-all work. Most of it would be finished within a year or two of the end of the war. When it had been finished, when devastations and decays had been made right and the community was again substantially as well furnished with durable goods, production goods and consumption goods together, as in pre-war days, what was to happen to the men and women who had been engaged in the work of rehabilitation ? Presumably the community would turn to increasing its regular output of immediately consumable goods and making additions on the pre-war scale to old and new forms of capital equipment. But the urgency of the need for these things would be less than that for immediate post-war replacements ; so that, just as there had been a contraction in the total amount of their work when the tension of war itself was relaxed, so there would be a second contraction on a smaller scale when the tension of replacement gave place in turn to the lesser urgencies of normal life.

Alongside of this second reduction in the aggregate volume of work and employment there would also come about a second shifting in the direction of work. There would thus arise a second transfer problem. But this time, since there would not be now, as there were the first time, obvious guiding lines to the new jobs wanting to be done in the shape of obvious deficiencies to be made good, the transfer problem, though smaller in scale, might well prove less tractable. There might be hesitancy about what private persons wanted, their demands, so to speak, hanging fire, with a consequent threat of large-scale unemployment. If this happened, in a well-managed State central and local authorities would be found standing by with carefully prepared plans for undertakings of general utility and other more complex fiscal devices, so as to offset, or, maybe, to prevent, the slackening of private demand.

When the difficult period following the completion or near-completion of the tasks of replacement and renewal had been passed through, it would be unreasonable to expect that economic life would go on just as though there had been no war. Inevitably people's relative demands for many sorts of goods and services would be substantially altered from what they were. In particular, an exporting country, such as this, would be bound to find that a number of other countries, once its customers, had, under the stress of war-time isolation, built up industries to provide for themselves some of the things that formerly they had bought from it. The world pattern into which our industry must be fitted would be different in important respects from what it used to be. Unless the need for adjustment to the new long-term conditions were realised quickly and acted on with decision, many persons, willing and anxious to work, would be left, maybe for years, clinging to occupations in which their services were not, and were not likely to be, wanted; an aftermath of prolonged industrial malaise.

If readers of the chapters that follow will bear this half-true, half-imaginary sketch plan in their minds, it may serve as a rough guide to the main features of the confused region, with its twisting paths and complex overgrowth, through which they will be called upon to travel.

CHAPTER II

DATES AND TIME DIVISIONS

FOR convenience of exposition we may divide our period into four parts, which I shall call respectively the Breathing Space, the Boom, the Slump and the Doldrums. In assigning dates for these four parts I shall rely on monetary data. Since, however, there are many such data and the various relevant indices do not all move up or down together, dates for the beginning and ending of the Breathing Space, the Boom, the Slump and the Doldrums are not given in nature; if we are to use them, it can only be through the exercise of a more or less arbitrary choice. In some circumstances, of course, the arbitrary element is less than in others, and in all circumstances, the looser the dating, the smaller is the part played by it.

The Breathing Space, of course, began at the Armistice. About the date at which it ended and the post-war Boom started there is no difficulty. During the first few months after the Armistice there was a slight decline in most British monetary indices. The volume of bank deposits showed no tendency to increase until March 1919. The three principal index numbers of wholesale prices, those of the *Statist*, *Economist* and Board of Trade, all tended downwards, the two first reaching minima in March, and the third in May. The Ministry of Labour's index of the Cost of Living and their index of retail food prices both reached their minima in May. The Metropolitan, Country and Provincial Clearings, when seasonally corrected, reached theirs in March. Dr. Bowley's index of weekly money wages was steady from January till April. Thus, for nearly half a year, there was in no sense and no degree a monetary

5

boom; rather the contrary. In the spring, however, there came a change. Both the *Economist* and the *Statist* index numbers of wholesale prices began to move upwards in April, the Board of Trade number in June, Cost of Living and retail food in June, money wage rates in May, Metropolitan, Country and Provincial Clearings in April, deposits of the London clearing banks in March. Thus we may say, without ambiguity, that the Breathing Space ended and the post-war monetary Boom started in the spring of 1919; if we are pressed to name a particular date, the best answer is 30th April. May was the month, as it so happened, in which the number of persons in receipt of out-of-work donation, which had so far been increasing, first showed a marked decline.

For the ending of the monetary Boom the witness of our several indices is less concordant. Thus the *Statist* and *Economist* index numbers turned down respectively in May and April 1920, and the Board of Trade number in June.[1] Cost of Living and retail food turned in November. Bowley's index number of money wage rates continued to rise until January 1921. Deposits of the London clearing banks showed no clear-cut turn till December 1920. But non-financial clearings turned down definitely in April 1920. There is thus a wide scatter among relevant data. Recognising the tendency of Cost of Living, retail food and money wage rates to be laggard and sluggish, in the exercise of my right of arbitrary decision, I decree that the Boom broke during the summer of 1920. As between the months of May, June and July, there is no obvious ground for choice. I shall, however, in so far as precise dating is needed, name

---

[1] " When the Board of Trade number is used, twice as much importance is given to food as to raw materials; with the others the proportions are nearly reversed " (Bowley, *Prices and Wages*, p. 15). The delayed fall in this index number is probably accounted for by the fact that minerals continued to rise for some months after other things had begun to fall; their final turn-down did not occur till November.

30th April. This has the convenient consequence of enabling us to reckon the period of Boom at exactly a year.

Between the breaking of the Boom and the beginning of the Slump there was only a short interval. Very soon after the rise was stopped a downward movement set in. The Slump began in the summer of 1920. To give a date for its ending, to say even in which quarter it ended, is more difficult. For in truth it did not so much end as peter out. Non-financial clearings had become fairly stabilised by the middle of 1921, but prices continued to fall till the end of 1922, and money wage rates did the same in a much more marked degree, and for even longer. I decree that the post-war Slump dragged on till the beginning of 1923, thus lasting for over two and a half years.

The ending of the Slump was the beginning of the Doldrums. In these we might well say the country remained more or less — not, of course, completely — becalmed until the Wall Street crash of 1929 heralded a second and greater Slump. But the pre-1925 Doldrums alone concern us here.

CHAPTER III

THE ARRANGEMENT OF THIS VOLUME

In the discussion that follows, considerable use will be made of the time divisions sketched out in the last chapter. But it would not be convenient simply to hang our material on a straight chronological line. The arrangement I shall adopt is as follows. After a brief introductory Part I, Part II will be devoted to Employment, Part III to Production, Part IV to Government Intervention in Industry and Part V to the Monetary Factor. This will be followed by a Concluding Chapter entitled " The Upshot for Real Income and Real Wages ". A Statistical Appendix brings together in four sections a number of important tables, supplementary to those embodied in the text and relating respectively to Employment and Unemployment, Production, Prices and Money Wages, and Currency, Bank Deposits and Clearings.

PART II

EMPLOYMENT

POST-ARMISTICE CONTRACTION IN EMPLOYMENT

As was indicated in the outline sketch of Part I, Chapter I, the substitution of peace for war meant, and was bound to mean, a substantial contraction in aggregate activity. There had, of course, to be a large expansion in civilian peace work, but this was much less than the reduction in military activity and civilian war work. The call to effort being less keen, the response was naturally smaller, just as it had been smaller in pre-war days. The purpose of this chapter is to discover how large the net contraction was. To that end I shall compare the situation immediately before the Armistice with that which obtained in the spring or early summer of 1920, the peak of the post-war Boom. Material is available for a comparison with either the end of April or the end of July 1920. As a study of the tables in the Appendix suggests, it makes no material difference which of these dates is used. Therefore, since April fits in best with other parts of this enquiry, I shall work with that month. In our most important sources of information, data are only available for persons in the employee category, *i.e.* salary- and wage-earners, or, if we prefer it, persons other than employers and men and women working on their own account ; and we must, therefore, confine ourselves to these.

It is necessary at the outset to make precise the meaning to be assigned to the term employment. First, employment means for us *gainful* employment ; so that the work done by women gratuitously in their own homes, for example, does not count as employment. This is in accordance with common usage, though, as will be indicated presently, we must be careful not to be led by it into wrong inferences. Secondly, in the British Censuses a person is scheduled as gainfully *occupied* in the job to which he is normally attached, even though he is not at the time actually at work in it. For the Armed Forces I propose to count as *employed* all who are thus gainfully occupied, even though at the time they are in hospital or prisoners of war in enemy hands. But among civilians our definition must be different. In the Z8 reports, of which an account will be given immediately, persons engaged in a strike or lock-out are included among the employed, but persons out-of-work as an indirect consequence of such disputes, *e.g.* through the industries in which they are engaged being unable to obtain materials, are not included. In the questionnaires issued to employers, upon which the Z8 reports are based, no specific instructions were given as to the way in which persons laid off on account of sickness were to be treated ; but in a note prepared for me in the Statistics branch of the Ministry of Labour the opinion is expressed that " workpeople temporarily absent owing to sickness would in most cases be included in the numbers returned". Owing to the large-scale influenza epidemic prevalent at the time of the Armistice, this point is obviously important. Thus, broadly speaking, the terms employed and unemployed in civil occupations are understood here in the same sense as in the British Unemployment Insurance Acts ; the employed comprise all gainfully occupied persons in the employee category minus the unemployed.

From the beginning of the war until November 1920 the Board of Trade — and in the later stages the Ministry of Labour — carried out periodical enquiries embodied in what are known as the Z8 reports into the state of employment in the main body of occupations other than the Armed Forces in the United Kingdom.[1] Forms were issued to selected employers asking in most cases for the number of males and females " in your employ " or " employed in the above establishment " at a particular date or in a particular pay-week. In the occupations covered by the enquiry the proportion of employers from whom returns were obtained were different in different occupations and at different dates. In the report for April 1919 it is stated (p. 2) : " For Government Establishments, the Civil Service and Coalmining, the returns are practically exhaustive ; for Local Government they cover 38 per cent, and for industries other than Coalmining 33 per cent of the workpeople employed ; while the percentage of workpeople covered falls to about 10 per cent for commerce and about 5 per cent for agriculture in Great Britain. The resulting figures, accordingly, are uncertain in different degrees." Thus, except for Government establishments, the Civil Service and coal mines, the Z8 figure for that date — and there is no reason to suppose that the data for other periods were better — depends on samples, in some cases very small samples. It follows that they are liable to very substantial error and should not at best be regarded as more than rough approximations. Moreover, after January 1920 agriculture in Great Britain was withdrawn from the Z8 enquiries ; and the figures given in the April return are stated to be " very rough estimates included for the sake of completeness only ". They appear to be obtained by adding to the January figures numbers approximately equal to those by which the figures for April 1919 exceeded those for January 1919.

---

[1] These reports have not hitherto been published nor have the returns of figures contained in them, except in respect of July 1914, November 1918 and July 1920. For these months the figures were printed in *British Labour, 1914–21*, by a committee of the British Association, edited by Professor Kirkaldy.

Unfortunately there is a considerable range of occupations which the Z8 returns do not cover. In the report for July 1918 these, together with an estimate of the total number of *males* occupied in them in 1914, are listed as follows :

Agriculture in Ireland	850,000
Mercantile Marine	125,000
Clergy, literary and other professions	270,000
Sundry minor commercial occupations	240,000
Costermongers, hawkers and sundry dealers	130,000
Domestic service (outdoor and indoor)	315,000
Gardeners (except market-gardeners, covered under "Agriculture" in Great Britain), seedsmen and florists	160,000
Other occupations	60,000
	2,150,000

These numbers evidently include employers and persons working on their own account as well as men belonging to the employee category. For females no corresponding table is provided. But female domestic servants are not covered by the returns, and these amounted, according to the 1921 Census for England and Wales, to 1,005,000. As will appear presently, women employed in very small dress-making establishments were also excluded. The number of these is not known. To judge from the list of excluded male occupations, it does not seem likely that any substantial number of women in civil work other than the above failed to be counted in the returns.

For the Armed Forces the totals of men demobilised at various dates after the Armistice from the Army, Royal Naval Division and Royal Air Force are available in statistics provided by the War Office. We have also information about the numbers who, though not technically demobilised till after the Armistice, had been passed to the Reserve and in effect returned to civil life before it.

The Admiralty have supplied figures for the Royal Navy. Information is also available about the number of women demobilised from the Armed Forces during the eighteen months following the Armistice. Unfortunately in all cases, though a distinction is drawn between officers and other ranks, we have no direct means of knowing what proportion of the men and women belonged to the employee category. However, as will be shown presently, it is possible to make a rough estimate of these numbers; which, of course, are what we need to combine with our data about civil employment.

With these preliminaries, we have to attempt a comparison between the numbers of males and females in the employee category that were employed in the sense explained above in the whole body of civilian work plus the Armed Forces in the United Kingdom at the Armistice and at the end of April 1920 respectively. For readers who do not care to follow the analysis in detail, a summary of results is provided at the end of the chapter.

MALES

Let us begin with males. The Z8 returns give 8,163,000 males in the employee category employed at the Armistice, and 10,736,000 at the end of April 1920 — an increase of 2,573,000. This needs no comment.

For the Armed Forces calculation is harder. According to the War Office, 4,029,000 officers and men of the Army, Royal Naval Division and Royal Air Force were demobilised between the Armistice and 30th April 1920. Of these 143,000 in reserve classes had already been released and returned to civil life before the Armistice. Therefore for our purposes they ought not to be counted; and the gross effective demobilisation is reduced to 3,885,000. Meanwhile recruits and re-enlistments of ex-soldiers amounted

to 178,000 ; which brings the net figure down to 3,707,000.
The Admiralty state that the net outflow from the Royal
Navy, exclusive of the Royal Naval Division, from November 1918 to April 1920 amounted to 267,000. The final
figure for *all* the Armed Forces is thus 3,974,000.

We have now to try to estimate how many out of this
total consisted of males belonging to the employee category.
There are two ways in which this question can be approached. First, the Z8 report for July 1918 estimates
that, of male employers and persons working on their own
account, some 250,000 enlisted. The Director of Statistics
of the Ministry of Labour judges this to refer to persons
previously engaged in the Z8 occupations. The corresponding number for the non-Z8 occupations I shall suggest in a
moment probably amounted to, say, 100,000. This gives
a total of round about 350,000. The same Z8 report
estimates that there were roughly 200,000 unoccupied
males (presumably, from the context, men of military age)
in the United Kingdom in 1914 ; and that there were " a
considerable number " of men who returned from abroad
to enlist. Obviously none of the unoccupied can have
belonged to the employee category. Let us put the total
enlisted from these two groups outside that category at
200,000. Thus we get a total enlistment of non-employees
of some 550,000. Allowing for killed, re-enlistments and
so on, we may estimate (or guess) the number who were
demobilised after the Armistice at, say, 450,000. The
alternative line of approach is simpler. At the time of the
1921 Census 11 per cent of the males in Great Britain
between 18 and 44 (*i.e.* roughly of military age) were unoccupied or employers or persons working on their own
account, *i.e.* were outside the employee category. Applying
this proportion to our final figure of 3,974,000, we obtain
437,000. This is practically identical with the 450,000
arrived at — the calculations were done independently —

by the other route : a very satisfactory result. We thus get, for the total number of males in the employee category effectively demobilised from all the Armed Forces between the Armistice and the end of April 1920, approximately $3\frac{1}{2}$ millions.

We have still to take account of post-war employment in the non-Z8 occupations. The list of these occupations and the numbers attached to them in 1914, that were given in the Z8 report for July 1918, have already been cited. That report states that, for various reasons, the proportion of enlistments from this group were substantially less than for the population as a whole, and puts them at 450,000. Taking account of the character of the group, we may expect the share of the enlistments drawn from employers and persons working on their own account to have been substantially larger than for most occupations, say 20 per cent, which gives roughly 100,000. This leaves enlistments from the employee category at some 350,000. Allowing for casualties and so on, we may thus estimate, though with a wide margin of error, the number of employee members of the Armed Forces, who passed from demobilisation into this group, at 300,000. There were also probably some persons who passed into it out of munition work, Government service and other Z8 occupations. I suggest, for what it is worth, an aggregate estimate of 350,000.

Thus, for employment of males in the employee category in all civil occupations and also in the Armed Forces, the changes between the Armistice and the end of April 1920 work out as follows :

Increase in the Z8 occupations	2,573,000
„ „ non-Z8 occupations	350,000
	2,923,000
Decrease in the Armed Forces	3,500,000
Net decrease, say	600,000

It is possible to attempt a check-up on this last figure from another angle. In the Z8 report for July 1918 it is estimated that during the war the Z8 occupations were increased by some 200,000 men returned from or postponing retirement. Some such number we may reckon as probably withdrawn from industry after the Armistice. The same report estimates that some 90,000 boys came into these occupations at an abnormally early age. Here again we may reckon with a post-war reduction in numbers. But this reduction should be put at more than 90,000. For in the Z8 report of July 1919 we read : " The provision of the Education Act (1918) keeping children at school till the end of the quarter (or in some districts half-year) after they are 14, instead of permitting them to leave on their birthday, has been enforced since February 1st, 1919. Moreover, during the war the numbers leaving before they were 14 after passing a requisite standard rose considerably, and it has since fallen very much " (p. 14). The Z8 report for April 1920 estimates that 132,000 fewer boys were then employed in the Z8 occupations than at the Armistice. Taking into account the non-Z8 occupations, we may reckon with a rough figure of 150,000. Moreover, there must have been a fair number of demobilised men who were incapacitated by wounds or sickness from subsequent employment. According to information provided by the War Office, " between November 11th, 1918, and May 31st, 1920, 335,000 men were discharged from the hospitals as disabled by War Service ". These men presumably were included in the demobilisation figures. No information is available as to the severity of their injuries or illness ; but we may perhaps reasonably guess that, say, 100,000 in the employee category were in this way withdrawn from employment. We thus get 450,000 withdrawals altogether. Against them must be set new entrants due to the normal growth of population. Now, between the Census years

1911 and 1921 the total *female* population of Great Britain over 10 years old — which was not significantly affected by war casualties — increased by 1,694,000 (from 16,789,000 to 18,483,000) ; which would give some quarter of a million in eighteen months. Of the population over 10 years old at the 1921 Census, 82·8 per cent of the males were returned as gainfully occupied. This percentage refers to *all* gainful occupations, not merely to occupations in the employee category. But that is not likely to make much difference. We may infer, for the eighteen months, a normal addition to gainfully occupied males in the employee category of some 200,000. Deducting this from our 450,000, we are left with a net natural decrease, so to speak, in gainfully occupied males in the employee category of some 250,000.

To get the corresponding decrease in *employment* we have to add the excess of unemployment at the end of April 1920 over what it was at the time of the Armistice. Now, in November 1918 the percentage of unemployed returned by the Trade Unions — this did not, of course, include salary-earners — was 0·5 per cent ; and that for males in the insured industries, 0·4 per cent. Since the total of males then employed in the Z8 occupations was 8,163,000, the unemployed in these occupations cannot have amounted to more than, say, 40,000 wage-earners, or 50,000 altogether, of males in the employee category. At the end of April 1920 there were 217,000 ex-Service men in receipt of out-of-work donation ; civil workers were no longer eligible. The Trade Union percentage of unemployment was 0·9 per cent and the insured-industries percentage for males was 2·6 per cent. Since the former figure suggests a total male unemployment less than the recorded number of unemployed ex-Service men, the latter is clearly to be preferred. On the basis of a Z8 return of 10,736,000 employed males in the Z8 occupations it may be conjectured that the total number of males unemployed was not far off 300,000 ;

which entails an excess over the figure for November 1918 of about a quarter of a million.

We thus get by this route, when the various items discussed above are combined, an aggregate contraction in employment among males in the employee category of round about half a million. This agrees reasonably well with the 600,000 reached by the other and less speculative method. I shall accept 600,000. Obviously, however, in view of the nature of the data and the large element of conjecture present in some of our estimates, this figure might easily be wrong either way by 100,000 or perhaps even 200,000.

FEMALES

Turn now to females. Between the Armistice and the end of April 1920 the Z8 returns show a decrease in numbers employed of 800,000. During the same period there were demobilised from the Armed Forces some 100,000 women.[1] These, no doubt, included some women not belonging to the employee category, but the number cannot have been very large. What of employment for persons in this category in the non-Z8 occupations ? In the Z8 report for July 1918 it is estimated that during the war some 400,000 women were drawn into the Z8 occupations from domestic service and very small workshops and workrooms in the dress-making trade. No estimate is made of the respective contributions of these two sources, but obviously that from domestic service must have been greatly predominant ; for in England and Wales at the 1921 Census the number of women in *all* dress-making and blouse-making establishments was only 146,000 as against over a million in domestic service. As we have already seen, other non-Z8 occupations are not likely to have played any important part. *Prima facie*, then, we might be inclined to reckon that

---

[1] Cmd. 565, 1920, p. 8, gives 96,700 by February 1920.

between the Armistice and the end of April 1920 something like 400,000 women would have been passed back into the non-Z8 occupations. There is, however, a consideration to be set against this. At the Census of 1911 the number of women returned for Great Britain as engaged in domestic service was 1,392,000 ; in 1921 it was 1,117,000, showing a decrease of 275,000. There is some doubt about the comparability of these figures. For England and Wales the corresponding figures, which Dr. Bowley accepts as comparable, were 1,261,000 and 1,005,000, showing a decrease of 256,000.[1] This fact suggests that many fewer women returned to domestic service during our period than left it during the war. It does not seem, therefore, that we should reckon on a post-war expansion in the number of women in the employee category in the non-Z8 occupations of more than, say, from 250,000 to 300,000. This will give a rough net figure for the aggregate contraction in all employments, including the Armed Forces, of some 600,000. That figure represents voluntary withdrawals plus excess unemployment, the latter item being, there is reason to believe, probably very small.

It is worth while, in passing, to review these voluntary withdrawals in the light of what happened in the course of the war itself. The influx of women into gainful employment between July 1914 and November 1918 amounted to 1,663,000 into the Z8 occupations, minus some 400,000 withdrawn from domestic service and small dress-making establishments, plus something less than 100,000 enrolled in the Armed Forces, say 1,350,000 ; of which not more than 150,000 at most could be accounted for by the normal growth of population. Voluntary withdrawal on a large scale was, therefore, to be expected, more especially because the war-time influx of women workers — which was most

---

[1] Compare Bowley, Special Memorandum 17A, London and Cambridge Economic Service, p. 10.

marked in the munition-making industries — was in the
main designedly temporary to meet a temporary demand.
An abnormally large proportion of it consisted of married
women. This is clear from the fact that, whereas, according
to the Census of 1911, only 15 per cent of those gainfully
occupied were married, in many munition works a general
proportion of from 40 to 60 per cent were married.[1] Such
women would for the most part have no wish to remain in
wage-earning employment after their husbands and sons
had returned from the war, and might be expected voluntarily to withdraw. Moreover, a number of girls had gone
into industry during the war at an abnormally early age ;
and we might expect at least an equivalent fall afterwards.
In fact the Z8 report for April 1920 estimates that the
number of girls under 18 employed in the Z8 occupations
was 74,000 less at that date than at the Armistice. In view
of these considerations it is *prima facie* surprising that the
voluntary withdrawal only amounted to about half of the
new entrants, other than those attributable to the growth
of population, into all occupations during the war period —
say half a million against a million. It would seem that
their experience of gainful occupations in war-time had
created a new attitude favourable to such occupations in a
large number of women. This is an interesting fact. The
new attitude, however, did not survive the 1920–21 Slump.
For, according to the Census (for Great Britain) taken in
April 1921, the proportion of females over 10 years old returned as gainfully occupied was slightly less than it was
in 1911 — 30·8 per cent as against 32·3 per cent.[2]

[1] Kirkaldy, *British Labour, 1914–21*, p. 30.
[2] Cf. London and Cambridge Memorandum 17A, by Dr. Bowley, p. 4. The
above fact is *prima facie* surprising, for we should expect *a priori* that, as a result
of male deaths in the war, the proportion of women who were single or widowed,
and, therefore, specially likely to seek gainful employment, would have been larger
in 1921 than in 1911. In fact, however, the number of these women per thousand
of those over 15 fell from 494 to 480 between these years. (Cf. Carr-Saunders and
Caradog Jones, *Social Structure of England and Wales*, First Edition, p. 10.)

SUMMARY

In sum, then, we find that between the Armistice and the end of April 1920 the number of males in the employee category who were employed in civil work and the Armed Forces together decreased by 600,000. The corresponding figure for females works out also at 600,000, making a grand total of some 1,200,000 persons. As already indicated, these figures are extremely rough approximations, subject, especially as regards males, to large error. Of the broad fact, however, that employment, as here defined, contracted very substantially between the Armistice and the end of the Boom period they leave no doubt. It must be remembered always that a considerable part of the drop in women's employment was undoubtedly offset by the return of women from gainful recorded employment to unpaid unrecorded employment as domestic servants to themselves and their families in their own homes ; a consideration against which is to be set the fact that a good number of the servant-keeping class, who in part fended for themselves during the war, returned after it to their pre-war habits. It should be added that during the eighteen months to which this discussion relates hours of work were reduced on the average by about 10 per cent.

CHAPTER II

THE TRANSFER OF WORK-PEOPLE FROM
WAR TO PEACE EMPLOYMENT

WHEN it became evident in the autumn of 1918 that peace must come soon, anxiety was naturally focussed on the problem of transfer, particularly of the transfer of wage-earners. Vast armies would have to be rapidly demobilised and work in war factories, which had been engaging several millions of men and women, would come abruptly to an end. Would alternative work be available for them ? Could their transfer to such work be accomplished without great masses of would-be employees being thrown for a long period into involuntary idleness, with resultant dangerous reactions upon our whole social and political life ? This question could not be answered beforehand with any assurance. It was the clear duty of the Government to watch over and, so far as might be, protect the process.

In the earlier stages of the Breathing Space there was considerable anxiety about the chances of a revival of private demand adequate to fill quickly the gap left by the cessation of Government orders — an anxiety which the figures to be given in Chapter III show to have been not without warrant. Thus in December Mr. Churchill stated : " We are making special efforts to obtain orders from Government Departments, from the Colonies and the Dominions and from public bodies, with a view to placing them to the greatest advantage . . . to develop alternative industrial production as a stop-gap pending the transition from war to peace industry ". Sir Auckland Geddes later referred to " public works, which in their execution will

give a wide range of employment and will spread employment through a large number of trades ". The Report
of the War Cabinet for 1918 spoke of authority having
been obtained to enable the Minister of Munitions to
place interim orders for certain standard products, and of
arrangements made with the Railway Executive and the
Board of Trade to place large orders, if necessary, for locomotives and waggons, " such orders to be placed with special
regard to the smoothing of the transition from war to
peace industry ". In December a recommendation of the
Machinery of Government Committee to institute a Ministry
of Supplies had been provisionally adopted ; and Mr.
Churchill's successor was actually appointed under the
title of Minister of Munitions and Supplies. Already during
the war the Ministry of Munitions had made enquiries from
other Departments and from local authorities as to their
requirements for steel for immediate post-war contracts
for work delayed on account of the war. But the response
had been meagre, and the result of a census of available
orders two days after the Armistice was not encouraging.
It was suggested that, in order to overcome the reluctance
to place orders at a high-cost level, the Government might
agree to bear the difference in cost of placing an order now
and a year later, or else relax the embargo on borrowing
by local authorities and adopt a more lenient attitude to
capital issues by commercial firms. The Ministry was
apparently prepared at the time to give advance-orders to
producers, even at the risk of being left with material on
its hands for disposal ; and the Treasury even gave consent
to this course of action, provided that offers of financial
assistance were not made before the orders were placed. But
in its operation this policy appears to have been cautious
and faint-hearted. A few small orders were placed among
steel-works and copper-smelters ; but Lord Inverforth, who
succeeded Mr. Churchill, was apparently hostile to the

placing of any advance-orders in anticipation of demands from other Departments and local authorities, chiefly on the ground that this " would leave the Government without an answer to the trade deputations who were pressing for the retention of national factories by the Government ". When several firms, that had previously been engaged on armaments, approached the Ministry with a request for orders for railway engines in view of a probable large demand for engines in the near future, it was decided not to place any such orders except against the stipulated requirements of the Railway Executive. Never very largely or boldly conceived, this policy seems to have been quickly submerged in the campaign to liberate private enterprise from control and from the rivalry of State enterprise.

The position at this stage, though fundamentally similar, was different in detail for persons engaged in civilian war work and for members of the Forces. For the former the return of peace had an indirect impact through the cessation of Government orders for the goods they had been making ; for the latter a direct impact through the act of demobilisation. The indirect impact turned out to be the more abrupt. On 24th October 1918 contractors were informed of a decision by the Ministry of Munitions that " contracts for such stores as will serve no useful purpose in peace should be terminated abruptly . . . instead of continuing deliveries for the period stated in the present form of Break Clause " ; and that claims for compensation for cancellation of the notice-period would be open to consideration at a later date. The policy of the Treasury was laid down in a communication to the Ministry a week after the Armistice, as follows : " Even if termination involves the sacrifice of expenditure already incurred, it may well be more in the public interest, on general economic as well as on financial grounds, to avoid further expenditure of money and the use of labour and materials, which will ultimately be urgently needed elsewhere, than to complete munitions of war that are no longer required ". In accordance with this policy, notice to terminate explosives contracts was given immediately after the Armistice ; and chemical contracts were liquidated within a few weeks. Machine-tool orders were cancelled immediately where the machines were of a special-purpose type ; but, where they were of a general-purpose type having a post-war market, some postponement was allowed, and deliveries were later passed to the Disposal Board for sale. At the Armistice the Ministry of Munitions had over twenty thousand outstanding contracts other than for aircraft, explosives and chemicals. By 21st January notice to terminate had been given in four-fifths of these ; so that work on munitions contracts had virtually ended by the early spring of 1919. The liquidation of aircraft contracts was longer delayed, owing to the unusual length of the notice-period that was necessary for them. But by the end of January arrangements had been made also for the tapering off of work on most of these. On the whole, the date at which the representative person engaged on war work lost his or her indirect Government employment was earlier than that on which the representative man in the Forces lost his direct Government employment.

Again, whereas every man demobilised from the Forces had to find a new job and a new employer, a number of persons in industry, who ceased to work indirectly for the Government, might hope to continue at very nearly the same job and with the same employer. Thus mechanical transport equipment had civilian uses, especially spare and semi-manufactured parts. Labour in the optical and glassware industry was easily adaptable to civil work. Certain of the constituents of explosives, like toluol and benzine, could be sold to private consumers. Small engineering firms could sometimes switch their plant quickly from

C

cartridge-cases and fuses to gramophones, from aero-engine sparking-plugs to commercial plugs, from aircraft components to motor parts. It was generally true that, as one travelled back from final to primary product, the possibility of adaptation increased, although the rate at which it did so varied greatly in different industries. Given the requisite demand, iron and steel could be switched over almost without any interval from war orders to the service of peace-time needs. In sum, of the total number of controlled establishments within the jurisdiction of the Ministry of Munitions, it was estimated that about half had been engaged in war-time on work the same as, or fairly similar to, their normal peace-time work. Plainly the difficulties of transition were likely to be less for persons employed by these firms than for demobilised soldiers.

As against this was the fact that demobilisation of civilian war workers could not easily be regulated with regard to the opportunities awaiting them elsewhere; whereas in demobilising the Forces the Government could, and did, in some measure, take account of these. Thus, by an order of the 16th December, 1918, it tried to secure priority of release for slip men, *i.e.* men with definite offers of employment, for men in certain trades and for men on leave producing written offers of employment.[1] Difficulties arose and, in order to prevent jealousy and ill-feeling, it was found necessary on the 7th January to stop preferential treatment of men on leave. On that date demobilisation was opened for all men in receipt of offers of immediate work. To release at an early stage key workers, whose presence in industry was necessary before others could be taken on, and men with definite offers of work, was a sensible way of helping ex-Service men to be absorbed into civil life. This purpose had, however, to be subordinated in some degree to conceptions of fairness between men of

---

[1] Dearle, *An Economic Chronicle of the Great War*, p. 235.

long and short service, between older and younger men and between married and unmarried men.

Besides differential demobilisation there were two other ways in which the Government tried to look after demobilised members of the Forces, but not demobilised war workers. Service men on demobilisation were granted twenty-eight days' furlough — they appeared in the statistics as demobilised men at the beginning, not at the end, of this furlough — with full pay together with a war gratuity. Privates of less than one year's standing received the lowest gratuity, namely £5. Further, the Government tried to help men whose training had been interrupted by the war, or who had suffered disabling injuries, to recover, so far as might be, what they had lost. Thus, in the middle of December, schemes for higher education and training were announced and students were given grants for University education. In the following February a scheme of State assistance to enable men to complete apprenticeships which had been interrupted by war service was announced. An Industrial Training Department of the Ministry of Labour was formally constituted to organise training for demobilised ex-Service men and civilian war workers, and to control, in place of the Ministry of Pensions, training, other than curative, of disabled men. In principle this arrangement also was obviously sensible, and something of the same kind would need to be done in any similar emergency.

These differences of treatment between civilian war workers and members of the Forces deserve attention. In the broad picture, however, they are secondary incidents. The dominant fact was that, as a result of the return of peace, an enormous number of persons were liable to be thrown suddenly on the labour market and so might have found themselves at a grave disadvantage in wage bargaining, and faced with serious difficulty in finding new employment. To obviate these things and the social unrest, which, if they came about, would inevitably follow, the Government adopted two lines of policy.

First, on 21st November it passed through Parliament the Wages (Temporary Regulation) Act. The main purpose of this Act was " to secure the maintenance, for a period of six months, of the minimum wages generally applicable at the date of the signing of the Armistice in each trade or branch of a trade or district to each class of workmen, except in so far as these minimum wages are varied by arbitration or by agreement ".[1] In the conditions immediately following the Armistice some such Act was undoubtedly a wise precaution. Nor does the fact that a few months later the tendency of wages was upwards prove that it was superfluous ; for immediately after the outbreak of peace untoward happenings might easily have taken place. In September 1920, after two renewals, the Act was allowed to expire.

Secondly, provision was made for out-of-work donation to be paid by the State both for ex-Service men and also for unemployed civil workers. In the *Labour Gazette*'s summary of the scheme the civilians envisaged are spoken of as " civil war workers ", by which apparently is meant persons employed by " factories and firms engaged on work for the Ministry of Munitions ".[2] But, in his evidence to the committee of enquiry into the working of the scheme, the representative of the Ministry of Labour said : " Owing to the concentration of all the nation's resources on the prosecution of the war almost every industry, in Great Britain at any rate, was dependent, to a greater or less degree, on the war effort, and would suffer dislocation when the effort ceased. It was, therefore, decided that the only way of meeting the situation was by making a free grant

---

[1] *Labour Gazette*, November 1918, p. 485.
[2] *Ibid.* December 1918, pp. 437-8.

of out-of-work donation for a limited period to unemployed civilian workers, as well as to demobilised men." [1] The test of eligibility for a donation was that the applicants should have been employed contributors under the Health Insurance scheme before 25th August 1918, or should give proof of employment before that date if between the ages of 15 and 18 or over 70. [2] It thus appears that, broadly speaking, all civil workers were counted as war workers and were eligible for out-of-work donation. For ex-Service men this donation was, in the first instance, made available for twelve months after each man's demobilisation, for civilians for six months from a date to be appointed. Ex-Service men were to be eligible for 26 weekly payments, civilians for thirteen. At a later date eligibility was extended for both classes. The rates of payment, originally 24s. a week for men and 20s. for women, plus children's allowances, were also modified. The scheme was intended as an interim measure pending the elaboration of a system of universal contributory unemployment insurance. In the circumstances some such scheme was essential if great distress and dangerous repercussions were to be avoided. Since, however, at the present time a general system of unemployment insurance exists, the situation against which it was intended to guard cannot arise again. Therefore, since the purpose of this volume is to study past history, not for its own sake, but chiefly for the guidance it may afford for action, the 1918 scheme need not be described in detail here. A clear account of it is given in the *Labour Gazette* for November 1918.

On the ground thus prepared and softened by State planning the task of ejecting as painlessly, but also as rapidly, as possible a great army of persons from the occupations in which they were engaged, and transferring them to others, had to be undertaken — and undertaken,

---

[1] Cmd. 407, 1919, p. 1.   [2] *Ibid.* p. 2.

not by any supervising autocrat, but, so to speak, by the invisible, or if we will, the blind hand of our interlocked economic system. As we have seen, a large number of the civilian workers displaced did not need to leave their trade or their factory, or even their job — a job, say, in metal-working or engineering that could be used in war work but was not specialised to it, and could equally well contribute towards making civilian goods. None the less, the number in the Armed Forces and in civil war work that had to be definitely transferred was very large. What happened to these men ? How far in fact were they thrown during a prolonged period of transition into involuntary idleness ?

Down to 1911 the only statistics of wide range available for measuring such idleness were the percentages of members unemployed returned at the end of each month by certain Trade Unions.[1] In spite of the fact that the membership of the Unions concerned was not large — until 1900 it was under half a million, and even in 1920, its maximum year, it only slightly exceeded a million and a half — there is reason to believe that these percentages, particularly when corrected to allow for the over-representation of engineers and ship-builders in the Unions making returns, provided a reasonably good index of the proportion of unemployment prevailing from time to time throughout industry as a whole. In a discussion before the Royal Statistical Society in 1923 Mr. Ramsbottom of the Ministry of Labour, after mentioning the chief considerations which might suggest that the statistics were unrepresentative, said that, in his own view, " before the war, in times of good trade the Trade Union percentage — crude percentage, as originally published,— approximated very closely to the actual level of unemployment among the wage-earning population ", but that, in times of bad trade, on account

---

[1] During the war the percentages were based on the number of men on a Union's books minus the number of men serving with the Forces.

of the undue weight given in it to the highly variable
engineering and ship-building trades, " it over-rated the
amount of unemployment ". [1] Under the Unemployment
Insurance Act of 1911 and the further Act of 1916 additional
statistics were collected ; but these, owing to the complicat-
ing effect of out-of-work donation, are not available between
the Armistice and November 1919. Hence for that period
they cannot be used to supplement the Trade Union figures.
Those figures were, November 1918, 0·5 per cent, April
1919, 2·7 per cent, May 1919, 2·1 per cent ; so that employment in April–May 1919 was about 2 per cent higher than
in November 1918. At this time the total number of
wage-earners seeking work can hardly have exceeded 16
millions. Hence, according to these figures, the number
of persons involuntarily out of work in April–May 1919
was not much over 300,000 ! In view of all the circumstances this figure is fantastically small and cannot possibly
be correct. The explanation *may be* that men in receipt of
out-of-work donation who had been serving in the Forces
did not, for the most part, as yet report themselves to their
Unions as out-of-work. The fact that the Trade Union
figures refer to skilled men is also relevant. But, whatever
the explanation may be, it is quite certain that these
percentages are worthless for a study of this period, and
ought not to be cited.

There are, however, available statistics published in
connection with the post-Armistice scheme for out-of-work
donation. This scheme, as already noticed, covered all
wage-earners, whether ex-Service personnel or others, and
whether male or female. At the end of April 1919, the
number of persons holding out-of-work donation policies,
who were registered as unemployed, were :

---

[1] *Statistical Journal*, March 1923, p. 200. Mr. Hilton's paper, to which this
discussion referred, furnished a corrected index eliminating this bias. Cf. Appendix,
Section I, Table VII.

Ex-Service men	.	380,000
Civilian male workers		239,000
Total males	. .	619,000
Female workers	.	474,000
Grand total		1,093,000

This was the largest total recorded in any month. It is, of course, much smaller than the difference between the numbers *employed* in November 1918 and April 1919 respectively, because that difference includes a large number of persons voluntarily withdrawn from gainful employment. At the same date there were some 350,000 men enjoying post-demobilisation furlough, most of whom, presumably, were not yet engaged in civilian industry.[1] From this time onward the number of persons in receipt of out-of-work donation rapidly and continuously fell, till in October 1919, the last month in which donation was paid to civil workers, the figures were :

Ex-Service men	.	340,000
Civilian male workers		101,000
Total males	. .	441,000
Female wage-earners	.	38,000
Grand total		479,000

It would be wrong to claim that the whole of the large reduction in the number of persons receiving out-of-work donation between May and November carried with it a corresponding decrease in unemployment. Part of it was due to changes in administration and to the exhaustion in the later months of the rights (13 weeks in six months for civilians) of some policy-holders. Nevertheless, there can

---

[1] Since post-demobilisation furlough was for twenty-eight days, the number of men on furlough in any month must be roughly equal to the addition made in the month before to the total number demobilised.

be no doubt that a large part of the reduction was genuine improvement. In November, too, the number of ex-Service men on post-demobilisation furlough had fallen to about 170,000.

The improvement continued for the remainder of 1919, and, apart from difficulties in the engineering trade due to a strike of iron-founders, during the earlier part of 1920. A summary account of the movement of employment in 1920 was given in the *Labour Gazette* of January 1921 as follows : "At the beginning of 1920 there was much un-employment in the engineering industry and in some other sections of the metal trade owing to the shortage of castings, resulting from a general strike of iron-founders, which had begun in the previous September and was still in progress. In other industries employment was good on the whole. After the termination of the strike in January, employment in the metal trade improved, and in nearly all the principal industries it was good until the summer." [1]

At the end of April 1920 demobilisation was practically complete ; at that date the number of ex-Service men in receipt of out-of-work donation was 217,000 (+ 2000 ex-Service women), falling in July to a minimum of 140,000.[2] Thus the great post-war transfer was substantially completed by the spring, or at latest the early summer, of 1920. Thereafter the state of and the fluctuations in wage-earners' activity that the country was to experience, though, of course, in large part an aftermath of the war, were incidents in the then established peace situation, not incidents in the transfer of men and women from war to peace employment.

The essential fact from the standpoint of this chapter is that at no time throughout the period covered by the trans-

---

[1] *Labour Gazette*, January 1921, p. 2.
[2] From this date onwards it rose ; standing at 338,000 in February and 279,000 in March 1921.

fer did the number of persons involuntarily out-of-work —
those on post-demobilisation furlough should not be
included in that class — rise appreciably above the million
mark. It only reached that mark during two months,
March and April 1919. Moreover, it may well be that the
high figures for these months exaggerate the amount of
true involuntary idleness then prevailing. For, as we have
seen, all civilian workers who were out-of-work were
entitled to out-of-work donation for 13 weeks per six
months. In these circumstances it is practically certain
that a number of persons, particularly married women,
who did not intend to resume work in industry, nevertheless
exercised their legal right to claim donation. In so far as
they did this, the number of workers whose unemployment
was really involuntary was less than the number recorded
as in receipt of out-of-work donation. The truth is even
more favourable — involuntary idleness during the course
of the transition was even smaller — than the figures cited
indicate. Scarcely anyone before the event would have
dared to prophesy that the great post-war transfer would
be carried through so smoothly and with so little pain.

CHAPTER III

THE COURSE OF EMPLOYMENT THROUGHOUT OUR PERIOD

In Chapter I, Part II, an attempt was made to measure the contraction in employment, the contraction in the number of persons gainfully occupied, and the scale of withdrawal from gainful occupation between the Armistice and April 1920 — the optimum date. I will now examine the course of employment throughout the whole of our period.

I. THE BREATHING SPACE AND THE BOOM

A broad distinction can be drawn between the happenings of the Breathing Space and those of the Boom. During the former period, down to April 1919, more persons were withdrawn from the Forces and munition-making than were absorbed into peace-time work, so that employment was declining to a minimum; during the latter, employment in some measure recovered, the recovery, of course, being much smaller than the previous decline.

In studying this process we have not the means of making direct estimates about what happened in the non-Z8 occupations.[1] The best we can do, therefore, is to base ourselves on certain *prima facie* reasonable assumptions and draw the appropriate inferences. For males we assume

---

[1] The following extracts from the Z8 reports are of some interest in this connection. In the report of July 1919, p. 7, it is stated : " The placing in domestic occupations [of women] by the employment exchanges, which were not apparently more numerous during the first three months of the Armistice than in the corresponding period a year earlier, were in the following six months about 40 per cent greater in 1919 than in 1918 ". The report for October 1919, p. 8, states that from March to June 1919 there were 46 per cent more placings than in 1918, but from July to October only 23 per cent more, " doubtless because the period of rapid reduction in the employment of women in other occupations was at an end ".

that the total number belonging to the employee category
in all civil employments changed in the same proportions
between the Armistice and the end of April 1919 and
between that date and the end of April 1920 as employment
in the Z8 occupations did ; and also that the 143,000 men
released from the army prior to demobilisation were demobilised at the same rate as the rest. For women we
assume that those in the forces were demobilised at the
same proportionate rates as men. For women in civilian
occupations the Z8 returns show a drop of 87,000 between
the two Aprils. Against this we have to set some proportion of the 250,000 to 300,000 women that we have counted
as returning to the non-Z8 employments between the
Armistice and April 1920. As the interval between April
1919 and April 1920 comes to two-thirds of this period,
our best guess is that two-thirds of these women returned
during the course of it. On this basis the women in non-Z8
occupations and Z8 occupations together show an increase
of, say, 100,000 as against a reduction of 30,000 for women
in the Armed Forces. Thus, we get the following table :

	(In thousands)		
	Males	Females	Persons
Change in civil employment between the Armistice and the end of April 1919 .	+ 1350	– 600	..
Change in employment of persons in the employee category in the Armed Forces between these dates . . .	– 2380	– 70	..
Aggregate change in employment from November 1918 to April 1919 . .	– 1030	– 670	– 1700
Change in civil employment between the end of April 1919 and the end of April 1920 .	+ 1550	+ 100	..
Change in employment of persons in the employee category in the Armed Forces between these dates . . .	– 1120	– 30	..
Aggregate change in employment from April 1919 to April 1920 . . .	+ 430	+ 70	+ 500

As we saw, in April 1919 the total number of persons
in receipt of out-of-work donation was 1,093,000 ; and we
have reckoned that in the following April the number of
males unemployed was some 300,000, to which, on the basis
of the insurance figures, we should, perhaps, add 140,000
women.   On this reckoning employment between the two
Aprils ought to have increased by some 650,000 persons.
It is certain, however, that a substantial number of those
who were drawing out-of-work donation, particularly
among married women, were persons not in transfer from
one occupation to another, but in process of abandoning
industry altogether.   We need not, therefore, on this account
push up our figure for the aggregate increase of employment between the two Aprils above the half-million mark.
Obviously, however, that figure is open to serious error.
Indeed, doubt is thrown on the whole of this statistical
manipulation by the fact that, when the methods we have
used are applied to the period April 1919 to October 1919,
they suggest that aggregate employment in civilian work
and the Forces together did not increase significantly between these two months, in spite of the fact that over the
same period the number of persons in receipt of out-of-
work donation fell, as was shown in the last chapter, by
some 600,000 — a circumstance which *must*, one would
think, have been associated with a substantial increase in
aggregate employment.   Again, according to this manipulation, from October 1919 to April 1920 employment appears
to have increased much more than unemployment decreased.   I cannot find any adequate explanation of these
paradoxes.   But my figure of half a million increase of
employment from April to April is not directly attacked
by them, and, for lack of a better, it must, with all reservations, be allowed to stand.   It appears then that, whereas
between the Armistice and April 1919 employment in all
fields together contracted by round about 1½ million per-

sons, the recovery during the year of boom which followed amounted to round about this half-million, that is to say, it was of the order of 3 per cent. It cannot, I think, have been *much* larger than that.

II. THE SLUMP

By the spring of 1920 the complications of demobilisation were over. Out-of-work donation continued to be paid to ex-Service men for another year, till March 1921.[1] But its disturbing effect no longer made it necessary for the Ministry of Labour to suspend the publication of the unemployment percentages under the 1911 and 1916 Insurance Acts. Those figures, and also the Trade Union percentages, become again reasonably satisfactory indices. Thus we are able to get a fairly clear picture of the subsequent course of industrial activity.

Till April 1920 according to the Trade Union figures, till June according to those for the insured industries, employment continued to improve, and at midsummer it was very good everywhere. Soon afterwards, however, a downward movement, which was to continue for at least a year and to gather great momentum, set in. The *Labour Gazette* describes the earlier part of this movement as follows : " In July, August and September a decline in employment, which had already become apparent in certain trades, especially boot and shoe manufacture, leather tanning and currying, cotton weaving, and the hosiery and jute trades, gradually spread to a considerable number of other industries, and by the beginning of October a depression was reported in most branches of the textile and clothing trades, and in the boot and shoe and leather trades. In

---

[1] The Eighteenth Abstract of Labour Statistics (p. 38) records a small number of payments (6630 in April) for yet another year, but for all practical purposes the donations ceased in March 1921.

October and November the shortage of fuel, caused by the general stoppage of work at the coal mines, which continued for over two weeks (18th October–3rd November), resulted in general slackness and much unemployment and short-time working in nearly all the principal industries. There was a partial recovery shortly after the settlement of the strike, but the improvement proved only temporary, and, after a renewed decline during December, employment at the end of the year was slack in most of the principal industries." [1] The percentage of unemployment, as recorded by Trade Unions, had begun to increase in May; as recorded in the industries insured against unemployment, in August. Thus we may safely date the down-turn as having set in in the summer of 1920, *i.e.* roughly at the same time as the down-turn in the monetary Boom — possibly a little later.

Between April and November 1920, according to the estimate set out in Table I, Section I, of the Appendix, the number of women in the employee category employed in the Z8 occupations other than agriculture — for which figures are not available in November — fell by 195,000 and the number of men by 89,000, *i.e.* a total of 284,000 persons. Thus, on a reasonable guess about the non-Z8 occupations, it seems probable that between April and November more than two-thirds of the whole recovery of employment accomplished during the Boom year was wiped out. Owing to the new 1920 Unemployment Insurance Act coming into force in November, a comparison between April and that month on the basis of the insurance figures is likely to be unreliable. The Trade Union figure for unemployment rose as between the ends of the two months from 0·9 to 3·7 per cent. This suggests something much bigger than the Z8 figure for the contraction in the number of men employed, and therefore, since in the Trade Unions making returns there

[1] *Labour Gazette*, January 1921, p. 2.

were very few women, in total employment. In any event, throughout the autumn of 1920 and the winter of 1921 unemployment steadily increased, till in March 1921 the Trade Union percentage had risen to 10. Under the influence of the great coal stoppage, which started in April 1921 and lasted three months, the situation steadily worsened. In June the Trade Union figure was 23·1 per cent and the insurance figure 22·4 per cent. When the stoppage came to an end there was, of course, an improvement. The Trade Union figure for July was 16·7 per cent, the other figure 17·9 per cent. During the latter half of 1921 and throughout 1922 there was a gradual, if small, improvement. In December 1922, the last month of what I have called the Slump, the Trade Union figure was 14·0 per cent, and the insurance figure 14·5 per cent for males and 8·1 per cent for females, working out at 12·8 per cent for both together. The monetary Slump was over, but employment was still, according to pre-war standards, extremely bad.

III. THE DOLDRUMS

In the first fifteen months of the Doldrums, according to the Trade Union figures, there was a substantial improvement in employment from January 1923 to May 1924; the percentage of unemployment fell from 13·6 to 7·0. According to the insurance figures the improvement continued till June 1924, the percentage in January 1923 being 13·3 and that of June 9·3. After that, employment worsened. In April 1925, when the Gold Standard was restored, the Trade Union percentage had risen to 9·4, the other to 10·9. Thus, as regards employment, the Doldrums was not a static period, but contained two parts : first a recovery till June 1924, and afterwards a relapse.

These, however, were minor movements. The fact

about the Doldrums of dominating interest is the very
much larger proportion of unemployment recorded then
on the average than had been customary in similar periods
of quiescence before the war. That matter will call for
careful study in the next chapter.

CHAPTER IV

THE DOLDRUMS AND THE INTRACTABLE MILLION

By the end of 1922, as we have seen, the immediate violent sequelae of the war were finished. The Doldrums was a period of relative stability and quasi-equilibrium. But the equilibrium was not a healthy one, because it was characterised throughout by a very large amount of involuntary idleness. It has sometimes been suggested that the marked excess of unemployment on the average since the war ended over what it was in pre-war times is in great part merely a statistical appearance, due to the fact that a larger proportion of workers involuntarily idle were recorded as unemployed. I have myself always been sceptical of this explanation ; and the fact that after two and a half years of the second war recorded unemployment had become practically nil has confirmed that scepticism. The Doldrums was not a period of slump, rather a period of recovery, in such wise that, on the basis of pre-war experience, the Trade Union unemployment percentage should certainly have been less than 4. Nevertheless, in 1923, starting at a maximum of 13·6 per cent in January, it still stood in December at 9·3 per cent, while in 1924 its best figure (in May) was 7 per cent and in December it was up again to 9·2 per cent. Throughout the whole of the period, January 1923 to April 1925, the percentage recorded for insured work-people in Great Britain and Northern Ireland was only once below 10 for men (9·9 in May 1924) and never below 9·3 for men and women together.[1] The absolute number of persons recorded as unemployed in the insured industries was never less than a million, only in four months,

---

[1] Cf. Appendix, Section I, Table VIII, and footnote 1.

in one of these barely, less than 1,100,000, and in nine
months less than 1,200,000. In this connection an interesting point is made by the Balfour Committee. On a basis
of reasonable assumptions they found that the extra unemployed in 1924 as against 1913 amounted to 800,000,
while the employable population had increased by some
900,000.[1] These rough estimates suggest that the number
of persons actually finding employment was still substantially the same as before the war, the additional employable population and the additional unemployed about
cancelling one another. The hard core of unemployment,
the intractable million as we may call it, though, of course,
it did not consist of the same persons throughout, but of
many different people, some of whom were only out of
work for a short time, was not a statistical fiction, but an
inescapable fact. It is our business here to elucidate it.

The most obvious fact about the post-war period, after
the preliminary upheavals were over-passed, is that the
demand of the community (the public and the Government
together) for soldiering and munition-making became
enormously less and was in great part shut down. Of ex-
Service men returning to civil life the great majority would
naturally try in the first instance to move back into their
pre-war occupations. Many of them, indeed, had had their
former jobs kept open for them. But, of persons who had
entered gainful employment for the first time during the
war and wanted to continue in it, the majority, having no
skill for any kind of job except the one they were actually
doing, would try to stay where they were. Hence, in the
Doldrums, we should expect to find the proportion of the
population seeking employment in industries that had been
swollen during the war to be somewhat larger, and the
proportion seeking it in those that had been contracted
somewhat smaller, than before the war began. Among

[1] *Survey of Industrial Relations*, p. 37.

the war-expanded industries iron and steel, electrical engineering, ship-building and marine engineering, cycles, motors and aircraft, miscellaneous metal trades, certain chemical trades, and Government establishments, dockyards, arsenals, etc., were especially prominent. According to the Z8 returns the number of men in these occupations increased from 1,115,000 in July 1914 to 1,706,000 in November 1918, *i.e.* by 591,000.

A wider setting into which these estimates may be fitted is provided by the facts about industry recorded in the Censuses of 1911 and 1921 for England and Wales [1]— difficulties of classification interfere with the construction of a table for Great Britain — and extracted by Dr. Bowley. The decline in agriculture and the expansion in coal-mining and in the metal trades were in line with the movement recorded between the 1901 and 1911 Censuses ; [2]

[1] Cf. *The Economic Position of Great Britain*, by A. C. Pigou and Colin Clark (London and Cambridge Economic Service, Special Memorandum No. 43), pp. 11-12. The tables are based on those given by Dr. Bowley in the London and Cambridge Economic Service, Special Memorandum 17A, pp. 8-10.

[2] The occupational tables in the Census of 1921 are not comparable with those of 1911 owing to changes in classification ; so that over that period only the industrial tables can be used. The figures below are taken from the occupational tables in the Censuses of 1891, 1901 and 1911.

UNITED KINGDOM : MALES AGED 10 YEARS AND UPWARDS OCCUPIED

	1891 (Thousands)	1901 (Thousands)	% Increase	1911 (Thousands)	% Increase or Decrease
Coal and shale mines .	596	749	26	1,016	35½
Metals, machines, implements and conveyances .	1,098	1,410	27½	1,672	18½
Ships and boats only . .	97	127	31	163	28
Building and construction .	953	1,333	40	1,208	- 9
All occupied males . .	11,463	12,951	13	14,308	14¾

(*Economic Journal*, vol. xxxiv, p. 6.)

though, as might be expected, for metals the rate of movement was much accelerated.

CONTRACTED INDUSTRIES

	1911	1921	Change	
	(Thousands)	(Thousands)	Absolute	Percentage
Agriculture . .	1230	1124	– 106	– 8
Cotton . .	628	596	– 32	– 5
Dressmakers, milli- ners, etc.* .	401	191	– 210	– 52
Building and con- struction . .	861	758	– 103	– 12
Private domestic service . .	1527	1232	– 295	– 19

EXPANDED INDUSTRIES

	1911	1921	Change	
	(Thousands)	(Thousands)	Absolute	Percentage
Coal-mining. .	971	1133	+ 162	+ 17
Chemicals . .	133	198	+ 65	+ 49
Iron and steel manufacture .	166	239	+ 73	+ 44
Engineering and ship-building .	637	887	+ 250	+ 39
Electrical apparatus	80	166	+ 86	+ 107
Cycles and motor cars . .	99	199	+ 100	+ 101
Gas, water, electri- city . .	109	163	+ 54	+ 49
Railways * . .	455	549	+ 94	+ 21
Shipping . .	144	193	+ 49	+ 34
National Govern- ment . .	414	647	+ 233	+ 56
Local Government	298	465	+ 167	+ 56
Entertainment and sports . .	71	116	+ 45	+ 63

* Comparison is affected by changes in classification.

Further light on this matter is thrown by a comparison

made by Dr. Bowley [1] between the shift of population into certain industries and the increase in population.

GREAT BRITAIN AND IRELAND

	1911 (Thousands)	1921 (Thousands)	Increase
Male population, aged 15–65	12,536	13,316 (estimated)	780
Males over 16 in engineering, ship-building, vehicles, iron and steel, and metal industries . . .	1,600	2,175 (Jan. 1922)	575

Thus over three-quarters of the total increase in the male industrial population between 1911 and 1921 was attributable to this small group of occupations.

The post-war allocation of would-be wage-earners that I have been describing was, as the reader will have perceived, mainly based on what the comparative demands for labour in different occupations were before the war and on what they had become during the course of it. But the states of demand — demand schedules — for labour in various occupations, when they had settled down after the war, were determined by the circumstances and the prospects visible then. In so far as these circumstances and prospects were different from what they had been before, with any given pattern of relative wage rates the relative quantities demanded would also be different. *A fortiori* they would be different from the relative quantities of labour that had become attached to various employments under the influence of pre-war and during-the-war happenings. More generally, any wide divergence between post-war and pre- and during-the-war conditions of demand might be expected *pro tanto* to create differences between the proportions in which wage-earners were wanted and the proportions in which they were offering themselves for various kinds of work.

[1] *Economic Journal*, vol. xxxiv, p. 5.

Without attempting to go into the subject in detail, we may distinguish four important developments that strongly affected demand conditions here. First, a number of countries, which had previously been accustomed to obtain manufactured goods from the great industrialised countries, notably from Great Britain, being shut off during the war from their sources of supply, started producing for themselves, and, after the war, naturally made strong efforts to maintain their new industries. Thus Japan and India became considerable manufacturers of textile goods ; with the result that British-made textiles were less needed. Secondly, war shortages in Europe had caused a very large acreage of land in the New World to be turned over to agriculture — a development which those who had undertaken it were unwilling after the war to undo. At the same time technical agricultural improvements had increased productivity. These changes led, when European agriculture began to recover, to very cheap prices for agricultural products. Since British demand for these products is not very elastic, we were able to get what we needed of them in exchange for a reduced quantity of exports ; or, to put the same point in other language, foreign producers of agricultural goods, having to sell them cheap, had not the means to buy so much of our exports as before. Lastly, in the period following the war the quantity of investment abroad in real terms undertaken by this country was substantially smaller than it had been before 1914. Mr. Colin Clark puts the money value of our overseas investments in 1907 at £138 millions, in 1924 at £72 millions.[1] Since prices were much higher in the latter than in the former year, the proportionate reduction in real terms was, of course, much greater than in money terms.

All these three influences, it will be noticed, struck specially heavily at those of our industries whose products

[1] *National Income and Outlay*, p. 185.

entered into the export trade.[1] It is not surprising,
therefore, to read Mr. Henry Clay's contemporary (1923)
comment : " The significant features in our foreign trade
are the reduction in the volume of our exports and the
steady trend back to the pre-war distribution by markets.
The volume of exports of United Kingdom products, as
measured by exports at 1913 prices, reached its highest point
since the Armistice in the June quarter of this year, when it
was just over 80 per cent of the 1913 volume. The trend
of trade is indicated in the following table of percentages :

BRITISH EXPORTS

Percentage of Total Value to	1913	1919	1920	1921	1922
	%	%	%	%	%
British Empire	32·7	20·0	30·6	34·9	33·8
Europe	37·6	57·0	40·4	35·1	37·6
Non-European foreign countries .	28·1	21·3	27·4	27·7	27·1
France	6·4	19·0	11·3	7·0	8·0
Germany	9·5	2·4	3·3	5·0	6·0
British India	11·3	7·5	11·8	13·8	11·3
U.S.A.	9·4	6·8	8·4	8·0	9·3

"It does not look as if there were any easy alternative to
our pre-war commercial relations ; it is a world with similar,
if diminished, wants that we have to work for. We may
have gained at certain points — Europe is probably more

---

[1] This general statement may be illustrated. The demand for coal for export
and, less markedly, for home use was badly hit in the nineteen-twenties on account of
technical developments. Alternative sources of power superseded coal in a number
of important uses. Thus ways were found for developing electricity from lignite
and — much more significant — from falling water. The internal-combustion
engine, using petrol, led to a substantial substitution of road transport, which did
not, for railway transport which did, depend on coal. Between 1914 and 1929 the
proportion of oil-burning as against coal-burning ships rose from 3·4 to 38 per cent.
As a consequence of these and other similar developments, whereas before the war
the world consumption of coal had been increasing on the average by 4 per cent per
annum, in 1929 it was only 9 per cent larger than it had been in 1914. But the
effects of these changes did not make themselves fully felt until the later nineteen-
twenties. The demand for British coal was specially good in 1923 on account of
the French invasion of the Ruhr and the consequent severe check to German coal
production. Unemployment in our coal industry did not become severe until after
the Great Strike in 1926.

dependent, not less, on British coal — but in the main the war has tended to reduce for the time being the country's real income from exchange, as it has reduced the resources with which it gains that income." [1]

The rift brought about by these and other causes between the quantity of labour wanted and the quantity offering itself for work over important parts of our industry is clearly shown in the following table from Sir William Beveridge's *Unemployment, a Problem of Industry*.[2] I have rearranged it so that the industries are set out in the order of the percentages of unemployment recorded for the year 1924.

The extremely unfavourable situation in the war-expanded industries is immediately apparent. So also is that of the textile industries, a large part of whose sales is normally made abroad ; and that of dock, harbour, river and canal service, which is also bound up with foreign trade. The heavy unemployment in this last group of occupations, as also in that of public works construction, is, however, in part accounted for by the disorganised manner, notorious long before the war, in which these industries engage their labour, casual methods which also prevail, though in a less degree, in the building industry.

The opening of the rift that I have been describing was naturally associated with alterations in relative wages ; money rates rising much less markedly in the overcrowded industries than elsewhere. For example, if we put wage rates ruling in August 1914 at 100, the corresponding figures for March 1923 were 176 for bricklayers, 260 for railway porters and 185 for wool and worsted spinners and weavers; but for ship-builders' riveters they were only 120, for fitters and turners in the engineering industry 145, for coal miners 130, and for cotton spinners and weavers 161.[3]

[1] *Economic Journal*, vol. xxxiv, p. 13.   [2] *Loc. cit.* p. 351.

[3] *Manchester Guardian Commercial*, European Reconstruction Issue, No. 16, p. 867. Cf. Appendix, Section III, Table III.

Industry	Numbers Employed (100)	Unemployed	
	1923	1924	1925
		%	%
Ship-building and ship-repairing . .	270	29·4	33·8
Dock, harbour, river and canal service .	191	25·6	29·9
Steel-smelting and iron-puddling furnaces, iron and steel rolling mills and forges .	211	21·1	24·5
Shipping service	127	19·5	20·8
Public works construction, etc. . .	128	17·8	17·7
Road transport not separately specified .	149	15·4	14·1
General engineering, engineers' iron and steel founding	667	15·2	12·6
Cotton	568	13·7	8·3
Textile bleaching, printing, dyeing, etc. .	115	12·7	13·0
Hotel, boarding-house and club services .	259	12·3	11·0
Metal industries not separately specified .	165	11·4	10·3
Building	716	10·6	9·8
Tailoring	186	9·5	10·3
Bread, biscuits, cakes, etc. . .	160	9·4	9·1
Boots, shoes, slippers and clogs . .	142	9·2	10·5
National Government . . .	181	9·1	7·7
Chemicals	104	9·0	9·0
Construction and repair of motor vehicles, cycles and aircraft	192	8·5	7·0
Dressmaking and Millinery . . .	117	7·5	7·3
Furniture-making, upholstering, etc. .	94	7·2	6·2
Local Government	242	7·2	8·6
Drink industries	100	7·0	6·7
Woollen and worsted	269	7·0	14·6
Hosiery.	90	6·9	8·7
Distributive trades	1,254	6·6	6·7
Laundries, dyeing and dry cleaning .	107	6·2	5·7
Gas, water and electricity supply industries	173	6·1	6·1
Railway service	190	5·8	6·3
Coal-mining	1,244	5·7	15·8
Printing, publishing and bookbinding .	228	5·4	4·9
Commerce, banking, insurance and finance	227	4·9	4·9
Professional services	109	4·0	3·5
Tramway and omnibus service . .	108	3·2	3·6
All industries	11,486	10·3	11·3

Note.—The numbers employed are taken from the *Ministry of Labour Gazette*, November 1929, and the annual unemployment percentages are calculated from the monthly figures given in the Gazettes.

More detail is provided in the following table prepared by Dr. Bowley :

INDEX NUMBERS OF WAGES [1]

	Rates of Wages for a Week's Work (as used in the Bulletin Index Number)			*Ministry of Labour Gazette*, Sept. 1923		Estimated Percentage for Hourly Rates, 1923 (Sept.)
	1914 (July)	1920 (July)	1923 (Sept.)	Percentage (1914 as 100)	Basis of Payment, etc.	
Bricklayer .	100	235	161	190	Hour	190
Bricklayer's labourer .	100	300	177	214	Hour	214
Compositor *	100	251	213	207	Week	226
Railwaymen	100	279	203	200	Week, minimum increase	230 approx.
Dock labourer .	100	265	167	172 to 200	Day	215
Engineering, fitter .	100	229	146	145	Week	165
Engineering, labourer .	100	309	178	176	Week	200
Coal . .	100	242	140	166	Shift	160 to 190
Cotton .	100	260†	157†	161	Week	181
Wool .	100	239	180	180	Week, minimum increase	214
Agriculture	100	254	168	156	Week	172
Average	100	264	174	170	Week, including several other industries	190 to 200

Notes.—The columns under *Ministry of Labour Gazette* are summarised from an article in its issue for October 1923. The first three columns show the average of the changes in a number of selected districts, except in the cases of railways, cotton and wool, where the original statistics relate to the whole or a great part of the industry. The final column is obtained from estimates of the reduction of the working week.

* The majority of compositors are paid on a time basis, the minority on daily newspapers or special work by piece.

† The numbers actually used in the Bulletin index for cotton were 300 and 181, which are based on piece rates and do not allow for the shortened week ; this excess is balanced in the average by an under-estimate for coal-miners, which does not allow for the additions described in the text.

He comments as follows : "As the figures stand, the index number for weekly rates of wages was nearly identical

[1] London and Cambridge Economic Service, 1923–6, Memo. 5, p. 2.

with that of the Cost of Living in September 1923, so that average real wages of those employed for the normal week were practically the same in 1914 and 1923. . . . There is considerable variation about the average. Unskilled labour (other than agricultural) has gained more than skilled. It is very noticeable that in those industries which depend to a great extent on export (engineering, coal and cotton) and in agriculture, which is affected by imports, the increases have been less than in building, in printing and on railways, which are nearly immune from foreign competition. The woollen industries have had, till 1923, a nearly secure home market, which is relatively more important to them than in the case of the cotton industry, and the increase in woollen is greater than in cotton wages." [1]

The relatively low levels of wages in the overcrowded industries, besides helping in some measure to close the rift between demand and supply by making it worth while for employers to engage more work-people there, also helped to do this in a more fundamental way by discouraging people from coming into the overcrowded industries, and encouraging some of those already there to go away. The expulsive power, even of relatively low wage rates and heavy unemployment combined together, worked, however, in a very slow and hesitating manner. For this there were three principal reasons. First, as everybody knows, when only small shifts in relative numbers are needed, these can be accomplished without any adult trained person moving, simply by a change in the direction of the stream of new recruits coming into industry every year. For example, if, as appears to be the case, the average period of a man's industrial life is about thirty years, a contraction up to 3 per cent per annum could, theoretically, be accomplished in a representative industry

---

[1] London and Cambridge Economic Service, Special Memo. No. 5, p. 3.

simply by no new recruits coming into it. In women's industries, where, owing to the custom of retirement on marriage, industrial life is on the average only about one-third as long, an annual contraction up to 10 per cent could be accomplished in that way. Obviously adjustments made by the diversion of new recruits have much less friction to overcome than adjustments by the actual shifting of adult wage-earners. But the adjustments needed to close the rifts in the post-war period were much too large to be made in this manner. To do that, very large numbers of adult workers would have needed to change their jobs, and, in many instances, their homes. This they were naturally very unwilling to do ; it entailed a tremendous wrench. Secondly, though, when one looks back afterwards, it is often easy to see that such-and-such a contraction of demand for labour in a particular industry was due to causes unlikely to be reversed, at the time it may well have been impossible to see this. Inevitably those affected hope against hope that the set-back is only temporary and that presently demand will revive. They prefer to face the hardship of unemployment for what they trust is only a little while, rather than uproot themselves and their families and start out on new and unknown ventures. In the period of chaos following the war, uncertainty about the prospects of demand in different occupations and consequent reluct-ance to take an initiative were of necessity very great. Thirdly and lastly, in periods when certain industries obviously need more workers — a war or a railway boom — a worker out of a job, who wants to move, has no difficulty in deciding where to go. But, when the only obvious thing is that his present industry needs less workers, such a man has great difficulty. In the period 1923–5 it was plain enough that ship-building and engineering, for ex-ample, were overcrowded occupations. But what occupa-tions were crying out for new workmen ? When a few industries need to contract a great deal, even though the rest in the aggregate are prepared to expand in equal aggregate measure, since the number of new workers that any one of them is able to take on is small, the openings are not easy to see. Candidates for work may be ready to move but have no clear guidance about *where* to move. If they do move, will they not merely find themselves unemployed in some other job or some other place ? The temptation to stay where they are in the vague hope that something will turn up is very strong. These three factors greatly impeded the adjustment of relative supplies to relative demands for labour in the period of the Doldrums.

The above causes in combination had powerful effects. In one instance they — or some other more hidden cause — led for a short time to a highly paradoxical result. " The Ministry of Labour's insurance figures show that the movement of labour into the overcrowded engineering industry was continuing through the worst of the depression ; the number of men and boys insured in this occupation group was 951,000 in July 1918, 1,044,000 in January 1922, 1,066,000 in September 1922." [1] This, however, is not a representative case. Unfortunately, full statistics for the number of persons insured in different industries are not available till 1923. But the tables published in the Nineteenth Abstract of Labour Statistics reveal that between the Julys of 1923 and 1925 the number of men insured in Great Britain in general engineering fell from 619,000 to 572,000, those in steel-smelting and iron-puddling furnaces, etc., from 206,000 to 193,000, those in ship-building and ship-repairing from 241,000 to 218,000, and those in woollen and worsted from 206,000 to 196,000 ; while the numbers in electrical engineering rose from 49,000 to 60,000, those in building and public works construction

---

[1] *Manchester Guardian Commercial*, European Reconstruction Issue, Section 15, p. 843.

from 817,000 to 883,000, and those in the distributive trades from 737,000 to 868,000. But these and other associated adjustments were not enough, as the table printed on p. 50 shows, to prevent the chief war-expanded industries from still suffering in 1925 from much more than average unemployment.

One comment remains to be made. Had it been feasible to reduce wage rates in the sheltered industries, larger quantities of labour would have been demanded there, so making it more apparent to people in the over-crowded industries where work was to be found. More of them, we may presume, would have moved across ; and employment in the two sets of industries together would have been larger than it was. Wage rates in the industries from which men moved might well on that account not have fallen so far as they did ; and it is even possible that the average rate of money wages in all industries together might not have been any lower than it was. Whether this would have been so or not we cannot be certain ; it is, I think, unlikely. In any case it is difficult to see how, in industries that were themselves prosperous, work-people could have been brought to accept wage reductions for an end so remote from their own interests as that of enticing into competition with themselves unemployed men from other occupations. Still, the considerations set out above make it plain that throughout the Doldrums wage-earners in those other occupations had a stronger economic case — not merely a stronger sentimental case — than their more fortunate colleagues for resisting further cuts in their already low rates of wages.

PART III

PRODUCTION

CHAPTER I

THE COURSE OF PHYSICAL PRODUCTION OVER THE BOOM, SLUMP AND DOLDRUMS

A LARGE part of any country's economic activity is, of course, always devoted to things other than physical production — transport, commerce, the professions, personal service, Government service, central and local, and so on. According to the Census of 1921, out of 12,113,000 men gainfully occupied, 4,887,000 were engaged in these occupations, and out of 5,065,000 women, 3,016,000 were so engaged. Thus among men gainfully occupied some 60 per cent were concerned with physical production, among women some 40 per cent, among persons some 53 per cent. The proportions were very much the same in 1911. These percentages are thus not very high, perhaps a good deal lower than some people would have been inclined to guess. Consequently, in spite of their stability as between 1911 and 1921, we must not expect movements in aggregate activity and movements in physical output to correspond very closely ; — though, since our employment figures also in the main exclude activities other than those connected with physical production, this does not matter much for comparisons between production and recorded unemployment. Further, changes in technical efficiency will affect physical production from given numbers employed ; so that even here we should not expect close correspondence. Nevertheless, movements in physical production are evidently of great interest, not only for their own sake, but also for their relation to other movements.

If the quantities of all the various types of goods and services produced in a year varied always in the same proportion, that proportion would show in an unambiguous way how far production as a whole had changed. But when, as, of course, happens in real life, the quantities of different types of goods and services alter in very various proportions, production as a whole becomes a shadowy concept. It is no longer a physical entity susceptible of direct measurement, but an arithmetical concoction, a sum of money divided by an index of prices, or a " quantity " obtained directly by weighting amounts of different kinds of stuff by reference to their prices or to the expenditures upon them over some selected period. Moreover, there are alternative ways of constructing indices of production, just as there are for indices of prices, between which it is not possible to say that this one is right, that one wrong. Over a considerable range the choice can only be arbitrary. Thus the figures, which are offered by statisticians as the best measure they can suggest of changes in production as a whole, are not something absolute, but should rather be regarded as shots, subject to considerable error, fired at a target whose outlines are blurred. None the less, when skilfully contrived, they can be made to provide a very useful, if very rough, picture of the broad trend of events. The discussion which follows must be read in the light of this preliminary caution.

Hoffmann has constructed an annual index for aggregate production in this country over a long period and Mr. Rowe has constructed one from the beginning of 1920. In the following table these two indices are set out along with an index of employment based on the Trade Union figures, the figure for 1913 being represented by 100 in each case. A fourth column gives an annual index of

E

British exports, as valued at 1913 prices, printed in the Balfour Committee's Report and corrected for 1923 and 1924 to allow for changes of quality. This is, in a sense, an index of the quantity of exports comparable with the indices of production.

Year	Employment Index	Hoffmann's Production Index *	Rowe's Revised Production Index †	Export Index ‡
1913	100·0	100·0	100·0	100·0
1918	..	79·0	..	..
1919	91·4	89·2	..	54·9
1920	99·7	90·5	90·4	70·9
1921	87·0	61·5	66·4	49·8
1922	86·6	76·6	82·5	68·9
1923	90·6	82·9	85·8	74·5 (79·0) §
1924	92·8	88·4	90·7	75·5 (80·0) §
1925	91·4	87·2	89·7	..

* From *Weltwirtschaftliches Archiv*, September 1934, p. 398. For a note on the relation of this index to Rowe's cf. *post* Appendix, Section II, p. 225.
† London and Cambridge Economic Service *Bulletin*, June 1925, p. 16, with the figures adjusted to 1913=100.
‡ Balfour Committee, *Survey of Overseas Markets*: adjusted by the Committee to allow for the changed status of Southern Ireland and in 1923 and 1924 for quality changes (pp. 3 and 658).
§ Adjusted for quality changes.

The figures so far set out, being for completed calendar years, do not permit us to take account of such facts as that the Boom began in April 1919 and ended in April 1920. It would clearly be useful to have statistics for shorter periods. Besides his annual index, Mr. Rowe has also constructed, from the beginning of 1920, a quarterly index of production. This is based on a narrower range than his annual index ; for example, no quarterly index for agriculture is possible, and among minerals only coal is available. Moreover, since the index is mainly based on raw materials imported and passing into the hands of manufacturers, Mr. Rowe suggests that this index may tend to measure the volume of production in the immediate future rather than in the quarter against which the figures are set.[1] Thus for comparison with other series it might

[1] London and Cambridge Economic Service, Memorandum 8, p. 11.

sometimes be best to put Mr. Rowe's figures three months forward. In the table below his index is set out alongside of (i) a corresponding quarterly index of employment, and (ii) a corresponding quarterly index of export quantities. Again, all the indices are worked so that the average of 1913 is 100.

QUARTERLY INDICES OF EMPLOYMENT, PRODUCTION AND EXPORTS [1] IN QUANTITIES

Year	Employment	Production	Exports
1913 (average) . . .	97·9	100·0	100·0
1919 1st quarter			
,, 2nd ,,	97·6	..	54·9
,, 3rd ,,			
,, 4th ,,			
1920 1st ,, . .	98·1	104·9	71·3
,, 2nd ,, . .	98·9	101·2	73·5
,, 3rd ,, . .	98·3	102·4	73·6
,, 4th ,, . .	95·0	92·2	65·4
1921 1st ,, . .	91·5	82·9	53·5
,, 2nd ,, . .	79·0	47·6	38·4
,, 3rd ,, . .	84·0	77·2	46·4
,, 4th ,, . .	84·0	62·5	60·7
1922 1st ,, . .	83·5	76·3	67·1
,, 2nd ,, . .	83·6	78·9	65·0
,, 3rd ,, . .	85·5	85·1	69·9
,, 4th ,, . .	85·9	83·2	73·3
1923 1st ,, . .	89·2	89·2	74·4
,, 2nd ,, . .	89·0	89·0	77·6
,, 3rd ,, . .	84·7	84·7	68·7
,, 4th ,, . .	92·1	92·1	77·5
1924 1st ,, . .	89·6	89·6	73·8
,, 2nd ,, . .	90·6	90·6	76·7
,, 3rd ,, . .	89·6	89·6	69·9
,, 4th ,, . .	93·9	93·9	73·3
1925 1st ,, . .	91·6	91·6	..
,, 2nd ,, . .	..	87·0	..

[1] The table for exports is taken from Pigou and Robertson, *Essays and Addresses*, p. 166, and continued for 1924. In it adjustment is made for the changed status of Southern Ireland after the first quarter of 1923. Professor Robertson's

I add the following table,— due to Hoffmann,[1] — which distinguishes between annual movements in output of producers' goods and of consumers' goods :

Year	Producers' Goods	Consumers' Goods
1913	100·0	100·0
1919	85·2	93·7
1920	90·6	90·7
1921	57·2	66·0
1922	72·5	81·0
1923	88·8	77·1
1924	94·4	82·6
1925	89·0	85·5

For this table Hoffmann's lists of producers' goods and consumers' goods are respectively as follows : [2]

PRODUCERS' GOODS	CONSUMERS' GOODS
A. *Mining*	F. *Textiles*
1. Coal	1. Cotton
2. Iron ore	*a.* Yarn
3. Tin ore	*b.* Cloth
4. Copper ore	2. Wool and knitted material
5. Lead ore	*a.* Wool yarn
6. Zinc ore	*b.* Woollen cloth and
7. Miscellaneous ores	knitted material

table is constructed in accordance with the method adopted by the Board of Trade. This method, which was a peculiar one, has been summarised for me by Mr. Corlett as follows :

" The method used by the *Board of Trade Journal* for 1920–22 was to value the trade of each year up to the end of the quarter on the basis of the average prices at the corresponding period in 1913. Thus, if a_1, a_2, a_3, a_4 were the quantities in the four quarters of 1920, and the 1913 prices of the commodity were p_1, p_2, p_3, p_4 in the four quarters, the estimate of the trade in the quarters at 1913 prices (b_1, b_2 . . . being quantities in 1913) would be

$$(1) \quad a_1 p_1 \qquad\qquad\qquad\qquad\qquad\qquad\text{(3 months)}$$

$$(2) \quad (a_1 + a_2)\frac{b_1 p_1 + b_2 p_2}{b_1 + b_2} - a_1 p_1 \qquad\qquad \begin{array}{l}\text{(6 months}\\ \text{−3 months)}\end{array}$$

$$(3) \quad (a_1 + a_2 + a_3)\frac{b_1 p_1 + b_2 p_2 + b_3 p_3}{b_1 + b_2 + b_3} - (a_1 + a_2)\frac{b_1 p_1 + b_2 p_2}{b_1 + b_2} \quad \begin{array}{l}\text{(9 months}\\ \text{−6 months)}\end{array}$$

From 1923 the trade of each quarter was revalued on the basis of prices in the corresponding quarter of the previous year and then related to 1913 through the index for that quarter."

[1] *Weltwirtschaftliches Archiv*, September 1934, p. 398. [2] *Ibid.* pp. 392-3.

Producers' Goods—*contd.*

B. *Iron, Steel and Machine Industry*
 1. Iron and steel
 2. Manufactured iron and steel products, machines, implements

C. *Metals and Metal Wares*
 1. Copper
 2. Lead
 3. Zinc
 4. Tin
 5. Aluminium
 6. Metal ware

D. *Vehicles, Ships, etc.*
 1. Ships
 2. Locomotives, etc.
 3. Tramways
 4. Motor cars

E. *Timber and Timber Products*
 1. Furniture
 2. Miscellaneous

Consumers' Goods—*contd.*

F. *Textiles* (*contd.*)
 3. Silk
  a. Yarn
  b. Cloth
 4. Artificial silk
 5. Jute and hemp
 6. Linen

G. *Food, Drink, Tobacco*
 1. Flour, bread, cake and pastries
  a. Flour
  b. Bread, cake, pastries
 2. Meat products
 3. Confectionery
 4. Sugar
 5. Beer
 6. Malt
 7. Alcohol
 8. Tobacco

H. *Paper and Printing*
 1. Paper
 2. Printing

I. *Leather Products*
 1. Leather
 2. Leather work

J. *Rubber Products*

K. *Chemicals*
 1. Alkali and bleaching material
 2. Soap and candles
 3. Oil
 4. Dyes

L. *Gas and Electricity*
 1. Gas
 2. Electricity

Hoffmann observes : " The grouping of industries by reference to producers' goods and consumers' goods encounters the well-known difficulty that products of technically homogeneous industries, as, for instance, the iron and steel industry, are not only sold to enterprises, but to private households as well. Since, in the absence of sales statistics, an exact grouping is impossible, the only way out is a grouping according to the preponderance of the one market or the other. The grouping in the present index is subject to this limitation. Therefore the calculated indices cannot claim complete unambiguity, but they may be taken as an expression of the growth tendencies of the two groups." [1]

I. THE BREATHING SPACE AND THE BOOM

The most striking fact about the foregoing tables is that, according to both Hoffmann's index and Rowe's annual index of production, even in the post-war Boom production was substantially, say 10 per cent, less than in 1913. Some doubt is thrown on this by the fact that Rowe's quarterly index makes 1920 output practically the same as 1913 output. Except for the year 1920, the movements of this index conform broadly with those of the annual index. The discrepancy for 1920 is, however, fully explained in Mr. Rowe's original memorandum as follows : " The quarterly average for Group III is considerably higher than the annual index, partly because no account can be taken of the production of tinplate and galvanised sheets, which was relatively low, but mainly because the tonnage under construction in ship-building yards was far greater than in 1913, while the tonnage launched was about the same (for the quarterly index the former had to be used, while for the annual the latter can be used, and seemed more appropriate). Agricultural production was low in 1920, and this important group is not, of course, included in the quarterly figures ; and the same is true of timber." [2]

---

[1] *Loc. cit.* p. 395.

[2] London and Cambridge Economic Service, Memorandum No. 8, p. 14. Group III contains iron and steel, galvanised sheets, railway locomotives, wheels and axles, tinplates and ship-building.

Clearly, where there is a difference the annual index is to be preferred.

Granted then that production really was lower in the Boom year than in 1913, that fact is *prima facie* surprising and calls for explanation. Can the explanation be that there was a transfer of activity from production, as defined in the index, to other forms of employment ? No. For on Bowley's figures it appears that between the Censuses of 1911 and 1921 the number of persons occupied in production proper, *i.e.* in occupations other than transport, commerce, Government service, etc., rose by some 4 per cent, and the number of males by some 7 per cent. The following considerations must, however, be borne in mind. First, while employment in 1913 was very high — the Trade Unions only recorded 2·1 per cent unemployment on the average — in the post-war Boom there was substantial unemployment till the beginning of 1920, and, though a high level of employment was attained in the spring of that year, the Slump followed very quickly ; so that, over the Boom year as a whole, April 1919–April 1920, there was a good deal of unemployment. Secondly, the length of the working day was cut down on the average some 10 per cent below its pre-war length, while it may well have been that war weariness reduced the energy of work, and industrial disputes on a heavy scale certainly interfered with it. Finally, equipment had deteriorated during the course of the war, and the shift-over to peace conditions was bound to entail some disorganisation and failure by some managements to arrange work in the most effective way. These considerations taken together will explain a substantial check to immediate post-war, relatively to pre-war, production.

Besides the question how aggregate physical production in the post-war Boom stood in relation to its pre-war level, it is also of interest for our enquiry to know how the contents of production in the two periods were related to one another. Was the recovery in the output of civilian goods, which followed the return of peace, mainly a recovery for the service of the export market or for the service of the home market ? In so far as it was for the service of the home market, what were the respective parts played in it by industries making producers' goods and those making consumers' goods ? In so far as the output of consumers' goods expanded, was this mainly for the service of direct consumption or for rebuilding stocks ? The data for a complete answer to these questions are not available, but it is possible, nevertheless, to throw some light upon them.

It has always been difficult to disentangle production for export from production for home use. But Sir A. Flux in 1929, in an article in the *Statistical Journal*, calculated, on the basis of the 1907 Census of Production, that at prices ex-factory and ex-farm the share of the gross value of agricultural and manufacturing output entering into exports amounted to 30·5 per cent ; in 1900 and again in 1924 the proportion, as reckoned for me by Mr. Rothbarth, seems to have been in the neighbourhood of 25 per cent. In view of the large size of these figures it is evident that a strong revival of the export industries would entail arithmetically, apart altogether from secondary reactions, a substantial revival in production as a whole ; a 10 per cent move in exports implying roughly a 3 per cent move in production for export and home use together. Moreover, in the immediate post-war epoch it was in fact to the export industries that many people looked as a dominant field of new civilian activities ; attention being focussed on the enormous needs for rehabilitation in many foreign countries alongside of the virtual disappearance of competition in exports from our pre-war rivals. In Part V, Chapter IV, some extracts from the *Economist* will be cited which illustrate very well this point of view. What actually happened ?

Our tables show that the volume of British exports, *i.e.* their money value recalculated at 1913 prices, was 45 per cent less in 1919 than it had been in 1913, and in 1920 nearly 30 per cent less — a much worse showing than is made by the indices of production as a whole. In this connection particular interest attaches to cotton piece goods, partly because exports of these goods constituted before the war a very large fraction — nearly a fifth [1] — of the aggregate value of our recorded exports ; partly because the proportion of our output of cotton goods that were exported was very large,— something like three-fourths of the whole,— and partly because the enormous expansion in the *value* of our cotton exports in the immediate post-war period may easily lead us into a serious mistake about quantities. The facts for 1913, 1919 and 1920, the figure for 1913 being put at 100, are as follows :

Year	Value of Exports of Cotton Piece Goods in £ millions	Quantities of these Exports in million yards of Average Width
1913	100	100
1919	183	50
1920	324	66
1921	141	43

Thus the volume of our exports of cotton piece goods exported in 1919 was half, in 1920 just over two-thirds, what it had been in 1913.[2] This is merely a particular illustration of a general truth. Another illustration is afforded by coal. The *value* of our exports in 1919 and 1920 was enormously higher than — in 1920 twice as high as — it had been in 1913, on account of the very high prices at which they were sold ; but the *volume* of exports,

---

[1] *Is Unemployment Inevitable ?*, pp. 307 and 318.
[2] For a fuller account of cotton exports cf. *post*, Chapter IV.

which had been 73·4 million tons in 1913, was 35·2 millions in 1919 and only 24·9 millions in 1920.

This summary of relevant facts shows that civilian industrial activity during the Breathing Space and the Boom was not directed to the export market in nearly so high a degree as in 1913. On the contrary, the export market, as compared with pre-war years, recovered substantially less than the home market. At the same time, as our tables show, as between 1919, three parts of which year was in the Boom, and 1920, one quarter of which was in the Boom, exports expanded much more markedly than aggregate production. During the war they had fallen to a very low level indeed. In the first part of 1919 they must have been much less than half, since in 1919 as a whole they were only a little more than half what they were in 1913. Thus, in spite of the fact that at the end of the Boom they did not stand nearly as high relatively to 1913 as aggregate physical production did, nevertheless *during* the Boom year their (geometrical) *rate* of expansion was very rapid, much more rapid than the rate of expansion of physical production as a whole. In this way during the actual course of the Boom itself recovery in the export market was in a sense a dominant fact.

To complete our account of this matter and to guard us against supposing that foreign tariffs were a main source of the misfortunes of our export industry, the following passage from the Introduction to the Report of the Balfour Committee's *Survey of Overseas Markets* (1926) may be cited : " Taken altogether, the average increase of import duties per unit of product has probably not exceeded 80 per cent — a rise not more than sufficient to keep pace with the average rise of price level of the exports. It is a legitimate inference that, taking British trade as a whole, tariff increases since 1913 have not, so far, been an important factor in retarding recovery. . . . While changes in the rates

of Customs duty have not in most cases played an important part in retarding the recovery of British export trade,
the same cannot be said of other forms of restriction and
obstruction at Customs frontiers." [1] The main forms of
obstruction noted by the Committee were Customs pro-
hibitions and restrictions, with the delay caused by licensing,
exchange control, and the doubling of the number of in-
dependent Customs administrations in Central and Eastern
Europe after the war, coupled with the fact that the administration was largely in the hands of comparatively new and
inexperienced authorities.

The next question we have to answer is whether the
resumption of civilian activity was predominantly in producers' goods, capital goods if we will, or of consumers'
goods. To distinguish these two kinds of activity statistic-
ally is as difficult as it is to distinguish activity devoted
to the home and to the export market. For the line between
producers' goods and consumers' goods is not clear.

As regards their relative importance for the country,
some guidance may be got from estimates that have been
made as to the amount of income that is " invested ".
Mr. Colin Clark, basing himself on Censuses of Production,
gives figures for 1924, which I have combined into the
following table : [2]

	£ millions
Investment in fixed capital (net)	235
Additions to working capital	20
Overseas investment (net)	72
Total net income	4035
Maintenance and repair of fixed capital	341

Payments to people making net investment in fixed capital
and also payments to those engaged on maintenance and
repair are clearly payments received by industries making
producers' goods. Together they come to £576 millions.

[1] Loc. cit. p. 15.
[2] Cf. National Income and Outlay, pp. 88 and 185.

Payments made for consumers' goods include costs of maintenance and repair of fixed capital. Payments made in respect of additions to working capital and of overseas investment may be regarded as distributed between producers' industries and consumers' industries roughly in the same proportion as other payments. Hence the proportion of payments made to producers' industries and consumers' industries respectively in 1924 works out on these estimates at £576 millions against £4035 millions – £576 millions, *i.e.* against £3459 millions. This suggests that in 1924 activity devoted to producers' industries would be somewhere about one-sixth of that devoted to consumers' industries, or about one-seventh of the whole. The corresponding figures for 1907 do not seem to have been seriously different.[1] At all events we have here a rough indication of the comparative orders of magnitude of the two sorts of activity.

There is some evidence, unfortunately not very widely based, to the effect that the upturn took place in industries making consumers' goods a little earlier than in those making producers' goods. This evidence is to be found in Table III of Section II of the Statistical Appendix. In that table Mr. Rothbarth has set out the months in which, according to returns provided by employers and published in the *Labour Gazette*, employment turned upward in a considerable number of industries in both categories. On the average of the dates it appears that consumers' industries turned about the middle of January 1919 and producers' industries near the end of March. Hoffmann's index also suggests that recovery in consumers' goods came first. Thus, with the figure for 1913 put at 100, his index for producers' goods was 85·2 and for consumers' goods 93·7 in 1919, while in 1920 both indices stood approximately at 90½. It is unfortunate that quarterly indices

[1] Cf. *National Income and Outlay*, pp. 94 and 179.

are not available. The implication of the annual figures is, however, fairly clear ; consumers' goods began to recover first, but producers' goods presently overhauled them and in the end recovered as far as they did. This order of events is slightly surprising, because, as is well known, output in industries making instrumental goods is in some degree geared, not to the *rate* of output in the consumers' industries, but to *changes* in the rate of that output, so that decreases in the rate at which industries making consumers' goods are decreasing, which in general occur before they have begun absolutely to increase, are liable to be associated with expansions in industries making instrumental goods.[1] What happened may perhaps be accounted for by the fact that the post-war reopening of activity needed a longer period of preparation for many sorts of producers' goods — this was not, of course, true of ship-building — than for most consumption goods.

In a privately printed memorandum, to which I have been given access, the broad relations between movements of industries making producers' and consumers' goods respectively have been described, on a basis, it must be admitted, of general impression rather than of detailed knowledge, as follows : " It is known that large investment was effected by firms, largely out of the amortisation and other reserves they had accumulated during the war, for the adaptation of their plant to civilian demand, to replace worn-out machinery and, in some cases, to expand productive capacity in order to meet an expected increase in demand, which, when it materialised, proved to have a brief span of life. If only on account of the technical difficulties of converting plant and the practical impossibility of anticipating the nature and extent of immediate post-war consumers' demand, this real investment got into full swing rather later than did the manufacture of

---

[1] Cf. my *Industrial Fluctuations*, Second Edition, p. 110.

consumers' goods." [1]   This, I think, probably gives a correct picture of the facts.

There remains the question how far the renewal of activity in industries making consumers' goods during the Boom period was represented by corresponding increases of consumption and how far by the accumulation of new working capital in the form of goods in process assembled inside the machine of industry and in stocks of finished goods in warehouses and shops. There are no statistical data of a general kind bearing upon this question. As regards food, it appears that, while the stocks of tea, coffee and cocoa rose greatly between 1st September 1918 and 1st September 1919 and were at the latter date much above their pre-war level, stocks of wheat (including flour) and barley were at that date decidedly lower both than a year before and than on 1st September 1914 ; while stocks of oats had fallen as against 1st September 1918, but risen relatively to what they were on 1st September 1914. [2] But this covers only a very small part of the field. On general grounds we can lay it down that an enhanced flow of consumers' goods made at home to consumers' hands can only have taken place on a basis of enlarged working capital in the machine of process and probably also in stocks held by wholesalers and retailers. I myself am inclined to suspect that, while a part of the raised activity in civilian industries during 1919 and the first part of 1920 must have gone to enlarge current consumption, a very large proportion of it was reflected in accumulations of working capital in a wide sense. If this is so, the Boom, in its real, as distinct from its money, aspect, might be described as a Boom in working capital. In view of the fact that business men are apt to rely largely on the banks to finance working, as distinguished from fixed, capital, the

---

[1] Memorandum prepared by Mr. Loveday, p. 12.
[2] *Ibid.* p. 15.

large increase in bank advances during the period gives some, though perhaps not very strong, support to this view.

II. THE SLUMP

Both Hoffmann's and Rowe's annual indices of production were very much lower in 1921 than in 1920. The low level was, no doubt, in large part due to the great coal strike from April to June. Their apparent recovery in 1922 was also, no doubt, largely due to the fact that in 1921 they had been on that account abnormally low. In 1922, as well as in 1921, they were both much lower than in 1920, indicating heavy Slump conditions. Rowe's quarterly index began to fall seriously in the last quarter of 1920, thus, as was to be expected, since employment does not yield its fruit immediately, lagging behind the fall in employment. The extraordinarily low figure for the second quarter of 1921 is, of course, accounted for by the coal strike already referred to. In comparing production figures with employment figures for that quarter, it is important to recollect that persons on strike are not counted among the unemployed ; a fact which partly accounts for the much slighter relative fall in the employment index. Throughout 1922 till the end of the period which I have called the Slump the quarterly production index remained, like the employment index, very low ; though in the last half of 1922 there was an improvement considerably more marked than the accompanying small improvement in the employment index. Throughout the period the larger sweep of the movements of the production index are partly explained by the fact that the employment index for the period, based as it is on the Trade Union returns, takes no account of short time.

In both 1921 and 1922 the annual export index was still substantially more depressed, as against 1913, than the

indices of production ; but the excess depression, especially
in 1922, was somewhat less than in 1920.[1] Over the course
of the Slump taken as a whole, the decline was predominantly a home market decline. Exports, so far from
aggravating, in some measure mitigated the general downward movement.

The evidence of Mr. Rothbarth's table of dates set out
in the Appendix, Section II, Table III, suggests that, just
as consumers' goods began to recover before producers'
goods, so also they began to decline first, on the average
by a little over a month. The fall in producers' goods,
while beginning later, was, however, more serious. Whereas
in 1920 Hoffmann's index (Cf. *ante*, p. 60) for these goods
stood at the same level, as against 1913, as his index
of consumers' goods, in 1921 and 1922 the two indices
stood to one another in much the same relation as in 1919,
i.e. with the consumers' goods index some 10 per cent
higher than the other. Thus producers' goods soon relapsed again after their good year. Throughout the main
part of the Slump, as during the earlier stages of the Boom,
they were in a substantially worse position as compared
with pre-war days than consumers' goods. As between
1921 and 1922 their relative position did not worsen further,
but remained fairly steady. Both indices make a substantially better showing in 1922 than in 1921, mainly, no
doubt, because in the former year there was no coal strike.

[1] If, instead of the Board of Trade export figures, we use an export index
employed by Dr. W. Schlote (*Entwicklung und Strukturwandlung des englischen
Aussenhandels von 1700 bis zum Gegenwart*, Statistical Appendix), this result is
more marked. Putting both production and exports at 100 for 1920, we have

Year	Hoffmann's Production Index	Schlote's Export Index
1920	100	100
1921	63	71
1922	80	100
1923	98	112
1924	104	116

There is no direct evidence about the state of working capital, including stocks in warehouses and shops, during the course of the Slump ; but it may be presumed on general grounds that the contraction in activity over this period only manifested itself to a relatively small extent in a reduction of current consumption. It was probably mainly associated with a cessation in the process of building up additional working capital.

III. THE DOLDRUMS

With the ending of 1922 the bottom of the depression was passed. Employment improved and, with it, aggregate production. But in neither case was the improvement large. Throughout our part of the Doldrums, including, if we will, the whole of 1925, Hoffmann's annual index never rose above 88·4 per cent (the figure for 1924) of its 1913 value. Rowe's annual index never exceeded 90·7 per cent (in 1924). His quarterly index reached 90·6 per cent in the second and, after a drop, 93·9 per cent in the fourth quarter of 1924 ; but quickly fell again. As a rough generalisation we may say that in our part of the Doldrums aggregate physical production was some 10 per cent below its 1913 level.

As compared with the Slump years of 1921 and 1922, exports were up somewhat relative to aggregate output, but, as against 1913, they were still relatively down. Thus, as against 1913, weakness in the exports market was still a direct aggravating factor in the general malaise. As already suggested, the relation of exports to production seems to have reverted to what it was in 1900. It is important, however, to realise that a low level of exports, when things had settled down after the Slump, was not something special to England. It was part of a world malady, from which this country suffered actually a little less than others.

F

The Balfour Committee found that, while the exports of the world reckoned in sterling rose between 1913 and 1923 from £4035 millions to £5299 millions, or 31 per cent, the proportion of British exports to world exports *rose* from 13 to 14 per cent.[1] The practical moral was drawn by Sir A. Flux as follows : " These figures appear to suggest that the restoration of world trade to its former dimensions and capacity of expansion can do more to restore our own export trade and revive the industries that depend on it than a struggle to secure for ourselves trade that has been carried on by some other nation, important as it is to maintain our competitive capacity ".[2]

According to Hoffmann's index, during the Doldrums the output of producers' goods expanded greatly relatively to that of consumers' goods. In 1922 the index for these had been 72·5 against a consumers' goods index of 81·0, but in 1923 it had risen to 88·8 per cent and in 1924 to 94·4 per cent, while the index of consumers' goods, after a drop in the intermediate year, stood only a little above what it was in 1922, namely at 82·6 per cent. A natural inference is that during 1923 and 1924 investment in fixed capital of various sorts was going forward strongly,— though it was destined to be checked in 1925, perhaps in connection with the restoration of the Gold Standard, or perhaps, with the tightening-up of bank policy, which, as will be shown in Part V, Chapter I, preceded it. If this is so, we should be inclined *prima facie* to expect a considerable expansion in new capital issues in 1923 and 1924. There was in fact no such expansion either of issues for the home market or in general. However, as Mr. Colin Clark has made clear,[3] these issues are an extremely unreliable index of what is happening to real investment. In

---

[1] *Survey of Overseas Markets*, pp. 2-3.
[2] *Economic Journal*, 1926, p. 554.
[3] Cf. *National Income and Outlay*, pp. 166-7.

spite of them, therefore, the inference suggested by Hoffmann's figures may, nevertheless, be right.

IV. CONCLUDING CAUTION

Throughout this discussion, when we have compared the parts played in aggregate changes of production by changes in different elements, notably in production for the export market and production of producers' goods, we have been careful to speak in terms of arithmetic, not of causation. Thus, when we found that a 10 per cent expansion in the export industries would carry with it roughly a 3 per cent expansion in the sum-total of all industries, this was on the understanding that expansion of the export industries left the activity of other industries unaffected. But, of course, in real life, when one branch of industry expands, repercussions on other branches are almost certain to occur. If the whole of a country's resources are fully occupied, an expansion in one branch is bound to entail a contraction in others. But, if substantial quantities of resources are standing idle, such an expansion is very likely to evoke, not a contraction, but an expansion, in other branches. Whether it does this, and, if it does, how large the secondary expansion will be, depends partly on the policy of banks and partly on that of wage-earners. If banking policy is directed to prevent money income from rising, or if, though it allows money income to rise, wage-earners force money wage rates up in equal proportion, repercussions cannot, indeed, occur. But, if bank policy permits money income to rise and wage-earners do not force up money wage rates in an equal proportion, they will occur. The expansion of one branch of industry gives more money to the persons engaged in that branch, while this is not offset, or is only partially offset, by contractions of income elsewhere. The wage-earners in export industries,

or industries making producers' goods, have more money
to spend, and thus create a market for the services of other
wage-earners. In this way the addition made to aggregate
activity may be substantially more than that made to
activity in the branch of industry which first started to
expand. In some circumstances a cumulative movement
may be set up and presently gather strong momentum.
The study of these matters lies, however, outside our
present scope.

CHAPTER II

SHIP-BUILDING

IT is well known that, when a boom is followed by a slump, the industries hit most severely are those engaged in making long-enduring products and particularly such of these as take a long time to manufacture. The reasons for this are plain. First, when the demand for the services rendered by a long-enduring product varies, the demand for new output of that product and, therefore, for work-people engaged in making it must vary in a much larger proportion, instead of, as with a quickly perishable product, varying in the same proportion. For with long-enduring products there is sure always to be an existing stock large relatively to the annual output, so that to increase the total stock sufficiently to add 10 per cent to its yield of service might well entail increasing the annual rate of output by 100 per cent ; while, if 10 per cent less of total stock were wanted, there might for some time be no need to make good wear and tear, and so the demand for new output might disappear altogether. Secondly, if demand all round is increasing with population and capital in a fairly steady trend, the occurrence of a boom must itself directly generate a subsequent slump in respect of durable products, though it has no such tendency in respect of those which are immediately perishable. For, if the stock is augmented at more than the average rate in one period, it must be augmented at less than the average rate in another. A boom in effect snatches up for itself a part of the demand that would normally become operative at a later date. Conversely, of course, a slump, if it is not merely the reflex of a preceding boom, by hampering additions to stock now, generates a need for enhanced additions presently. Thirdly, when a product takes a long time to make, the fact that a large amount of it, started in a preceding boom, is coming to completion may easily be ignored, so that its unlooked-for emergence startles people and discourages them from beginning work on any further new output.

Ships are outstanding examples of products that are both long-enduring and also take a long time to make, and it is, therefore, to be expected that in any period of violent industrial fluctuation the ship-building industry should experience exceptional disturbance. Its post-war history is thus a very good illustration of a general economic rule. It is also very important, so to speak, as a thing in itself. In the latter part of Mr. Fayle's *The War and the Shipping Industry*, which carries the story down to 1925, an excellent account of it is given. The paragraphs that follow are based on that work.

On 31st October 1918 British tonnage available was less by nearly 18 per cent than it had been at the beginning of the war, while in vessels of ocean-going size the decline was no less than 25 per cent.[1] At the same time there was a change in the proportions of different types of ships. Replacement of lost shipping had mainly taken the form of the construction of comparatively large ships. Thus there was an increase in the number of ships between 5000 and 10,000 tons of 191, while for all ships there was a decline in numbers of 951. There had been a decrease in the proportion of faster steamers, compensated by an increase in the proportion of those of moderate speed. There was an increase in the number of large tankers ; but the only other specialised type built in large numbers was the frozen-meat ship, and even here the loss had not been made good. Most of the standard ships lacked the specialisation needed for the liner trade or even that demanded by tramp owners

[1] *Loc. cit.* p. 323.

before the war.   There was also a higher proportion of old ships in service.

World tonnage did not decrease in the same ratio as British tonnage. In fact, between June 1914 and June 1919 the gross tonnage of steam and motor vessels of 100 tons gross and up, recorded in Lloyd's Register, had risen from 45·4 millions to 47·9 millions (*i.e.* 5%). This was largely due to the great ship-building programme of the United States, whose sea-going steam tonnage rose in this period from 2 million gross tons to 9·8 million.   To a less extent Japan, the Dominions and Holland had increased their tonnage.

In October 1918 detailed instructions were sent to loading officers throughout the world as to what supplies should be left behind and what shipped if an Armistice was concluded.   These instructions were carried into effect when the occasion arose ; so that space was not used for war supplies which were no longer considered essential. At the same time the convoy system, with its incidental delays, was stopped, sinkings ceased, and ships allocated for the transport of American troops to France were released.   As a result there was a large amount of extra tonnage available for normal requirements.   The full demand for civilian purposes did not come into operation immediately.   For a time there actually seemed to be a surplus of tonnage, so that liner freights in the North Atlantic fell in some cases to one-sixth of the rates in force immediately before.

It was not long, however, before a shortage of shipping began to develop once more, and by March 1919 it was as serious as in the worst period of the war.   In view of the fact that the world tonnage was not below that at the beginning of the war, and that it is world tonnage which should determine the available supply of shipping, this is *prima facie* surprising.   It must be remembered, however, that some of the world's shipping was not very suitable for peace requirements. This was particularly true of some of the American shipping — and not only the wooden ships. Again, owing to failure to agree on the terms of surrender of the German ships, these ships were held in German ports until after the Brussels Agreement of 14th March 1919. Thus the shipping statistics do not show the true amount of shipping available for trade purposes. It was after the release of the German ships that the position began to improve.

More important than the actual shortage of tonnage was the fact that the tonnage which was available was not as efficient as it had been before the war. The change in the age and type of ships has already been mentioned, but, since there were some compensating improvements, it is doubtful whether there was any marked decrease in efficiency on this score. The most vital factors were the need for repairs and congestion at the ports. Owing to the urgent need to keep all possible tonnage constantly employed during the war, small repairs and refits had been postponed. In addition, it had been necessary to use shipping for work for which it had not been intended, with natural resultant damage. It had sometimes been necessary to use inferior coal for bunkers. Many of the most skilled seamen and firemen had been withdrawn for naval work. There were complaints that damage had been caused to requisitioned ships by the use of unskilled labour in loading and discharging. Fayle reports that by February 1919 nearly 12 per cent of the available ocean-going tonnage was in the hands of the repairers, but that there was still a tendency to postpone repairs because of the high cost.

Possibly, however, the most serious cause of the drop in efficiency was the port congestion both at home and abroad. The main reasons for this were —

(1) The railways had been allowed to deteriorate and there was a shortage of rolling stock.

(2) Stocks of imported commodities were allowed to pile up in the warehouses at the ports, with the result that there was no room for new imports.

(3) As a result of the high freights for coasting trade as compared with railway charges, coasting traffic was almost stagnant and there was increased pressure on the railways. In August 1919, in an attempt to overcome this difficulty, the Government agreed to refund to merchants sending their goods coastwise the difference between railway and coasting rates.

(4) Hours of labour at British ports were reduced and, as a reaction after the war years, the efficiency of work had decreased. Also there were difficulties through labour troubles in many countries.

(5) The regulations of July 1919, which restricted the use for bunkers of any coal except that coming from South Wales and the Northumberland-Durham coalfields, caused serious delay. The Liverpool bunkering facilities, for example, were intended for coal brought by rail from the Cheshire, Lancashire and Yorkshire fields, and not for water-borne coal from the Bristol Channel. As a result the majority of ships for Liverpool either had to bunker abroad for the round trip, and so lose cargo space, or to lose time going to the Bristol Channel and waiting their turn at the crowded coal ports.

(6) There was also some bunkering abroad for the round trip on account of the threat of a strike of coal miners, dock labourers and transport workers.

The annual report of the Chamber of Shipping for 1919–20 estimated that these obstacles to quick turn-round had decreased the annual carrying capacity of the available shipping by 30-40 per cent as compared with 1913 : and this in spite of the fact that, according to Prof. D. H. Robertson, there was an increase in the imports per net ton per voyage since 1913 of 15 per cent in 1919 and 9 per cent in 1920.[1]

So far we have been discussing the available capacity of the shipping. The demand for shipping space must next be considered. At the end of the war the stocks of food and raw materials were very low in most European countries. The result was an urgent need for imports both for current consumption and to build up stocks to a normal level once more. The attempt to re-establish industries contracted during the war resulted in a demand for increased importation of their raw materials as compared with the war period. While, too, the demand for shipping space for the import of munitions ceased at the end of the war, ships were still needed for the repatriation of prisoners of war and troops from overseas. Moreover, there was a change in the distribution of shipping between different routes. Owing to the disturbed economic conditions of a large part of Europe, and, in particular, of Germany, Austria and Russia, and to the serious reduction in the output of the Northern neutrals because of the blockade, it was necessary to bring imports from more distant destinations than before the war. For example, Europe had to import coal from the United States because of the continued low level of output in the United Kingdom.

When all these factors are taken into consideration it is not surprising that the shipping position became stringent and that there was, at all events in the earlier part of 1919, an acute shortage of supply relatively to demand.

This situation was reflected in the state of the freight market. The partial index of shipping freights prepared by Dr. Isserlis, which stood at 87 in February 1919, had

[1] Cf. *Economic Fragments*, p. 119.

risen to 157 in August and September, relapsing to 126 in January 1920.[1] From that date there is available the Chamber of Shipping freight index. This, after an upward wobble, was in May 1920 at nearly the same level as in January ; so that, in a general way, the index stood much higher than in the post-Armistice Breathing Space.

These high freights — they were only available, of course, in the open market, while many freights were still controlled, — the recollection of war profits, the prospect of release from control, the general expectation of a world-wide boom in trade, the Chancellor of the Exchequer's announcement in May 1919 that the Excess Profits Duty would be reduced from 80 to 40 per cent, the natural desire to restore the United Kingdom's *share* of world shipping, which had dropped from 41·6% in June 1914 to 34·1% in June 1919,[2] all acted together to stimulate British ship-building. In spite of the enormously high costs of building at the end of 1919, nearly 3 million tons of merchant ships were under construction in British yards, 1 million more than in December 1913. The tonnage of merchant vessels of 100 tons gross and upwards launched in the United Kingdom in 1918, 1919 and 1920 were respectively 1,348,000, 1,620,000 and 2,040,000.[3] There was thus a substantial increase in the first, and an enormous increase in the second, peace year over the best accomplishment during the war itself. Since, according to the Z8 returns, the number of men employed in ship-building and marine engineering was slightly less — 433,000 against 435,000 — in July 1920 than in November 1918, this is, on the face of it, curious. The explanation presumably is that a large number of men, who at the Armistice were engaged in work on warships, presently became available for employment on merchant ships.

---

[1] Private Memorandum by Mr. Corlett.   [2] *Ibid.*
[3] Cf. Appendix, Section II, Table IV.

To anyone looking back on this period from the vantage-ground of a later time it is apparent that this Boom was being pushed forward in the face of a clear writing on the wall. Already, as we have seen, in June 1919, in spite of war losses, world tonnage was greater than in June 1914 by some 5 per cent, — largely, of course, as a consequence of American ship-building efforts. Everywhere facilities for building had been increased and were in use. More-over, the withdrawal of British ships from trade between foreign ports during the war had led to the development of foreign, particularly American and Japanese, services there, which it would not be easy to supplant. Yet again, world trade had been dislocated, and it was not reasonable to expect that, once the immediate requirements of de-mobilisation and re-stocking were satisfied, the trade needs for sea transport would reach their pre-war level for some considerable time. Nevertheless, not in England only, but all over the world, ship-building boomed. "By June 1920 the steel and iron steam and motor tonnage of the world was greater than in 1914 by 7 million tons, or 14·2 per cent."[1] British tonnage (of 100 tons gross and upwards), which in June 1919 was down to 16·3 million tons, had by that time recovered to 18·1 million tons, as against 18·9 millions in June 1914.[2] Between June 1920 and June 1921 world tonnage rose further from 47·8 to 53·9 million tons, and British tonnage from 18·1 to 19·3 millions, its peak level. World tonnage, it may be noted, continued to expand till 1923, when it reached 62·3 million tons.

The breaking of the Boom made itself manifest in shipping freights at about the same time as in general prices. From a maximum of 141 in March 1920 the freight index had fallen to 84 in August; by March 1921, a year after the maximum, it had crashed to 37, and in the last quarter of 1921 and throughout 1922 it stood in the region from 33

[1] Fayle, *The War and the Shipping Industry*, pp. 381-2.   [2] *Ibid.* p. 415.

to 27.[1] Thus the fall between March 1920 and March 1921 amounted to 74 per cent, and between March 1920 and December 1921 to 77 per cent. The corresponding contractions in the general index number of wholesale prices were 35 and 48 per cent. The large excess fall in freights as compared with other prices is in accord with what the considerations set out at the beginning of this chapter should have led us to expect.

In the first quarter of 1920, before freights had begun to fall, the tonnage of new ships *begun* in the United Kingdom was 708,000. In the second quarter it fell to 589,000 tons, in the third it was 594,000 and in the fourth 506,000 tons. Then a great fall began. In the four quarters of 1921 the figures were 393,000, 69,000, 51,000 and 55,000, and it was not till the last quarter of 1922 that they again topped 100,000.

Tonnage *launched* — this is not, of course, identical with tonnage completed — only fell substantially many months later than tonnage begun. In the second, third and fourth quarters of 1920 it was greater than in the first, and, though in the intermediate quarters it had been less, in the last quarter of 1921, when tonnage begun was very low indeed, it was actually larger than in the first quarter of 1920 ; — this in spite of the fact that between January 1921 and July 1921 the tonnage laid up in the principal ports of the United Kingdom had leapt up from 940,000 to 1,852,000 tons.[2]

In like manner tonnage *under construction*, a better measure of ship-building activity than either tonnage begun or tonnage launched, continued to expand for a year

---

[1] Cf. Appendix, Section III, Table VII. In February 1920 freights are said to have stood at 500 per cent above the level of July 1914, as against an excess of a little over 200 per cent in general wholesale prices (*Is Unemployment Inevitable ?*, p. 290).

[2] Fayle, p. 434. This high figure was no doubt largely due to the coal strike, but in January 1922 it still stood at 1,307,000.

after freights had started to fall, reaching its maximum
only at the beginning of the second quarter of 1921. This
long delay of effect behind cause is obviously due to the
fact that ships take a long time, maybe nine months or a
year for a fair-sized vessel, in building.

By 1922 the end of the Slump had made its full impact
on the industry. In that year some one-sixth of the world
shipping was laid up in the ports.[1] In the United Kingdom
the average quarterly launchings in 1922 were 263,000
tons, and in 1923, 162,000, as against 510,000 in 1920. If
we subtract from tonnage under construction tonnage
suspended (first recorded in June 1921) [2] in consequence of
cancellation of contracts or inability of owners to pay
instalments, the following figures for tonnage actually
being constructed emerge :

Date		Tons
1921	1st April	3,302,000
,,	1st July	2,795,000
,,	1st October	2,552,000
1922	1st January	1,918,000
,,	1st April	1,619,000
,,	1st July	1,439,000
,,	1st October	1,198,000
1923	1st January	1,121,000
,,	1st April	1,311,000
,,	1st July	1,208,000
,,	1st October	1,029,000
1924	1st January	1,231,000
,,	1st April	1,373,000
,,	1st July	1,465,000
,,	1st October	1,431,000

Thus there was a continuous decline from April 1921 till
January 1923, when the volume of tonnage actually under

---

[1] Cf. G. C. Allen, *British Industries*, First Edition, p. 153.
[2] Fayle, p. 425. Since at that date 497,000 tons under construction are recorded
as suspended, while no figure is given for tonnage suspended three months before,
at which date the under-construction figure was 90,000 tons less, it may be that the
true maximum was at the beginning of the *first* quarter of 1921.

construction had contracted by two-thirds. The arrest in the decline at this date coincided with what we have agreed to regard as the end of the Slump.

During the first stage of the Doldrums, throughout 1923, the figures, as the table in the Appendix [1] shows, moved irregularly ; they were wavering about at the bottom of a depression. By the beginning of 1924 a definite and continuous, though not very rapid, upward movement had begun. Nevertheless, neither within our period nor indeed ever until the new war started, was the British ship-building industry to attain again its pre-war scale. The main reason for this, no doubt, was the fact that the physical volume of world trade was substantially less than before the war — in consequence of the general dislocation of international economic relations for which the war had been responsible. Writing in 1933, Professor Allen paints this picture : " The additional capacity created during the war has been idle for the last ten years and the profits earned have been small. Throughout this period unemployment has never fallen much below 20 per cent of the labour force, although the number of insured workers has been reduced from 320,000 in July 1924 to 265,000 in July 1930. Real wages are lower than in pre-war days and ship-building can no longer be considered a high wage industry, as it was then. At present the outlook is gloomy." [2]

[1] Cf. *post*, Appendix, Section II, Table IV.
[2] Cf. G. C. Allen, *British Industries*, First Edition, p. 156.

CHAPTER III

CONTRASTS OF SHIP-BUILDING
AND HOUSE-BUILDING

I AM not able to attempt any adequate summary of the complicated history of house-building during our period. It stands, however, in such striking contrast with the history of ship-building, whereas *prima facie* the two might have been expected to be similar, that a brief comment on it seems to be called for.

With houses, as with ships, though for different reasons, there was at the end of the war a very great shortage. The shipping shortage, as we have seen, was largely due to the destruction of tonnage during the war and the difficulty of at once making effective use of the tonnage that remained. The housing shortage was due to the fact that during the war house-building had been almost entirely, and house maintenance to a large extent, suspended, while the population had continued to expand, and, with the falling birth rate, the number of families had grown in a still larger proportion. In 1919 returns from local authorities indicated a need for 400,000 houses, a figure which was raised shortly afterwards to 800,000. There was great hardship because a number of people, who would have liked to set up separate establishments as separate Census families (in the main private domestic households, including resident servants), were " obliged to live in the closest domestic contact with other persons from whom they desired to separate themselves ".[1] Some 300,000 or 400,000 Census families, which would have normally come into existence, were prevented by the shortage from doing so. While,

[1] *Housing Report of the 1931 Census*, pp. x and xx.

however, the shipping shortage led, as the last chapter showed, to an immediate and enormous boom in ship-building, the housing shortage had no such effect. It was not till the period in which we are interested was over that activity on a really large scale began. There are no estimates for houses under construction at different dates, but the following table shows the number of new houses completed in England and Wales (other than those built before October 1922 by private enterprise without State assistance) between 1st January 1919 and 31st March 1920, and thereafter in successive half-yearly periods : [1]

NEW HOUSES PROVIDED IN ENGLAND AND WALES UNDER
IMPROVEMENT AND RECONSTRUCTION SCHEMES, AND
HOUSES OVER £78 RATEABLE VALUE
(£105 IN GREATER LONDON)

Period	With State Assistance	Grand Total
1st January 1919 to 31st March 1920	715	
1st April 1920 to 30th September 1920	5,412	
1st October 1920 to 31st March 1921	23,137	210,237
1st April 1921 to 30th September 1921	44,808	
1st October 1921 to 31st March 1922	56,263	
1st April 1922 to 30th September 1922	49,902	
1st October 1922 to 31st March 1923	17,951	41,751
1st April 1923 to 30th September 1923	8,038	36,987
1st October 1923 to 31st March 1924	10,626	49,223
1st April 1924 to 30th September 1924	25,833	60,268
1st October 1924 to 31st March 1925	41,836	76,621
1st April 1925 to 30th September 1925	50,455	82,405

The facts are brought out very clearly in the following diagram reproduced from Mr. Connor's article : [2]

[1] Connor, " Urban Housing in England and Wales ", *Statistical Journal*, 1936, p. 8. For houses built by private enterprise without State assistance the number completed between 1st January 1919 and 31st March 1922 is estimated at 30,000 ; but no estimate is available for the distribution of this building over different parts of the period.

[2] In the diagram the total of 30,000 houses produced without State assistance between 1st January 1919 and 1st October 1922 are assumed to have been distributed evenly over the first six columns. The part of the diagram referring to the later years is not, of course, relevant to our discussion.

HOUSES PROVIDED IN ENGLAND AND WALES, 1920–35

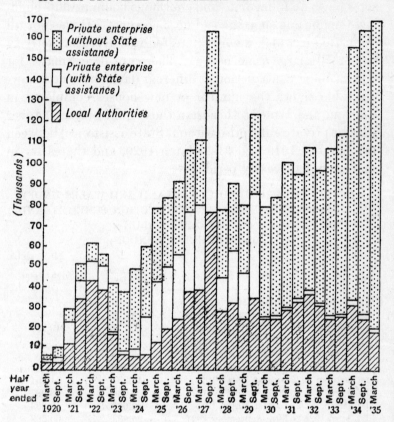

Thus it is apparent that house-building can have contributed very little to the activity of the Boom. Its expansion on a substantial scale was reserved for the Slump and the Doldrums, when it served in a small measure to offset, instead of, as with ship-building, to aggravate, depression in other industries.

Now nobody has ever pretended that this fortunate, so to speak anticyclical, order of events in building was the result of deliberate policy on the part of either the central or local authorities. If evidence to the contrary is needed,

we have only to note that in the spring of 1921, when the
Slump was very deep and unemployment was rapidly increasing, the Government, as a part of its economy drive,
cut down its original plan for 500,000 houses in three
years to 216,000, the number which by that time had been
finished, or were in course of construction, or for which
tenders had been approved.[1] Why, then, did the sequence
of events take the form it did ?

It has been suggested that an important part of the
explanation can be found in the fact that immediately
after the war building materials were abnormally expensive
— in consequence, as some say, of anti-social activity on
the part of " rings ". This explanation, however, does not
fit the facts. Calculations made by Mr. Rothbarth show
that down to the end of 1920 the rise in building materials
was less than the rise of materials in general. After that,
indeed till the end of the Slump, when all prices were falling,
the prices of building materials lagged behind materials in
general, and so were, in a sense, abnormally high. But this
was the very period in which building activity was substantially larger than it had been in the Boom year.[2]

A much more important obstacle on the supply side
to quick expansion was the serious shortage of building
labour, particularly of skilled labour, due to heavy war-
time withdrawals and lack of new entrants. One authority
writes : " Even after tenders had been approved it was
difficult to start actual building owing to a great shortage
of building labour. Only in 1924 did the Building Unions
relax their admission requirements in return for an undertaking on the part of the Government to continue building
subsidies for fifteen years." [3] Here there is a great contrast
between house-building and ship-building. Whereas at
the Armistice, according to the Z8 returns, the number of

---

[1] Memorandum privately prepared by Mr. Loveday, p. 27.
[2] Cf. Statistical Appendix, Section III, Table VI.
[3] Memorandum prepared by Mr. Loveday, p. 26.

men employed in ship-building and marine engineering, in consequence, of course, of urgent war needs, had risen to 435,000 from 289,000 in July 1914, in building the number had fallen from 920,000 to 438,000, and as late as July 1920 had still only recovered to 796,000.

In spite of this, however, there can, I think, be little doubt that the dominant influence which made the immediate post-war history of house-building so greatly different from that of ship-building operated from the demand side. Whereas expanded desire for new ships translated itself readily in the hands of monied men into correspondingly expanded demand, expanded desire for new houses, since the vast majority of them were needed by relatively poor wage-earners, could not do this. Recognising the wage-earners' difficulty in the matter of housing, the Government in 1915 had passed an Act which in a general way forbade the rents of existing working-class houses being raised above what they were in 1914. In 1919, in view of the all-round rise in prices, a 40 per cent increase in rents was allowed. Very soon, however, prices and wages had risen by much more than this above their pre-war level. Unless, therefore, people were prepared to hire new houses at much higher rents than those ruling for equivalent old ones, it would not pay to build them ; and naturally wage-earners were very unwilling, even if they were financially able, to pay for new houses substantially higher rents than those which were being paid for the main mass of already existing houses. The only way out was for the Government to intervene.

Before the war house-building was almost entirely carried on by private enterprise. Expenditure on housing by local authorities, whether out of rates or by way of loan, in 1913–14 was only £1·27 millions, and there was no expenditure at all by the central authority.[1] Thus the

---

[1] Sykes, *British Public Expenditure*, p. 33.

situation after the war was a new one and action was not
rapid.   It was not till eight months after the Armistice
that an emergency Housing, Town-planning, etc. Act was
passed.   This Act required local authorities to conduct
surveys of their districts and prepare and carry out housing
schemes for working-class needs, so far as they were not
likely to be met in other ways.[1]   All and any deficits
arising out of this in excess of a 1d. rate were to be charged
to the Treasury.   At the end of 1919 another Act was passed
extending the subsidy system to private builders.   Eight
months later, in March 1920, only half of the local authorities had submitted satisfactory plans.[2]   As the table on
p. 89 shows, no appreciable amount of building can have
begun under these Acts till well on in 1920.   By the spring
of 1921, however, a fair number of new houses were coming
forward ;   in spite of a general Slump, building was
expanding.

But the cost to the Treasury was considerable.   Confronted with slump conditions, the Government reacted
with a campaign for economy.   The Treasury grant for
housing was cut down from a quasi-limitless figure to
£200,000 per annum — to be devoted for preference to
slum clearance ;   so that the programme of assisted construction was much reduced.   In consequence the aggregate
rate of building again declined, though building by private
enterprise without State assistance was increasing.   The
Doldrums thus began with a low level of building activity.
But, with the rapidly growing number of private families,
the housing shortage was now causing serious anxiety.   In
1923 a new Act, the Chamberlain Act, was passed, the
principal feature of which was the provision of a national
subsidy of £6 a year for twenty years on houses of specified
types and sizes, whether built by local authorities or by

[1] Connor, *Statistical Journal*, 1936, p. 4.
[2] Sykes, *British Public Expenditure*, p. 34.

private enterprise.[1] At the same time, as a result of lowered wages (following a dispute in 1923), an agreement by the Building Unions to accept some degree of dilution and reduced costs of materials, building costs fell. A definite and strong up-swing began. In 1924 the advent of a new Government and criticism of the adequacy of past policy led to the passing of yet another Housing Act, designed to promote the building of houses to be let rather than sold. " This provided for a much larger national subsidy of £9 for forty years, with a special subsidy of £12 : 10s. for houses erected in agricultural parishes. The response to this generous and more widespread offer was large ; and the more so as by then building costs had materially declined." [2] The really large building Boom, however, occurred in 1926 and 1927, after our period had closed.

[1] Connor, *Statistical Journal*, 1936, p. 34.
[2] Cf. Sykes, *British Public Expenditure*, p. 35.

CHAPTER IV

COTTON EXPORTS

The cotton industry illustrates aspects of post-war history quite different from those brought up in our studies of ship-building and house-building. Before the war it supplied, broadly speaking, the whole of our domestic needs ; " but for the absorption of at least three-fourths of its production it was dependent upon its export markets ".[1] Hence for our present purpose the interest of the cotton industry is focussed upon its activity for exports, and this chapter will be concerned only with that.

Before the war cotton exports were the most important among the exports of the United Kingdom. In 1913 the value of exports of cotton piece goods was £97·8 millions out of total exports of United Kingdom produce of £525 millions. Exports of yarn amounted to a further £15 millions. The following tables, given by Daniels,[2] show approximately the variations of the exports of the different kinds of cotton piece goods and of yarn, by quantity and value, for the war and post-war years, as a percentage of the 1913 figures.[3]

The lines in these tables most important for our purposes are, of course, those giving aggregate quantities, particularly the one in the piece goods table. In what follows, attention will be confined to piece goods, no further reference being made to yarn, which is comparatively unimportant.

---

[1] *Is Unemployment Inevitable ?*, chapter by Daniels, p. 306.

[2] G. W. Daniels, London and Cambridge Economic Service, Special Memorandum, No. 8.

[3] The trade statistics were given in square yards from 1920, but after 1921 the linear yardage was also given, to enable comparison to be made with previous years. It is linear yardage which has been used in making these comparisons. Since the average width of cloth exported increased, particularly in exports to South America, this is not a completely satisfactory basis.

EXPORTS OF COTTON PIECE GOODS
(In millions of linear yards and £ thousands)

Description		1913	1914	1915	1916	1917	1918	1919	1920	1921	1922	1923	1924
Grey	Q.	2,357	86	70	57	48	32	36	39	38	61	51	60
unbleached	£	27,408	84	64	65	78	90	128	191	101	132	116	146
White	Q.	2,045	82	74	90	84	59	53	71	48	65	63	69
bleached	£	27,054	78	68	99	124	152	180	327	143	145	134	154
Printed	Q.	1,230	76	56	76	79	66	56	85	42	52	60	58
	£	16,744	76	58	96	130	164	193	392	160	136	146	146
Dyed in	Q.	1,151	76	61	81	80	65	64	90	44	64	71	74
the piece	£	21,759	81	70	110	139	173	243	422	160	168	170	154
Coloured	Q.	290	72	69	74	77	65	61	89	46	60	79	62
cottons	£	4,817	74	74	93	126	160	205	400	182	157	183	153
Total	Q.	7,075	81	67	74	70	52	50	65	43	61	61	65
piece goods	£	97,776	81	66	91	115	142	182	323	140	146	142	157
Average price per yard	..	3·32d.	100	99	119	164	271	367	496	326	239	234	239

EXPORTS OF COTTON YARN
(In millions of lbs. and £ thousands)

		1913	1914	1915	1916	1917	1918	1919	1920	1921	1922	1923	1924
Yarn	Q.	210	85	90	82	63	48	77	70	69	96	69	78
	£	15,006	79	69	89	111	143	226	317	159	176	140	185
Average price per lb.	..	17·14d.	93	76	109	176	294	292	453	230	184	203	239

It should be noted that the heavy fall recorded in the post-war period is in some measure illusory ; because, as a partial offset to reduction in quantity, there was some improvement in quality. Daniels and Jewkes, in a paper before the Manchester Statistical Society in 1927, estimate that, when allowance is made for this, the average export of piece goods in 1922–4 should be put at 72 per cent of the 1913 quantity, instead of at the 62 per cent which is shown when change in quality is ignored. Part of this change in quality was due to the fact that exports fell off more in markets which had been taking cheaper cloth than in those mainly interested in the finer types. Obviously, however, when full allowance has been made for quality changes, the broad effect of the figures in our table is only mildly mitigated.

To interpret the significance of this post-war history it is necessary to consider separately the different principal markets in which our cotton exports are sold ; for they were not all affected by the same influences. The most important group of markets are in the Far East — India, China and the Dutch East Indies, India holding easily first place. In 1913, of our total exports of cotton piece goods measured in linear yards, 43 per cent went to India, 10 per cent to China, 4 per cent to the Dutch East Indies, making 57 per cent to the Far East as a whole. The two next important groups of markets are in the Near East, comprising Egypt and Turkey, which in 1913 took respectively 3 and 5 per cent of our piece goods exports, and South America, which took 9 per cent. The remaining principal markets, the Dominions, Europe and Africa, took round about 5 per cent each.

The post-war collapse in the Indian market was very serious. For quantities in linear yards of cotton piece goods, with the 1913 figure written as 100, we find for British exports to India, according to the Annual Statement of Trade of the United Kingdom :

1919	1920	1921	1922	1923	1924	1925
25	42–43	34	43	44	51	44

Three main factors were responsible for this development: decreased consumption in India, increased home production there, and increased importation from countries other than Great Britain. The decrease, as against 1913, in consumption was presumably due to war-induced poverty, though it should be noted that consumption in 1913 was at an abnormal level, some 17 per cent more than the average of 1910–14. Home production, which was already expanding before 1913, was stimulated by the difficulty of obtaining imports during the war. The following table prepared by Mr. Corlett shows for fiscal years (April to March) Indian mill production, total imports, imports from the United Kingdom, and net balance available for consumption after allowing for exports and re-exports. A final column is added for British exports to India per calendar year, as given in the Annual Statement of the Trade of the United Kingdom. The table makes no allowance for the production in India by hand-looms. An estimate by Daniels and Jewkes puts this for the average of 1910–14 at 1056 million yards and for 1922–6 at 1226 million yards annually.

COTTON PIECE GOODS
(Millions of linear yards)

Year (Fiscal years April–March)	Indian Mill Production	Total Imports	Imports from United Kingdom	Net Balance available for Consumption after allowing for Exports and Re-exports	United Kingdom Exports to India (3 months earlier)
1913–14	1164	3197	3104	4210	3057·4
1918–19	1451	1122	867	2310	935·4
1919–20	1640	1081	976	2435	767·8
1920–21	1581	1510	1292	2883	(1300)*
1921–22	1732	1090	955	2587	1038·6
1922–23	1725	1593	1453	3087	1307·6
1923–24	1700	1486	1319	2960	1337·0
1924–25	1970	1823	1614	3557	1553·2

* A rough estimate since the statistics for this year were only given in *square* yards.

Comparing columns 3 and 4 of this table, we find that in no single post-war fiscal year did the fall of Indian imports from Great Britain exceed the aggregate fall of Indian imports by more than 125 million yards ; and in none would the contraction of imports from Britain have been as much as a tenth less than it was, even if there had been no substitution of imports from other countries for British imports. It is thus apparent that the *main* cause of our loss of trade to India was contraction in Indian consumption

and growth in Indian production — not the ousting of our
exports by foreign competition. That cannot at the most
have been responsible for more than a very small proportion
of the total decline.

Nevertheless, competition, mainly competition from
Japan, had considerable significance, more especially as a
prelude of things to come. The following table, taken
from the *Review of the Trade of India*, shows the share of
the United Kingdom and Japan in the imports of cotton
piece goods into India and gives separate figures for the
main types :

Year	Total		Grey		White		Coloured	
	U.K.	Japan	U.K.	Japan	U.K.	Japan	U.K.	Japan
1913–14	97·1	0·3	98·8	0·5	98·5	..	92·6	0·2
1918–19	77·3	21·2	64·3	35·4	95·9	3·7	88·5	9·1
1919–20	90·3	7·0	87·1	11·8	96·6	0·9	89·9	5·0
1920–21	85·6	11·3	72·4	25·9	96·9	0·9	91·8	3·3
1921–22	87·6	8·3	82·8	13·1	97·8	0·6	88·0	3·6
1922–23	91·2	6·8	89·5	9·6	98·2	0·6	86·9	6·3
1923–24	88·8	8·2	85·2	13·7	97·0	0·6	87·4	6·7
1924–25	88·5	8·5	86·0	13·0	97·1	0·8	83·1	10·0

The " Total " column in this table shows the proportion
of the trade in cotton piece goods for India that was lost
to Japan. The other columns show that the loss was not
general to all types of cotton goods, but had been particularly heavy for grey goods. In whites the Japanese trade
still continued very small. The grey class, however, had
been the most important in the Indian imports before the
war ; for in 1913–14 the imports of greys were 1534 million
yards out of the total of 3197 millions. It still remained
the most important in the years after the war. Thus in
1919–20 imports of greys were 533 million yards out of a
total of 1081 ; in 1922–3 they were 931 millions out of 1593.

The success of the Japanese in the post-war period was

due partly to the fact that during the course of the war, when exports from this country were severely handicapped, they had succeeded in establishing business connections. In 1918–19 the imports of cotton piece goods from Japan were well over one-fifth of the total imports into India. For greys the imports from Japan were 35·4 per cent of the total.   As can be seen from the table above, there was a tendency to return to the old source of supply in the prosperous year 1919–20, but some of the ground regained then was lost again in the following year.   A second reason was the post-war poverty of India and, in particular, the unfavourable terms of trade, with which she, like other mainly agricultural countries, was confronted.   This made it difficult for her to pay for high-quality British cotton goods, so that lower grade Japanese goods took their place. A third reason is the fact that in the Japanese industry a large proportion, perhaps 50 per cent, of the raw cotton used was Indian grown, whereas this country, of course, depended almost entirely on American and Egyptian cotton.   In 1913–14 the price per pound of Indian No. 1 fine cotton was 5·62 pence, 77 per cent of the price of American Middling ; in the post-war period it was somewhat smaller, only a little over 70 per cent.   This, for what it was worth, made things easier for the Japanese.   The great scale on which their cotton industry expanded is shown by the fact that, whereas in 1913 they had 24,224 looms (already more than double what they had in 1907), in 1918 they had 40,391 ; in 1920, 50,588 ; in 1922, 60,765 ; and in 1924, 64,225.   It must be remembered further that in Japan, after the war, working hours were twenty-two a day in two shifts, so that their machinery, when compared with that of Europe, was equivalent to more than double the figure shown.

In China, to which, as we have seen, some 10 per cent of our total exports of cotton piece goods went before the

war, the course of our post-war trade is shown in the
following table of indices :

1913	1919	1920	1921	1922	1923	1924	1925
100	42	67–8	32	47	36	45	27

The same sort of decline as we saw in India is visible
here ; in the first few years it was not quite so serious, but
in the last three it had become worse. The causes, however,
were in part different. The factory industry in China,
though absolutely small, showed a very great proportionate
increase in size during the war and early post-war years,
the number of looms increasing between 1915 and 1923
from 4564 to 22,477. Daniels and Jewkes, in the paper
already cited, estimated the mill production of cloth to be
27 million pounds in the post-war period, as against 10
million before the war. For the same period they estimated that the hand-loom production in China had risen
from 570 million pounds to 870 million pounds. This kind
of production seems to have been greatly stimulated when
the price of imported piece goods rose, because the population were too poor to pay the higher prices. The increase
in consumption as a whole was substantially less than that
of home production. Nevertheless, Daniels and Jewkes
estimate that, after allowing for imports and exports, it
had risen from 887 million pounds to 1162 millions — a
development very different from that of India. As with
all statistics used for China, partly on account of the
difficulty of estimating hand-loom production and partly
because of the imports via Hong-Kong, the figures must
be treated with great caution. It seems, however, that, far
from decreased consumption having been a cause of lost
trade in China, consumption actually increased by something like 275 million pounds.

The estimate made by Daniels and Jewkes of the excess

of imports over exports was 307 million pounds in the pre-war period and 265 million pounds after the war — a drop of 42 million pounds, or about 14 per cent. This is very much less than the drop in exports of cotton piece goods to China from the United Kingdom, and can have had little to do with it. Competition from rival sellers, particularly Japanese competition, was the main factor at work. The following table shows the percentage share of the United Kingdom and Japan in the imports of China reckoned by weight :

Exporter	1912	1913	1921	1922	1923	1924
United Kingdom	55	50	27	32	28	30
Japan . .	18	23	57	54	59	58

Thus the United Kingdom had lost its predominant position in the Chinese market, and that place had been occupied by Japan. The main reason was once again that the inhabitants could only afford to buy the cheaper Japanese goods. Mr. Barnard Ellinger, in a paper before the Manchester Statistical Society on 12th January 1927, held that the Japanese advantage lay, not so much in their closeness to the market, as in the fact that they concentrated on the mass production of one type of article.

The other main Far Eastern market was the Dutch East Indies, to which 304·9 million yards had been exported from the United Kingdom in 1913. The comparative figures for the post-war years, as percentages of 1913, were as follows :

1919	1920	1921	1922	1923	1924	1925
41	80	62	52	53	53	75

There is once again the same tendency to fall off, but it is not as bad as in the other two Far Eastern markets. Before the war the imports into the Netherlands East

Indies had been shared almost equally by Great Britain and the Netherlands. There had been negligible imports from Japan. After the war Great Britain had gained slightly on the Netherlands, but the imports from Japan had risen to about 20 per cent of the total.

The Near East markets comprise in the main Egypt and Turkey. Our exports to Egypt in 1913 were 266·6 million yards, and to Turkey they were 360·7. The following table shows the post-war percentages :

Importer	1919	1920	1921	1922	1923	1924	1925
Egypt	69	126	94	89	92	86	105
Turkey	92	84	62	68	72	64	75

Although there was a decrease in this region, the post-war situation was not nearly as bad as in the Far East. Our exports to Egypt had remained on practically the pre-war level, and, while those to Turkey had declined rather more, they were still fairly high. In this area the main source of increased competition had been Italy. The percentage of imports into Egypt of cotton piece goods from Italy had been about 6 per cent before the war and had risen to about 20 per cent by 1923–5. Most of the rise took place in the early 'twenties. The reason is to be found in the disturbed state of the market and also in the greater cheapness of cloth from Italy.

The other main area for our piece goods exports was South America, to which 672·9 million yards were sent in 1913, 199·1 millions of these going to the Argentine. The post-war percentages, as against 1913, for the Argentine and for the whole area, were as follows :

Importer	1919	1920	1921	1922	1923	1924	1925
Argentine	54	89	57	80	96	82	87
South America	42	78	53	101	82	80	83

Thus, except in 1921, our exports to this area kept up fairly well after the war. In the Argentine, where there was very little production, the main source of imports before the war had been the United Kingdom, which had supplied about half of the total, and Italy, which had supplied about a quarter. These proportions were almost maintained after the war, but imports from the United States had increased to about 15 per cent from under 1 per cent. A large part of that gain was lost in 1923 and 1924. Imports from Japan also increased slightly. Similar conditions prevailed in the other South American markets.

Little need be said of the other main groups of markets. The following table shows our exports to them in million linear yards in 1913 and the percentages of the 1913 quantities which were exported in the post-war years :

Importer	1913	1919	1920	1921	1922	1923	1924	1925
Dominions .	393·2	39	74	53	101	82	80	83
Europe .	369·7	200	102	46	149	89	120	139
Africa .	333·2	..	81	53	71	80	82	105
U.S.A. .	44·4	92	234·6	126	217	389	355	197

Thus our exports to Europe after the war were larger than before, but this was partly due to the export of some grey goods to be finished there. The African markets suffered through the reduction of the relative export prices of some of the main African products, causing the purchasing power of the inhabitants to be reduced. The most striking feature of the table is the increase in our exports to the United States, in spite of tariff increases. The total quantity was not large in relation to our total exports of piece goods, but what were sent to the United States were mainly goods of high quality. The purchasing power of the inhabitants being high, they were able to afford this class of goods and so to buy more from Great Britain.

It remains to summarise with a somewhat closer dating

the movement of our exports of cotton piece goods in the aggregate. During the war these had inevitably been much contracted ; at its close it would have been natural to expect an immediate improvement. In fact, however, in the early part of 1919 depression deepened. This was attributed by some writers to cable delays with Eastern markets causing contracts to be lost. But there was probably a more important cause at work. Purchasers were hopeful that the high prices then ruling would fall and that, if they held off the market a little longer, they would get the advantage of that fall. On later happenings the following table throws light. It gives, by quarter years, the quantities of exports of cotton piece goods in millions of linear yards for 1919 and millions of square yards for the later years.[1]

Quarter	1919	1920	1921	1922
I	647·6	1123·9	726·0	894·9
II	830·4	1272·9	485·0	955·9
III	885·1	1143·9	655·3	1217·4
IV	1160·6	894·7	1035·9	1115·5
Year	3523·7	4435·4	2902·2	4183·7

These figures show that, after the first quarter of 1919, during the year of Boom, April 1919–April 1920, there was a strong expansion, though aggregate exports of cotton goods were still very much less than in 1913. During the Slump there was a heavy fall, beginning in the third quarter of 1920 and covering the second quarter of 1921. For 1921 as a whole the table on p. 96 shows exports as less than half what they were in 1913. From the third quarter of 1921 over the next stage of the Slump there was a recovery.

[1] The approximate rate of conversion from linear to square yards is 1 square yard = 1·04 linear yards. Thus the total for 1921 in linear yards was 3018, and for 1922 was 4351.

H

This was maintained and continued in the Doldrums, so that exports in 1924 were as good as in 1920. In no completed year throughout our period did they attain to as much as two-thirds, or, allowing for changes in quality, say three-quarters, of their pre-war volume.

PART IV

GOVERNMENT INTERVENTION IN INDUSTRY

CHAPTER I

THE RISE AND FALL OF INDUSTRIAL CONTROLS

I

THE fundamental purpose of the Government's war-time controls in the munition industry, textiles, shipping, food and so on was a positive one ; namely, to secure to itself for use in the war effort great quantities of specialised services and goods. It is true, of course, that, when there is an abnormal demand for anything — and the Government was naturally in a position to force up demand indefinitely — this fact of itself always tends to stimulate people to direct their efforts to producing things to meet the expanded demand rather than other things. But the reaction is usually a slow one ; and during the war the essential requirement was speed. The Government was concerned to surmount at once by direct attack obstacles which in the ordinary course could only be turned by a slow and gradual movement. The need for direct attack was, of course, intensified in industries where the Government itself, by artificially keeping down prices, removed what would normally have been the main stimulus to private initiative. To achieve its fundamental purpose, therefore, it had to *act*.

Its action was of a double character, partly positive, partly negative. On the positive side it directly conscripted men, commandeered certain species of property, compelled farmers to plough up arable land, bought the whole of the

Australian, and afterwards of the English, wool clip ; and so on. On the negative side it forbade its citizens to use in their private service, except under licence, or after prior Government claims had been satisfied, certain sorts of things. For example, nobody might redecorate his house on an extensive scale without permission from the Board of Trade, and, under the food rationing scheme, nobody might eat more than a specified quantity of certain sorts of food. The negative side of the State's action was, it is true, mainly directed to securing an orderly distribution among the civil population of what the Government left over for them, rather than to enabling the total so left over to be kept down with a view to expanding the share available for the war effort. Plainly, however, if there had not been an orderly distribution of food, for example, among civilians, or of iron and steel among civilian industries, the total amount provided for them would have had to be substantially larger than it was on pain of serious damage to morale. Thus the positive purpose envisaged by the State was helped forward in some measure by its negative, as well as by its positive, action. The following brief history of war-time developments, within the sphere of what I shall call " industrial controls ", bears out and illustrates these general statements.

II

The industrial section of war-time controls — industrial controls — falls into three main spheres, corresponding to the main buying departments of the war machine. First, there were the controls operated by the War Office over the various commodities covered by army supplies (other than munitions). Textiles and leather came within this category and also certain foodstuffs and medical supplies.[1] Secondly,

---

[1] The frontier between the Ministry of Munitions and the War Office in its control over army supplies was not always clearly defined. But, broadly speaking,

there were the controls operated by the Ministry of Munitions, chiefly affecting the iron and steel and non-ferrous metal industries, engineering and aircraft, chemicals and explosives. Thirdly, there was the control over shipbuilding and naval accessories and munitions, which remained within the province of the Admiralty. These industrial controls are the subject matter of this chapter. The control of meat, fats, dairy produce and grain, which came under the Ministry of Food and the fortunes of which have been fully discussed by Sir William Beveridge in his *British Food Control*, will not be considered here ; nor will the control of imports through allocation of shipping tonnage operated by the Board of Trade (after 1916 by the Ministry of Shipping), the growth and decline of which Mr. Fayle has described in *The War and the Shipping Industry* ; nor yet the coal control, or the international controls operated since 1917 through the allied programme committees under the Allied Maritime Transport Council.

The growth of war-time industrial controls falls into several clearly marked stages. At the outbreak of war the Government had taken three important measures. It had come to the assistance of banks and discount houses by guaranteeing approved commercial bills payable by enemy and other insolvent debtors ; it had taken over control of the railways in return for a guarantee to the companies of their pre-war dividends ; and it had made the purchase and import of sugar a Government monopoly. Presently it requisitioned certain scarce supplies of key materials for munitions manufacture or prohibited their export, for example, the constituents of T.N.T. ; and in December 1914 it imposed an obligation on all distillers to recover from benzine or naphtha all toluene in excess of 3 per cent. But for some time these measures stood alone. For

it corresponded to the division between the requirements of the Master-General of the Ordnance and those of the Quartermaster-General. (Cf. E. M. H. Lloyd, *Experiments in State Control*, p. 24.)

industry and trade in general the watchword was " business as usual ". The War Office continued the practice of competitive tendering to supply its requirements ; and prices were left to find their own level, supposedly guarded by the magic of business competition. Twelve months after the outbreak of war a Cabinet Minister was outlining the view that the consumer was sufficiently protected against high prices by competition among producers, so that price controls were otiose ; and even in 1916 a Departmental Committee argued that a system of export licences was undesirable because " methods of private trade were better adapted than a Government scheme to avoid financial loss ".

But by the spring of 1915 it had become clear that the pressure of demand was such as to make a competitive market essentially a " sellers' market ", in which buying departments were faced with serious shortages of supplies and a tendency for prices to rise steeply. Competitive tendering not only involved delay in the allocation of contracts, but in an indirect way it often enhanced the rise in price of materials by encouraging forward-buying on the part of all the firms submitting tenders. In turn, the uncertainty concerning raw material prices made impossible any firm basis for contract prices. Moreover, there was much complaint, especially in the armaments trade, about inadequate use of the industrial capacity available. The Contracts Department of the War Office was inclined to deal exclusively with the larger firms, with which it had had connections in peace-time and which were familiar with War Office requirements. Orders that these firms could not themselves fulfil were sub-contracted to smaller firms, with which they had business connections ; and the main contractors were naturally jealous of their leading position in the trade. Complaints arose from smaller firms, unfamiliar with munitions work but eager to adapt themselves to it, that they could not get orders and that they were even being drained of labour for transfer to armament firms whose equipment was already loaded to capacity. Rivalry between different buying Departments (*e.g.* between the War Office and the Admiralty in shell contracts) tended to strengthen the upward pressure on prices and to add to the prevailing chaos in sub-contracting, with consequent delays in delivery, that in certain directions assumed alarming proportions. Prices quoted for armaments contracts were subsequently found to have been extraordinarily high in relation to costs ; and grave bottlenecks in productive capacity, especially in shell-filling, threatened to dislocate the whole military programme. To ease the situation, the method of collective agreements as to supply and price with associations or groups of firms was adopted. One of the earliest examples of this was the agreement entered into by the War Office with the Wholesale Clothiers' Association for the supply of uniforms at an all-round flat rate for manufacture ; the War Office purchasing and supplying cloth to the trade at fixed issue prices. This was followed in the boot industry by negotiations with the United Tanners' Federation to secure a reduction in the price of leather supplied for army contracts. About the same time, in agreement with the Dundee jute trade, the price of jute for sandbags was fixed at a figure considerably below the market price. On 9th June 1915 a new Department, the Ministry of Munitions, was set up to take over from the War Office the duty of munitions supply to the army. One of its first acts was to arrange for the placing of munitions contracts with local Boards of Management, acting on behalf of groups of local firms in their district.[1] At the same time the Ministry instituted a number of national factories to meet the excess demand for

---

[1] This was supplementary to, and not a substitute for, the contracts traditionally placed direct with the large armament firms. Actually the groundwork of the

shells. To safeguard supplies of non-ferrous metals, and, in particular, to prevent them from passing to the enemy, a system of voluntary control was at first exercised through the committee of the London Metal Exchange.

This elementary stage of control, representing, as it did, little more than the substitution of collective agreements between the Government and business associations for competitive tendering and individual contracting, fairly soon proved insufficient. A good example of this insufficiency is provided by the negotiations with the Brass-Makers' Association in the autumn of 1915 to secure a reduction in price of supplies to ordnance factories, the prevailing price being deemed excessive. The brass-makers were supplying, not only Government factories direct, but also armament firms ; and, since the latter were willing to pay the higher prices, the Association was able to resist the Government proposal for a reduction. A transition accordingly had to be made to a higher stage of control, which consisted of compulsory price-fixing on the basis (so far as circumstances allowed) of costing estimates of the manufacturing process by the buying Departments. Once started for final products, price-fixing inevitably travelled back to intermediate and primary products. This control of price was usually associated with Government control of dealings by licence ; dealing at no more than the given price being made a condition of licence. Already in the autumn of 1915 the Ministry of Munitions was successfully controlling the price of certain metals in this way ; first of shell steel, and then later, by extension, of all classes of steel. In December 1915 the first of the non-ferrous metals controls was introduced in the shape of regulations governing the price and the destination of all aluminium supplies.

local organisation had been laid by the Armaments Output Committee, instituted by the War Office at the end of March, but then subordinated to Mr. Lloyd George's Munitions of War Committee, the immediate precursor of the Ministry of Munitions, whose creation as a Department of State was announced on 26th May.

A yet further stage was reached when Government Departments undertook the bulk purchase or requisition of raw materials, and allocated these to manufacturers at fixed prices, with compulsory fixed margins for processing or making-up. In June 1916 the War Office decided to requisition the domestic wool clip and to supply it to the trade at fixed prices through authorised merchants acting as commission agents ; and in the following year the War Office purchased the whole of the Australasian wool clip and prohibited all private dealings in wool. In addition, the output of mills was requisitioned and paid for at prices built up from the fixed raw material prices by adding a series of margins, assessed on the basis of costing estimates ; so that in the end the manufacturer was virtually working for the Government on a commission basis. In 1916 the War Office, in face of a shortage of flax, similarly prohibited private dealings in Russian flax, requisitioned unsold stocks in dealers' hands, and proceeded to import Russian flax through firms specially appointed to be Government buying agents inside Russia. In allocating raw material to the fine linen industry in Belfast and Scotland, special committees acting under the Flax Control Board carried out a rationing policy by a system of licences, manufacture being prohibited except by licence. The Ministry of Munitions, having fixed metal prices at the end of 1915, found itself confronted with the consequential task of allocating steel supplies between competing users by means of a priority system. The system of requisitioning all visible stocks of a commodity was adopted as early as July 1915 for glycerine, and soon after for dormant printers' metal, to relieve the shortage of lead. Responsibility was undertaken by the Government for buying all the acetone needed by trade makers of explosives for the 1916 programme, on condition that private firms refrained from entering the market on their own account. All by-products of the gas,

coke, soap and dye industries were purchased in advance
for the duration of the war, as was also the whole of the
British output of non-ferrous metals. In January 1917 the
Ministry of Munitions took over all stocks of copper and
became the sole importer. At first no statutory authority
existed for requisitioning the productive capacity of a firm
to divert it from work on private orders to work on Government orders. But, voluntary methods having proved
" insufficiently effective ", powers were obtained to requisition any firm's output and to fix the price at which it
should be sold.[1] Regulation 30A of DORA empowered
the Ministry of Munitions, by order, to forbid the purchase
or sale of material except by licence, to require returns to
be made of all stocks held by private firms, and to impose
conditions of sale and of price ; while Regulation 30B
gave powers to prohibit speculative dealings in commodities. Finally, in February 1918 the Non-ferrous
Metals Industry Act made it necessary for anyone engaged,
not only in dealing in, but in smelting or refining, any
non-ferrous metals, to be licensed by the Board of Trade.
Moreover, by the end of the war the Ministry of Munitions
directly controlled some two hundred and fifty national
factories, in addition to the twenty-thousand-odd " controlled establishments ", covering in all some two million
workers, over which the Ministry exercised indirect control.

By the end of the war the industrial controls were
fairly extensive. " No one could start a new business or
enlarge an old one except for war purposes ; everyone was
liable to have buildings, plant or machinery requisitioned
for more urgent work ; while none of the industrial metals
and few raw materials . . . could be used without a licence
from one Government department or another." [2] The
State owned an appreciable part of the ordinary shares
of some private companies and nominated directors to the

[1] Memorandum on War Office Contracts, 1917, Cmd. 8447.
[2] *History of Ministry of Munitions*, vol. vii, Part I, p. 2.

Boards of a few. It had subsidised investment in plant and buildings, and in the case of iron and steel it subsidised current production itself. In certain instances it owned and operated factories direct. The War Office purchased the wool clip, allocated it to firms through recognised merchants operating on a commission basis, and controlled the price at every stage of manufacture. Even so, by the end of the war " control of material and industry was only just getting to the stage reached by Germany when the war began ".[1] The controls which had developed had often been introduced some considerable time after the need for action had appeared. The general attitude was one of reluctance to depart from normal business practices ; and control, when it came, came generally under pressure of an urgent situation and assumed the patchwork shape of a series of *ad hoc* improvisations. The verdict of an official historian is that " State control was slow in its development and unscientific in its application. It was never extended until the necessity for it became clamant." [2]

III

So soon as the Armistice was signed the Government's need of services and things was enormously contracted. The fundamental positive purpose, which had underlain the whole system of war-time control, disappeared. In theory it was then open to the Government to hold on to its dominating position and switch over the resources of the country to some new fundamental purpose — some tremendous five-year plan of social reconstruction. In practice, however, there was never any question of the Government continuing to control industry in order to secure services and goods for itself. If it was to maintain its dominating position, it would have had to be for a

[1] *Ibid.* p. 2.   [2] *Ibid.* p. 1

different purpose, namely, to regulate in a manner that
it deemed appropriate the operation and distribution of
resources for the separate, as distinguished from the joint,
services of its citizens.

Now, that it might be for the general interest that
Government should intervene on these lines in some fields
had been generally recognised long before the war. For
some services would not be performed effectively, or would
not be performed at all, *e.g.* the working of lighthouses, if
left to private enterprise. But to what extent and in what
fields Government action was desirable had been a matter
of keen controversy. The experience of the war had
relevance here in two respects. On the one hand, it brought
out the importance of maintaining at home certain sorts of
production to ensure that, in the event of a new war,
enemy action should not deprive us of essential means of
defence. Hence the claim for protection to key industries
and for large subsidies to home-grown sugar. These
claims won wide assent, and the Government did step in to
regulate the distribution of resources, not indeed directly,
but through the machinery of tax and bounty. Secondly,
war experience showed that in certain fields Government
action could promote operational efficiency. A good
example is the management of railways. During the war
these had, practically speaking, been worked as a single
concern under Government supervision with a view to
securing priority for military requirements. Before the
war the economies to be looked for from this kind of unifica-
tion could only be guessed at. Afterwards, in spite of the
peculiar character of war traffic with its immense train-
loads of munitions and troops, there were available some
guiding facts. Some authorities held that these facts
pointed clearly towards a unified State railway system.
It may be, indeed, that they concentrated attention unduly
upon immediate results ; taking too little account of the

deadening effect which such a system might, in the long run, produce upon railway enterprise and development. That is a matter for debate. The practical outcome was a characteristic British compromise. Under the Railways Act of August 1921 the railways of the country were compulsorily amalgamated into four main groups, and the Railway Rates Tribunal was established to control their charges ; but there was no nationalisation.

For a broad view, however, these are secondary matters. Upon the theory, long dominant in this country, that in the main the operation and allocation of productive resources are best left to private enterprise, the experience of the war could throw little light. As regards operation, when it was urged on the one side that Government Departments during the war had frequently been guilty of incompetence and unconscionable delays, it could be answered that in the rush and hurry of the time this was inevitable and gave no ground for distrusting Government Departments in peace. When, on the other side, it was urged that in certain spheres, e.g. in the production of shells, Government factories had shown themselves much more competent and economical than private concerns, it could be retorted that capacity for producing munitions of a uniform type in enormous and ever-expanding demand for a single customer was no evidence of capacity for the quite different task of normal peace-time production. As regards allocation, the relevance of war-time experience was still more dubious. For the allocation of resources to different uses in war there is a definite schedule to which to work. Food and munitions and the support of the Armed Forces must take precedence over everything else ; and, though, as the rivalry between the demands of munitions and ships for steel made plain, it is difficult, still it is not impossible, by conferences between representatives of the various Ministries, to work out a fairly satisfactory scheme of priorities. The reason for this is that everything is subordinated to a single relatively simple end. Under a régime of established peace there is no single end of this kind. We have no longer to deal with the Government's wants for war service, but with the wants of an immense and varied population for necessaries, comforts and luxuries. In war-time it is obviously more important to bring steel into the country than it is to bring bananas, and to manufacture army baking ovens than private kitchen ranges. But in peace-time none of these simple propositions can be laid down. Those things ought to be made which are most wanted and their proportion ought to be so adjusted that, given people's relative incomes, they will yield in combination the greatest sum of satisfaction. But the Government has no yard-stick with which to decide what these things are or what are their appropriate proportions ; and, even if it could decide what they are at one moment, before its decision had been put into effect, conditions would very probably be changed and they would have become something entirely different. The task of peace being thus quite other than the task of war, what was accomplished in war gives no guidance for peace.

Thus the broad issue of the part proper for Government to play in the operation and allocation of resources in normal times stood after the war much as it did before. But this broad issue was not the one at stake when the war came to an end. That was something much narrower and more practical. Should the Government divest itself of its war-time industrial functions immediately — as the phrase went, " at the earliest practicable moment " — or should it adopt a more cautious policy, keeping the organs of control in hand, or at least in reserve, over what might prove a not inconsiderable period of readjustment to peace-time conditions ?

On this matter the main drift of opinion among persons

in authority in the United Kingdom, as also in the United States of America, was not in doubt. A major concern was to conserve raw materials for peace-time production; and any continuance of Government enterprise was treated with suspicion as likely to divert materials from private firms that were striving to regain their pre-war markets. Continued Government enterprise, or Government orders, and continued Government control over supplies were, of course, distinct things. But the two were inevitably associated in men's minds; the latter was regarded as a handmaid to the former; and the conclusion was drawn that restoration of trade to its normal channels would be best promoted by rapid release of raw materials from restrictions and by allowing prices to find their " natural level ". What applied to sales of raw materials applied *a fortiori* to the output and sale of finished manufactures. Only in a few cases, where shortage looked like being so acute as to threaten an unbearable inflation of costs if prices were immediately freed, was business opinion anxious for the continuance of control. This, for example, was the reason for the decision of the Wool Council in November 1918 to recommend the prolongation of the control of wool until the following spring or summer; and it was only after the chairman of the Wool Council had announced, a few months later, that " the danger of short supply " had now been " definitely put behind us " [1] that raw wool was decontrolled in April 1919, and the London wool auctions reopened. Similarly, the leather trade had hoped that Government purchases in the United States of America and Canada would relieve the anticipated shortage of upper-leather in the first half of 1919, and that in the meantime prices would continue to be controlled. But the attempt in November to set up an international Leather and Hides Executive was frustrated (as were other attempts

[1] *Board of Trade Journal*, 28th November 1918, 30th January 1919.

at continued inter-allied control of raw materials) by the refusal of the United States of America to participate. Thereafter as late as June 1919 the Tanners' Federation and the Boot Manufacturers' Federation were pressing for a continuation of control of cattle and horse hides until the end of September.[1] Again, control was retained for a time over sales of platinum, in view of the cessation of Russian supplies, and over some acids and fertilisers, pyrites and phosphate rock. But these were exceptions.

In the great majority of instances, while Labour pressed for a continuance of control, trade interests were " almost unanimously in favour of the re-establishment of private dealings with the least possible delay ". Thus, five days after the Armistice, the *Economist* wrote : " The vital factor in procuring abundance of productive employment is not raw materials but freedom ; the first requisite of industry is the restoration of freedom " (16th November 1918). Again in February : "As soon as the merchant gets his hands free, we shall see trade begin to revive, but until the Government controls are taken off, he is tied hand and foot. . . . The world, starved of goods for four years, is capable of exerting a demand which will fully employ our working classes on productive work at good wages for a long time to come " (1st February 1919). The policy desired of Government was thus summarised in the Final Report of the Committee on Commercial and Industrial Policy after the War. Policy " should be so framed as to keep within the narrowest possible limits the restrictive measures which it may be necessary to continue, and should be directed towards the restoration of normal industrial conditions within the shortest possible time. . . . We entirely concur in the opinion expressed by the Trade Committees that State control of, and restrictions upon, industries will be found to be detrimental under normal

[1] *Board of Trade Journal*, 6th February 1919, 19th June 1919.

conditions, and we strongly urge that they should be removed so soon as possible after the conclusion of peace . . . the early restoration of unrestricted dealings in the markets of our country and the world at competitive prices is essential to the re-establishment of British industry and commerce on a sound basis." The Committee had, indeed, made certain specific reservations. Continued control of scarce tonnage might be necessary for a time " to secure the country adequate supplies of foodstuffs and raw materials for industry and their fair distribution ". " In addition, where supplies of raw material are not likely to be available on a sufficient scale to meet all internal demands, some arrangement for joint purchase and apportionment will be required." " Similarly, in view of the extent to which renewals and repairs to machinery will be needed, it may be desirable at the outset to regulate the execution of orders by means of a system of priority certificates." But these reservations were essentially reservations, subordinated to a broad policy of quite different type.

The Government found itself fully in agreement with that policy. Four days before the Armistice, Mr. Churchill assured a gathering of representative employers : " I am very anxious for you to realise that, although it will undoubtedly be necessary for the Government of this country to intervene in industry and to control and regulate aspects of industry . . . our only object is to liberate the forces of industrial enterprise, to release the controls which have been found galling, to divest ourselves of responsibilities which the State has only accepted in this perilous emergency, and from which, in the overwhelming majority of cases, it had far better keep itself clear ".[1] Similarly, a few days before the Armistice, the Standing Council appointed by the Cabinet Committee on Post-War Priority to survey stocks of leading raw materials were said to be

---

[1] Cit. Report of War Cabinet for 1918.

giving " urgent consideration to the question of releasing such materials from any form of control at the earliest possible moment ". Immediately after the Armistice Dr. Addison announced to the House of Commons that the Government proposed " to release iron and steel forthwith ", and to ensure the import of " as large a quantity of foreign ore as was imported prior to the war ". As regards other metals, there appeared to be sufficient supplies to make it possible " to release some from control now, and nearly all the rest we hope to release within six months ".[1] At the same time it was officially announced that, pending decontrol, manufacturers were at liberty, subject to the existing Priority of Work Order, to make immediate use of any iron or steel or non-ferrous metal in their possession, and to accept private orders for manufacture subject to existing regulations as to price. All restrictions on the purchase or manufacture of machine tools were removed in the course of November. Control orders limiting the manufacture of wire rope, forgings and castings, motor and aero engines, were withdrawn ; and on 25th November stocks of non-ferrous metals were released for general industrial purposes without special priority permits. After 23rd December iron and steel could be ordered and supplied without priority classification, although exports were still subject to licence owing to the blockade, and special priority was retained for urgent national and allied requirements. Industrial alcohol and glycerine were also released in December, and Control orders for shellac, benzol, naphtha, tar, acetic acid and chlorine were suspended. Just before Christmas Mr. Churchill was able to announce that, " save in a few exceptional cases, all priority classifications for the execution of contracts for Government Departments had been abolished. Ordinary civil orders may now be placed and executed without priority permits

[1] *Board of Trade Journal*, 7th November 1918, 14th November 1918.

or certificates." He promised that the large stocks of non-ferrous metals in the hands of the Government would be " put on the market at prices which we believe will have a direct effect in encouraging trade ", and expressed the belief that " there ought to be a period of great activity following this transitional period, and everyone should look forward to the future in the spirit of hope and confidence, for by that process they will more or less stimulate the revival which they desire ".[1]

As a general rule, materials were released from control earlier than finished products, and controls over metals, which were in the province of the Ministry of Munitions, were terminated sooner than controls over things like wool, cotton, jute and leather, which were administered by the War Office. The shortage of these materials was greater in the winter months of 1918–19 ; and Government orders came to an end more slowly than with munitions. But even here control was seldom prolonged beyond a period of six months. For manufactured goods all priority permits and certificates ceased to be operative on 1st March 1919, and the Priority Department of the Ministry of Munitions was closed on 16th April. Among other restrictions that were suspended in the course of March were those on the sale and delivery of building bricks and on the manufacture of small tools.

The prices of iron and steel at the Armistice were abnormally low (about £10 per ton below cost) owing to the operation of subsidies. These subsidies had been given to iron ore, pig-iron, limestone, etc., to enable products to be contracted for over a period and to obviate frequent revisions of contract prices as wages, etc., rose. To enable the trade to adjust itself gradually to " economic prices ", it was decided to continue the subsidies for a short period and to remove them in two stages : steel subsidies at the

[1] *Ibid.* 26th December 1918.

end of January 1919, and pig-iron subsidies at the end of April. " By these measures," said Mr. Churchill, " the steel and iron trades have been steadied and have gained confidence." [1] While dealings in iron and steel were released from control forthwith, maximum prices for iron and steel were continued, pending the removal of the subsidies. A proposal was made that, to avoid a scramble for steel at low prices, the Government should for the time being place orders for standard articles with steel-works up to their full capacity ; but this was rejected on the ground that it would hinder steel-works from accepting commercial orders. Instead, it was left to the trade itself to organise an equitable distribution of pig-iron and steel among buyers. The tinplate and galvanised sheet trades arranged among themselves an agreed price for the home market and for export, but otherwise were freed from control, Government priority only being insisted on for such part of their output as was still considered necessary for home and allied needs. [2]

Of the 250 national factories existing at the Armistice, nearly all were transferred to private ownership, either reverting to their pre-war owners or being put up for sale. The Committee on Demobilisation and Reconstruction had recommended that 20 of them should be retained permanently as Government munition factories, and another 25, which it classified as not suitable for ordinary industrial purposes, for temporary use as Government stores. Of the remainder, it was suggested that 115 should revert to their original owners, and 85 were classified as suitable for disposal to private firms as industrial concerns. In January 1919 the Cabinet decided that the Ministry of Munitions should proceed with the sale of these 85, giving preference in the sale of them to co-operative societies and local

---

[1] *Board of Trade Journal*, 26th December 1918.
[2] *History of the Ministry of Munitions*, vol. vii, Part I, chap. v ; *Board of Trade Journal*, 14th November 1918, 5th December 1918, 26th December 1918, 6th March 1919.

authorities. Labour representatives had pressed for their retention as national factories for peace-time production in order to reduce unemployment. But the advocates of de-nationalisation argued that, "if firms were threatened with Government competition, . . . they would be discouraged and the recovery of industry would be checked ", whereas, if they were used on products that did not compete with private enterprise, each factory would need to be employed on an uneconomic variety of articles, since things of which the State was the sole buyer were purchased by the State in too small quantities to keep a highly specialised factory fully employed.[1] The Labour Co-partnership Association and the Co-operative Productive Federation advanced proposals for operating the factories on a profit-sharing basis ; and the Ministry of Munitions decided to make the Ailsa Craig National Projectile Factory available for an experiment along these lines. The Government declined, however, to advance capital to finance the experiment, and the proposal lapsed owing to the difficulty of raising capital in other ways. Of the sites retained as Government stores, one of the largest, at Slough, was maintained as a repair depot for Government cars and lorries until April 1920, when it was sold to a private syndicate.

Thus, in broad summary, the industrial controls developed during the Great War of 1914–18 in the early days of renewed peace died and were buried. In part because control in war-time had developed as a series of improvisations to meet particular circumstances of emergency, the assumption that, with the passing of these circumstances, these improvisations would lose their rationale went practically unchallenged. Because controls had been the creature of departmental needs and departmental autonomy in war-time, departmental interests were left to determine

[1] Cf. *History of the Ministry of Munitions*, vol. vii, Part I, chap. v.

their fate when the war had come to an end. In so far as sectional views were guided by any general policy, it was by a negative policy — the instruction to liquidate war-time encumbrances with the least delay.

IV

To argue in detail about what would have happened if the death and burial of particular controls had been held up for a while in a cannier wait-and-see temper would be idle. But one broad conclusion can hardly be resisted. With a less impetuous abandonment of them the Government would have had the power,— though not necessarily the will — to enforce some evening-out of industrial activity during the three years that followed the Armistice, and so might have rendered the distresses of the great post-war depression less serious than they were.

CHAPTER II

PRICE RESTRICTION

BEFORE the 1914 war it was a general rule that prices should be left for settlement by the play of the market. There were, indeed, exceptions in respect of public utility concerns in a position to exercise monopoly power, *e.g.* railways and gas companies; also in certain instances where market imperfections put private purchasers at a special disadvantage, *e.g.* with cabs plying for hire. But the main trend of practice was plain. In contrast to this, during the course of the war a very large number of prices were regulated, or subjected to legal maxima. This was done both for goods sold to Government and for goods sold to private persons. Moreover, the range of regulation tended to expand; for it was soon seen that, if the price of a raw material or preliminary service was restricted and that of the finished article into which this material or service entered not restricted, the only result was to benefit intermediary manufacturers or dealers without doing any good to the final buyers. Nobody has ever doubted that, in principle, a wide use of authoritative price restriction was in the general interest.

Clearly, however, it was necessary, in deciding what price maxima to impose, for the authorities to guard against the risk of driving away supplies — except, of course, for commodities the consumption and manufacture of which they deliberately intended to discourage. Thus price maxima had to be fixed with careful regard to costs. In particular it would have been futile to fix for imports maxima appreciably below the prices ruling in the country of origin plus cost of transport. Hence, when it was desired to keep the price of an article to the public, or, indeed, to the Government, below cost and yet not to drive it off the market, the State was compelled to supplement its restrictive rule by the grant of a subsidy. Such subsidies were paid on wheat flour so as to enable the price of bread to be kept low, and on iron and steel to maintain price stability.

The most obvious purpose of price restriction was to prevent fortunately-situated sellers, when aggregate supplies were short, from making outrageous profits. So far as sales to the Government were concerned, to pay market prices to sellers and then to mulct them of 100 per cent Excess Profits Duty would have had much the same effect as to fix prices by authority at a level that prevented excess profits from coming into existence. But with sales to private persons the latter method alone was practicable ; the former would have left the poorer classes of buyers in an intolerable position. There was also a second ground for price restriction, which applied equally whether or not the restriction had to be associated with a subsidy. For, besides serving as a means to prevent profiteering by fortunately-situated persons, it also indirectly served to check demands for wage increases, which in war-time, when no labour can be allowed to stand idle, must, if granted, lead to a rise in prices, which in turn induces further demands for wage increases ; and so on in a continuing spiral. Even when, to keep down prices in the first instance, subsidies have to be paid and the funds for them raised by creations of bank money as large as would have been required to finance the first up-swing of wages had the price rise not been prevented, the secondary cumulative up-swing of wages and prices that constitute the spiral may be prevented, and inflation of income held in check.

After the war there was a general movement towards abolishing price restrictions as soon as practicable, along with the controls with which many of them were associated.

It is difficult to discover the exact dates at which the various price restrictions were removed. The following examples, which do not include munition materials, have been extracted for me from various issues of the *Board of Trade Journal*:

1919

January 11th	Tobacco
March 24th	Tea
March 31st	Imported and home-grown timber other than pitwood
April 1st	Cakes and meals (except linseed and cotton)
April 30th	Paper
May 1st	Bones
May 7th	Motor spirit and lamp oil (maximum retail prices), petroleum products (wholesale prices)
May 8th	Silver bullion
June 1st	Chocolates and other sweetmeats
August 1st	Glass
September 11th	Caerphilly cheese
September 25th	Swedes
October 13th	Vegetables (other than imported onions)
November 13th	Stilton and Wensleydale cheese

1920

January 8th	Pitwood
February 1st	Milk
	Canned condensed milk
March 1st	British native cattle hides
March 3rd	Home-grown pigs and pork
March 8th	Imported grain, flour and meal (importers' prices)
April 5th	Home-produced bacon, ham and lard
June 3rd	Coal
July 19th	Bacon and ham
August 2nd	Dried fruits
August 31st	Jam
September 23rd	Resumed Control of imported bacon, ham and lard *reimposed*
October 17th	Bread and flour (retail prices)

1921

January 3rd	Eggs
February 3rd	Home-grown wheat (wholesale prices)
February 10th	Pure lard
February 28th	Sugar
March 31st	Butter

In August 1919 a Profiteering Act was passed, which made it an offence punishable by fine or imprisonment to make, on selling any article, " a profit which is, in view of all the circumstances, unreasonable ".[1] During the eighteen months of the existence of this Act the 1800 profiteering committees set up by it accomplished practically nothing ; 202 prosecutions resulted in fines and costs amounting to £2241. As Sir William Beveridge observes, the Act was not business, as the controls had been, but window dressing.

In conditions of strong and effective competition, the withdrawal of price maxima need not lead to a fall in supplies, if the maxima have been judiciously arranged, nor yet to a rise in prices. It may even have the opposite effect ; for, when a maximum price is imposed by law, it tends to be regarded by sellers as a minimum also. Thus, when in May 1920 the Government abolished retail price maxima for bread, " competition between grocers and bakers was relied on to protect the consumer and did so. According to an official memorandum prepared in June 1920, the removal of flour and bread price control in April benefited consumers, the current price of bread being lower than it would have been possible for the Food Controller to fix by order as a maximum price." [2]

The war, however, had brought together into close association the producers of a number of commodities in a

---

[1] Cf. Beveridge, *British Food Control*, p. 288.

[2] *Ibid.* p. 300. " Retail prices of bread and flour were controlled again from 25th August to 16th October 1920, but only as a temporary expedient to prevent the increase of prices due to the abolition of the subsidy being made too soon " (*ibid.*).

way that tended to promote informal price agreements
among them. In these circumstances the removal of price
restrictions might well lead to the exercise of monopoly
power in a form threatening diminished output and augmented prices to the detriment of purchasers. It has been
alleged that this happened with certain materials used in
building; but I have not been able to investigate that
charge.[1]

The removal of price restrictions did not carry with it
the disappearance of subsidies. Thus the subsidy on wheat
flour was maintained for two years after the Armistice, for
fear lest its sudden withdrawal should lead to a sharp rise
in the price of bread. It was abolished in November 1920
after the harvest, when wheat prices were declining.

The problem presented by subsidies left standing at
the end of a war, which it is not desired to continue into
peace, is well illustrated in the iron and steel industry.
During the war, when the State was the ultimate user of
most of the steel produced, and when a rise of prices must
have led, under the sliding-scale system to an upward
movement of wages, and under the cost-plus-percentage-
profit system to a similar movement of profits, to stabilise
iron and steel prices was obviously in the general interest.
To this end a system of subsidies was introduced to offset
increases in production costs, of which some were real
" war " costs (*e.g.* high freights on imported ore), while
others were due to the fact that the policy of price stabilisa-
tion was not universal. By the end of the war the cumulative amount of the subsidy on heavy steel — such as ship
plates — was approximately £5 a ton, which was over 40
per cent of the price; and of this over one-quarter represented subsidies to cover increases in wages and in the

---

[1] It is an easy exercise in economic analysis to show that in conditions of rising
supply price (diminishing returns) the imposition of an effective maximum price
limit is likely to reduce output under conditions of competition, but to increase it
under monopoly. (Cf. my article in *Economic Journal*, December 1918.)

price of coal. After the Armistice the National Federation of Iron and Steel Manufacturers wished the subsidies to be continued for fear that a sudden rise in prices should check demand and decrease employment " at a critical moment ", and further increase wage costs. A Committee of the Ministry, on the other hand, advised that subsidies should be dropped at once to prevent economic development being affected by " artificial prices ", and to enable public expenditure to be reduced. The course actually followed was a compromise. It was decided that the fixing of maximum prices should be continued till June 1919, that the direct subsidy on steel should be removed at the end of January, and the subsidy on pig-iron (which was an indirect subsidy on steel) at the end of April, subject to the proviso that, if costs had not fallen by that date, the question might be reopened. Export prices were fixed, the prices being specific, not merely maxima, to cover prices plus subsidy, with a view to meeting American objections to subsidised competition and allaying the suspicions of some Allies that others might get special advantages.

It was seen that to delay the raising of prices and then to raise them in two jumps " might result in two evils — an unfair distribution among consumers during the period of subsidies, and the undue accumulation of stocks by those who had the means of storing material ". In order to cope with the former difficulty a Committee of the industry, composed of one representative of the makers in each area, was set up, with area committees representing both the iron- and steel-makers and the consumers. These bodies were to consider complaints of unfair distribution and advise the Minister of Munitions; but no record of what they did has come to hand. As regards the latter difficulty, an order was issued forbidding anyone to increase stocks by more than 100 tons above a datum line (viz. the stocks held by him in October 1915 or October 1918, whichever were higher) without a permit from the Minister, the permit to be given readily, but on condition that a sum equal to the subsidy was paid by the stockholder to the Government. This must have been a difficult policy to implement, but again no report about it has been found.

The Official History suggests that the price policy adopted had the effect of encouraging a quick placing of orders for peace-time products. It may be that this was so, but it was certainly not a matter of much significance. Demand for steel was high in relation to supply at this time ; for the scope for investment in capital goods to make up for the wastage of war was very obvious. The Continental industries were suffering either from the destruction of their works in the war or the dismemberment of their firms by the peace ; and the difficulties to be encountered by them in returning to a peace economy were very great. In such conditions rising prices would normally be found in a free market, and, once control was removed, the steel-makers, who had at first argued that it was desirable to keep prices down, were quickly successful in raising them to levels not touched before or since. Had there been no general inflation and had steel prices not been under such strong pressure, the delaying policy might have proved to be a sound means of readjustment, preventing prices from being raised to cover the remnants of transitory increases of cost due to war contingencies, *e.g.* high costs of imported ore, which were bound to disappear quickly though not immediately. The State's policy as regards subsidies was not, however, part of an effective integrated price policy, and it is doubtful whether on balance it was beneficial. It did, indeed, delay the inflationary effect of increases in steel prices operating through the sliding-scale system of wage adjustments. But in April, when prices did rise, the upward movement of wages, now once again fully hitched to the pre-war scale, was *pro tanto* larger.

It has to be added that, after peace had been restored, *new* subsidies were introduced. The Sugar Commission deliberately sold below cost, making a large loss. " When the war ended the fear of industrial unrest filled the minds of the Government ; the consumer was placated by receiving sugar, meat, bacon and cheese below cost. Here an argument against State trading comes at last to light. The officials could and would have conducted State trading at a profit after the war, as during it, but were overruled. The wartime courage of political leaders dependent on popular support declined in peace, and perhaps must always do so."[1] The post-war housing subsidies, discussed in Part III, Chapter III, were on a different footing from the others.

[1] Beveridge, *British Food Control*, pp. 331-2.

RATIONING OF CONSUMERS[1]

DURING the course of the war the supply of many articles in common use and in inelastic demand became very short. If nothing had been done by the Government, demand would have been adjusted to the short supply through a great rise in prices. This would have meant that better-to-do people would have substantially maintained their previous consumption, while poor people were unable to satisfy elementary needs. State action to limit prices unaccompanied by anything else would have broken the equilibrium between demand and supply, but it would not have secured fairness in distribution. At the restricted prices more would have been asked for than was available, with the result that the sharing-out would have been determined by favouritism, pull, accident or capacity to stand for long periods, without fainting, in queues. That would have been an intolerable arrangement. Consequently the State restricted by law the amount of the most important commodities in short supply that any individual was allowed to purchase. The idea was in this way to reduce the total quantity demanded, account being taken of the fact that some people would buy less than their permitted ration, so that it equalled the amount which, at the regulated price, was being supplied.

In order for this to be achieved the permitted rations had to be *small enough*. If they were not, some people would find that they could not get the ration, or such part of it as they wanted to get ; and distribution would still

---

[1] For a discussion of rationing in general cf. my *Political Economy of War,* 1940 edition, chap. xi.

be governed in part by luck and pull. Obviously the scale of ration that *is* small enough depends, given the scheme of various people's demands and the supply conditions, upon the size of the maximum price that is established. The higher this price is, the larger the ration that people can be allowed ; till, in the limit, when the maximum price reaches the price that would be charged if there were no price regulation and no rations, the ration allowed may be infinite, *i.e.* no rationing is needed.

Given that the ration scale established is small enough in relation to the controlled maximum price, the market will be exactly cleared, and there will be no question of queues or anything of that kind. Thus the establishment of an effective maximum price below the price which would rule in the absence of State interference, accompanied by an " appropriate " system of rationing, will enable anybody who does not want to buy more than his ration to buy what he does want ; while people who, at the established price, want to buy more than their ration will be prevented from doing this and will be tied exactly to their ration. As compared with what would have happened if the maximum price had been established unaccompanied by rationing we have thus orderly arrangement instead of chaos in distribution. As compared with what would have happened if there had been neither price limitation nor rationing, poorer people, encouraged by the lower price, buy more of the rationed goods than they could have done otherwise, while better-to-do people, restrained by the rationing, buy less. In the conditions of war-time it is unlikely that output will differ appreciably when price is controlled to stop exploitation from what it would have been otherwise. Therefore the whole effect, apart from stopping exploitation, of establishing price control plus an appropriate ration scale is to secure that poorer people obtain at the expense of richer people a larger share of the commodities in short supply than they would do otherwise. Moreover — a very important matter — this circumstance frees the Government from the need of securing an enlarged production or importation of a number of important commodities in short supply. It could not, for political reasons, avoid doing this if the alternative were to deprive poor people of those commodities almost entirely ; and that would be the alternative if prices were not controlled and rationing not imposed.

It is not difficult to see that in a *perfect market* a level of ration for any article could be chosen which would so reduce demand that, in the only sort of supply conditions which are of interest to us here, price would fall of its own motion, without any control, to any desired level within reason. Thus, if the Government wished the price to stand at such-and-such a level, it could bring this about by establishing an appropriate scale of ration without also controlling price : and, if it acted in this way, no question of queues and so on could possibly arise. *Prima facie,* therefore, it seems that, once a policy of rationing had been decided on, there was no point in maintaining a policy of price control also. Rationing having made price control unnecessary, price control is a fifth wheel in the coach. The answer to this is, of course, that in actual life — particularly the actual life of war-time — we have not to do with perfect markets, and that, therefore, if there were no price control, exploitation by particular fortunately-situated sellers might still take place. Hence price control is not in fact superfluous. None the less, rationing is more essential and of deeper significance.

During the war rationing to consumers — as distinguished from priorities to firms — was mainly concerned with staple articles of food, though from 1917 it also affected coal. Experience of it abundantly proved that in an atmosphere of good-will the many and various technical

K

difficulties involved could be successfully overcome. The detailed history of the complex and highly successful administrative work accomplished in this matter by the Ministry of Food has been fully set out by Sir William Beveridge in his book *British Food Control*.

During the first few months of peace the rationing of tea, jam and margarine was abolished, and in May 1919 the issue of ration books was discontinued, such rationing as remained after that time being operated without coupons. The de-rationing of meat, which had been planned for June 1919, had to be postponed on account of shortage in supplies ; and, as a general safeguard, during August and September " the whole population of Britain was once again recorded and required to register with the appropriate retailers for butcher's meat, butter and sugar ".[1] Meat rationing was soon found to be unnecessary, since people did not purchase up to their ration limits, and was abolished in December 1919. Butter rationing ended in May 1920, and sugar rationing, the last to go, in the following November. Throughout the immediate post-war period State policy had been directed to getting rid of all kinds of rationing at the earliest practicable moment.

[1] *British Food Control*, p. 297.

CHAPTER IV

FOREIGN TRADE POLICY

THIS country entered the war in 1914 as a Free Trade country. Nor, when the war ended, was there any suggestion on the part of the politicians then in power that a fundamental change in fiscal policy should be made. Foreign trade was to be left, as it had been before the war, to the unhampered discretion of private traders. Thus by 1st September 1919 the main body of the import restrictions, which had perforce been imposed during the war, were removed by the issue of a general licence for free import, except for a limited list of key products ; and restrictions on trade with enemy countries generally were relaxed.[1] But the experience of the war and the highly disturbed conditions prevailing throughout the world during the early days of peace led to our *laisser-faire* policy being modified in certain secondary respects.

First, the difficult position of would-be customers in a number of impoverished countries, their need for long credits, and uncertainty on the part of British exporters about their ultimate ability to pay, seriously impeded the revival of our export trade. The Government tried to smooth over these difficulties. What was done is described in the Report of the Balfour Committee, in their volume on *Factors in Industrial and Commercial Efficiency*, as follows : " In order to assist in promoting employment in this country, and originally with the concomitant object of helping in the economic restoration of certain States in Central and South-Eastern Europe, State schemes for export credits were initiated in 1919, and the Overseas Trade (Credits and Insurance) Act 1920 was passed to

---

[1] Dearle, *An Economic Chronicle of the Great War*, p. 282.

provide the required statutory authority. Under the first
scheme the Board of Trade could make advances, up to an
amount outstanding at any time of £26 millions, in respect
of goods wholly or partly produced or manufactured in the
United Kingdom and exported to the countries referred to.
This scheme, not having been much used, was amended in
1921 : instead of making advances it was decided to adopt
the method of guaranteeing bills drawn by traders in
respect of exports to the countries (now including the
British Empire) covered by the scheme. Later in 1921 the
scheme was further widened to cover all countries, except,
for the time being, British India, Ceylon, the Straits Settle-
ments and the Far East (where there were large unabsorbed
stocks), and Russia ; and in 1925 it was opened to all
these countries except Russia in respect of machinery and
similar goods, for which long-term credits may be required.
. . . Under the old advances scheme, advances were made
amounting to £1,752,150. Under the old guarantee
scheme, between 1921 and 30th June 1926, 2806 sanctions
for guarantees, to the value of £29,814,724, were given.
The guarantees actually used by exporters amounted only
to £6,140,852, the number of new bills guaranteed being
8899. In consequence of renewals, the Department
guaranteed, in all, bills to the amount of £19,261,875." [1]
Thus very little came out of all this. After an enquiry by a
Committee, a new and supposedly improved scheme was
introduced in 1926.

Secondly, as mentioned above, when a general licence
for free importation was given in September 1919, certain
commodities were excluded. Towards the end of the year,
however, Mr. Justice Sankey delivered a judgment which
declared prohibition of imports by departmental authority
to be illegal. In 1920 an Act was passed forbidding the
importation of dye-stuffs into this country except under

[1] *Factors in Industrial and Commercial Efficiency*, pp. 391-3.

licence, and in 1921 the Safeguarding of Industries Act was passed, designed to provide similar protection for other key products. Under this Act (1st October 1921) an import duty of 33⅓ per cent *ad valorem* was imposed for a period of five years on the importation of a number of listed " key " articles. Of these articles some, " such as synthetic dye-stuffs and drugs, gauges, scientific glass-ware, tungsten and hosiery latch needles ", had been found to be essential in large quantities for the purposes of war. Others were articles the manufacture of which did not, as a rule, employ a large number of hands and which did not have a large value of output, but which were an essential requisite of some other and considerable industry — as dyes for the textile industry, optical glass for photographic and scientific work, or magnetos for motor cars. Protection for some of these articles was defended, not only on the ground that the articles were key articles, but also on the ground that the industry making them was an infant industry, which, if artificially supported for a few years, would prove well suited to the country and capable of prospering without assistance. Infant industries, however, are notoriously unwilling to shed their swaddling clothes.

Thirdly, in the currency chaos following the war, it was feared that countries whose currencies were depreciated would, because of that, be able to sell here at abnormally low sterling prices, prices which they could not possibly maintain permanently, but which might, nevertheless, seriously disorganise our industries. There would, no doubt, be a temporary gain to British consumers, but, on account of the damage done to our productive powers, they too would suffer in the long run. On these grounds, protection against " exchange dumping " was strongly advocated. Part II of the Safeguarding of Industries Act 1921 provided that a duty of 33⅓ per cent *ad valorem* might be imposed on goods imported from a foreign country

whose currency was depreciated more than 33 per cent,
when, owing to the depreciation, goods were being offered
for sale within the United Kingdom at low prices, and
when, in consequence, employment in a British industry
was, or was likely to be, seriously affected : provided that
production of similar goods in the United Kingdom was
being carried on with reasonable efficiency and economy,
and that other industries using these goods as materials
would not be too hardly hit by duties imposed upon them.
No duty was imposed under this clause of the Act except
on goods coming from Germany.   For these, by order of the
Board of Trade, 33⅓ per cent *ad valorem* was charged in
August 1922 on fabric gloves, glove fabric, domestic and
illuminating glassware and domestic hollow ware ; and in
October on gas mantles and parts thereof.   The provision
of the Act relating to these duties expired in August 1924.
Evidently its practical significance had been very small.
Unfortunately, moreover, the principle underlying it was
thoroughly confused.   The ability of a foreign country to
sell here at abnormally low sterling prices does not depend
on the relation between the present and the pre-war value
of its money in terms of sterling, but on the relation between
the present value of its money in terms of sterling and the
present level of its domestic prices.   If a pound became
worth twice as many marks, while at the same time mark
prices in Germany became twice as high, Germany's competitive position here would not be strengthened at all ;
if mark prices became more than twice as high, in spite
of the fall in the exchange, it would be weakened.   This
elementary truth was not apparently appreciated by those
who framed the clause of the Safeguarding of Industries
Act that dealt with imports from countries with depreciated
exchanges.[1]

---

[1] This blunder was carried to its logical conclusion in the New Zealand Customs
Amendment Act 1921. By this Act a special duty was imposed at the rate of 2½ per

Fourthly, under this same Safeguarding of Industries Act it was sought to make provision against imports, which, in the disturbed post-war period, might be dumped here below cost of production, and so, again, while tempor arily benefiting consumers, might disorganise and cause lasting damage to British industries. " Cost of Production means the current sterling equivalent of 95 per cent of the wholesale price at the works charged for goods of the class or description for consumption in the country of manufacture, subject to the deduction of the amount of any excise or other similar internal duty leviable in that country and included in the price " (Clause 8). On goods imported for sale at less than cost of production in this sense a duty of $33\frac{1}{3}$ per cent might be imposed, subject to the same provisos as those described above in respect of goods imported from countries with depreciated currencies. A League of Nations document prepared by Professor Tredelberg for the Geneva Economic Conference of 1927 concludes its account of this British enterprise with the following words : " In spite of the care with which this law is framed, no case is yet known in which the Board of Trade has made use of its power to levy a dumping duty ".[1]

Much more important in practice than all these, as we might say, fancy arrangements, were the McKenna duties on imported motor cars (and certain other associated articles). These duties, at $33\frac{1}{3}$ per cent, were imposed in 1915, not for protective purposes, but in order to maintain the foreign exchange and to cut down expenditure on luxuries. But they were renewed annually during the next eight years, despite the ending of the war. No corresponding excise duties were imposed. After the war

cent when the importing country's exchange was between 10 and 20 per cent below the pre-war par, and one of 5 per cent when its depreciation was between 20 and 30 per cent (League of Nations Documents for the Geneva Economic Conference, 1927, paper by Professor Tredelberg, p. 27).

[1] *Loc. cit.* p. 22.

they thus became substantial protective duties grafted on to a Free Trade economy, but incapable of being intelligently defended by upholders of Free Trade. As was to be expected, therefore, in spite of vehement assertions that our motor-car industry would be ruined, Mr. Snowden, on becoming Chancellor of the Exchequer, repealed them in his 1924 Budget. The industry, of course, was not ruined. On the contrary, if export statistics may be taken as a guide, it became more prosperous than ever before. Nevertheless, in the following year, the Conservative Government, which had meanwhile come into power, reimposed the duties. This battle was one of politics, not of economics.

It has seemed to me proper to give this brief account of British fiscal policy between the Armistice and 1925, for otherwise I should be leaving a rather obvious gap in the history. Plainly, however, since England entered the second war no longer as a Free Trade country, but as one enjoying, or if we prefer it, suffering from, an elaborate protective tariff, its problems were bound to be quite different at the second return of peace from what they were in 1918. Knowledge about what happened then cannot, therefore, be expected, in 1946, to help statesmen much.

PART V

THE MONETARY FACTOR

CHAPTER I

THE MONEY LINK WITH AMERICA

WHEN once the war was over, it was obviously impracticable to continue for long pegging the American exchange by means of dollars borrowed from the United States Government. On 20th March 1919, therefore, it was announced that the exchange would no longer be officially supported — that the peg at 4·76 dollars to the pound would be removed. During the war the export of gold by private persons had been stopped by the fear of enemy action at sea and the refusal of the Government to insure gold cargoes. After the Armistice, for the first few months export was still " practically prohibited by the power of the Bank of England working through the patriotism of those through whom the export would be carried out ".[1] With the prospect of very high profits from exporting gold, which would appear should the exchange, once unpegged, fall seriously, it would not have been feasible by indirect methods to prevent a large gold outflow. But, if such an outflow took place then, in spite of the fact that as yet no limit was imposed on the issue of fiduciary notes,[2] the Bank could hardly have refrained from protecting its gold reserve by imposing a high discount rate, and so bringing about a severe restriction of credit. To allow such a state of things to develop in the dawn of peace, with

---

[1] *Economist*, 5th April 1919, p. 553.
[2] On 15th December 1919 a limit was fixed by Treasury Minute ; cf. Chapter V.

a substantial part of the army still being demobilised, would have been very dangerous. On 31st March, therefore, an Order in Council (valid till the ratification of the Peace Treaty, but thereafter needing renewal by Parliamentary action) was promulgated, prohibiting the export of gold coin and bullion. The Gold Standard was thus formally abandoned, and the sharp rein which its maintenance might, indeed must, have imposed on a liberal credit policy was cut. Nobody has questioned that, in the circumstances, the Government was bound to take this step. Mr. Hawtrey has put the case conclusively : "If notes remained convertible into gold and all obstacles to the export of gold were removed, the exchange would be supported by a limited gold reserve instead of by an unlimited supply of dollars. It looked as if, in that case, only a very severe restriction of credit would save the gold reserve from early exhaustion. To start peace with a trade depression seemed an appalling prospect." [1] Though, however, the Government decision was, on the facts, undoubtedly a wise one, it was responsible for some unfortunate consequences, the nature of which and the way of their happening we shall have presently to describe. The dilemma in which the Government was placed is not, as will be realised, one that could recur. Since Great Britain had been off the Gold Standard since 1931 and the Bank of England was no longer under obligation to give gold in exchange for notes, the Government could not at the end of the second war be confronted with the situation which obtained in March 1919. Should, however, a strong opinion have grown up that the rate of 4·03 dollars to the pound, which was maintained throughout the course of this war, had somehow become sacrosanct, a new very similar dilemma might have to be faced.

At about the time when the hesitancy of the Breathing

---

[1] *Currency and Credit*, p. 407.

Space ended in this country, it ended also in the United States. There prices turned gently upwards in February 1919. In England, according to the *Statist* index number, the turn came a little later, but was more marked. In general terms, in both countries prices turned upward in the spring. In June the United States embargo on the export of gold was removed, so that the Dollar Standard and the Gold Standard were henceforward the same thing. During the Boom that followed, English prices ran considerably ahead of American prices and, in general, the monetary Boom was more intense here. Thus between April 1919 and April 1920, while the American Bureau of Labour index number rose by 34 per cent, the *Statist* number rose by 44 per cent. If we use the Federal Reserve Board indices, which are specially designed to facilitate international comparisons, we find the American aggregate index rising 33 per cent, against 56 per cent for the English aggregate index. This relative price movement was accompanied by a fall in the New York exchange between the two Aprils from 4·65 dollars to the pound to 3·91, *i.e.* in the ratio of 100 to 84.[1] Plainly, if the Gold Standard had not been abandoned, this lapse in the exchange would have had to be resisted by a more stringent credit policy, which would have prevented the monetary expansion, and so the price rise, from being carried in this country so far as they were in fact carried. Thus the prohibition of gold export, which had been imposed to safeguard us against the risk of enforced monetary contraction, turned out, in consequence of the American Boom, to have been unnecessary for that purpose. It removed a restraining influence, which would not in fact have enforced contraction but would have limited expansion — would have

---

[1] The normally excellent series of statistics printed in the London and Cambridge Economic Service contains large errors for the New York exchange in respect of a number of months in 1919 and 1920.

prevented it from outstripping, as actually it did, the con-
temporaneous expansion in the United States. Thus the
abandonment of the Gold Standard here, in March 1919,
was responsible for the post-war monetary expansion
being extended further, and the price level rising higher —
perhaps some 15 per cent higher — than would have
happened had the Gold Standard been retained. The
breaking of the monetary link with America had that
immediate consequence.

But this is not the end of the story. Though in March
1919 the British Government deliberately broke that link,
it only did so with the firm intention of forging it again in
the near future. Its avowed policy was to re-establish our
country on a gold basis at the pre-war parity as soon as
that should prove practicable. This policy, which at the
time was endorsed by nearly all persons of authority,
dominated the outlook of the Treasury and the Bank of
England over the whole of our period, until in April 1925
it was finally carried into effect. This meant that the
state of the American exchange, rather than the industrial
situation at home, was their principal preoccupation. A
necessary preliminary to the restoration of the Gold
Standard was to bring the exchange back to the neighbourhood of par. When it began to run away, measures had
to be taken to arrest it ; when it tended to stand still,
further measures to improve it. These measures took the
form of operations on the discount rate and Bank dealings
in securities aimed at reducing the English, relatively to
the American, price level. When that price level was itself
falling, this entailed reducing our own price level in an
absolute sense and in a greater degree. Any restrictive
action which the Americans took we must take also ; and,
even when they did not take any, we, to make up our
leeway, had, nevertheless, to take some.

Already in November 1919, when the exchange rate

was down nearly to 4 dollars, the British authorities had raised the Bank rate to 6 per cent. In January 1920 the New York Federal Reserve Board put up its re-discount rate to the same figure. Neither rise proved effective in stopping monetary expansion. The Bank of England discount rate was raised to 7 per cent on 15th April, and the New York Federal Reserve Bank's re-discount rate again followed on 1st June. These rises were the immediate prelude to a down-turn in prices. As Mr. Hawtrey has put it : "America and England alike were involved in the inflation of 1919–20, and resorted, almost simultaneously, to a ruthless credit restriction in 1920–21 ".[1] Prices in both countries fell rapidly. But nevertheless, in spite of a mounting volume of unemployment, the high rates were not relaxed in either country for a year. At last, on 28th April 1921, the Bank of England reduced its rate to 6½ per cent, and the New York Federal Reserve Bank re-discount rate followed in May. From now onwards both the English and the American rates were reduced by steps. But England presently began to lag behind. In November the Federal Reserve Board's re-discount rate was down to 4½ per cent, but the Bank of England did not follow in full measure. On 3rd November our rate fell to 5 per cent, and finished the year at that figure.

The lag in the fall of our Bank rate, coupled with the fact that during the Boom the up-swing of prices had been substantially larger in England than in the United States, naturally suggests that the subsequent down-swing in reaction from it would be more than proportionately larger. But things did not work out so. According to the index numbers prepared for international comparisons by the United States Federal Board, English wholesale prices turned down in May or June, United States wholesale prices in June. The down-swing of American prices had

[1] *Trade Depression and the Way Out*, p. 21.

carried them, by April 1921, to 27 per cent below their level in April 1919, while as yet English prices had only passed below their then level to the extent of 4 per cent. However, between April 1921 and the end of the year, English prices fell more rapidly than American, so that in December 1921 they were 20 per cent below their April 1919 level, American prices being now down to 29 per cent below theirs. The relative fall in English prices which this movement implies was accompanied by a substantial improvement in the exchange during the latter half of the year.

During the first half of 1922 American prices recovered, while English prices remained substantially steady, with the result that, by July 1922, both price indices stood at about 80 per cent of their level in April 1919. With American prices thus rising and the exchange improving, the Bank of England discount rate, as we have seen, was reduced to 5 per cent in November 1921, fell further to $4\frac{1}{2}$ per cent in February 1922, and then by steps to 3 per cent in July ; at which level it remained for a year. Between July 1922 and the end of the year, English prices fell to 77 per cent of their April 1919 level, while American prices remained steady. In December 1922, the last month of what I have called the Slump, the New York exchange stood at 4·61 dollars to the pound. Thereafter for two and a half years the two sets of prices did not alter much, either relatively to one another or absolutely.

At the end of 1922, when this country entered the Doldrums, credit in the United States was expanding, with a good employment situation. Memories of the post-war Boom bred anxiety, and the Federal Reserve Board of New York in February 1923 raised its re-discount rate to $4\frac{1}{2}$ per cent. From March 1923 the exchange, which in that month had reached the high level of 4·70, began to fall ; in June it had reached 4·61. Thereupon in July the Bank rate was put up to 4 per cent. " In the following months, however, Bank rate was not made effective. The market rate of discount dropped almost to 3 per cent. . . . On the whole, despite the rise of Bank rate in 1923, the exchange had been sacrificed to the trade revival." [1] This policy justified itself when, by successive stages in May, June and August, the New York re-discount rate was brought down again to 3 per cent. For, to have followed the rate up and then immediately afterwards down would have created an unnecessary disturbance. Now, however, the goal of a restored Gold Standard was in sight. In July 1924 pressure was applied by the Bank of England, which drove the market rate up to $3\frac{5}{8}$ or $3\frac{3}{4}$ per cent. Very little effect seems to have been produced on our price indices. But this was the month in which partial recovery in employment gave way, as was shown in Part II, Chapter III, to renewed depression. The exchange at the same time rose, helped up by speculative anticipations of a return to par. At the end of February 1925 the New York re-discount rate was raised again to $3\frac{1}{2}$ per cent. Thereupon the Bank rate here was put up to 5 per cent to prepare the way for the — as it was thought — final return to the Gold Standard in April. On the 27th of that month the Chancellor of the Exchequer announced that the Bank of England would sell gold for export without restriction at the coinage price of £3 : 17s. $10\frac{1}{2}$d. a standard ounce. Early in May the Gold Standard Act was passed. With subsequent happenings we have not here to do.

[1] Hawtrey, *Currency and Credit*, p. 437.

CHAPTER II

MONETARY MOVEMENTS IN OUR PERIOD

In studying post-war monetary movements we should wish, if it were possible, to have free use of three sets of statistics : (1) statistics relating to the quantity of money (*a*) in the form of currency, and (*b*) in the form of bank deposits : (2) statistics relating to non-financial clearings, that is total clearings minus those chiefly concerned with Stock Exchange transactions ; and (3), most important of all, but probably not moving very differently from the last, statistics of money income. Satisfactory data are not available under all these heads and we shall have to make shift with estimates.

I. THE BREATHING SPACE AND THE BOOM

For the early stage of the Breathing Space from the Armistice till January 1919 there is no information about currency in the hands of the public, *i.e.* notes and coin held outside the banks. From that month onward the Bank of England has compiled estimates which have been in part published in its monthly Statistical Summary.[1] On the basis of these estimates it appears that currency in the hands of the public rose by 8 per cent between January and April 1919. Over the year that followed — what I have called the Boom year — from April 1919 to April 1920 it, somewhat surprisingly, rose by only 1½ per cent ; the explanation presumably being that a number of notes privately hoarded during the last stages of the war and the uncertainties of the Breathing Space came out into use, so that extra currency was not needed in spite

---

[1] Cf. Appendix, Section IV, Table I.

of rapidly rising prices. Between April 1920 and July 1920 there was a further rise, with the result that a comparison of April 1919 and July 1920, the maximum month for currency, shows a rise of 6 per cent. Even then, this is still very small compared with the Boom year's increase in deposits set out in the next paragraph.

Before January 1919 there are no monthly records of deposits. From then onwards, however, for the London clearing banks, which do some three-quarters of the business done by all the commercial banks in the United Kingdom, monthly figures are published in Appendix I to the Macmillan report on Finance and Industry. Between January 1919 and March 1919, in the latter half of the Breathing Space, they dropped about 1 per cent ; to be more exact, they dropped some 3 per cent between January and February, recovering two-thirds of that over the next month. Thereafter in the course of the Boom from April 1919 to April 1920 they rose by 19 per cent. It is of interest to compare this figure with the movements recorded in the war years. For the successive Decembers of these years statistics of deposits (excluding the Bank of England) of joint-stock banks plus private banks in the United Kingdom have been extracted from the *Economist* in *British Finance, 1914-21*, edited by Kirkaldy. The percentage increases between the Decembers work out as follows : [1]

Year	Per cent
1914–15	9
1915–16	16
1916–17	18
1917–18	16
1918–19	18

These more general figures may be presumed to have moved roughly in line with those of the London clearing

[1] *Loc. cit.* p. 74.

L

banks. It appears, therefore, that the percentage increase
for the post-war Boom year was of the same order as —
only slightly larger than — the percentages of the war
years themselves. The figure of 19 per cent for the London
clearing banks is very nearly the same as the percentage
increase in their current accounts, what Messrs. Phelps-
Brown and Shackle call the " cheque-paid non-financial
circulation of these banks ".[1] After April 1920 deposits
continued to expand, till in January 1921 — a dubious
peak, or rather perhaps, the start of a fairly long plateau —
they were 25 per cent above what they were in April 1919.

For non-financial clearings we have a fairly good index
in the sum of Metropolitan, Country and Provincial Clearings, as studied by Messrs. Phelps-Brown and Shackle,
from January 1919 onwards. Between that month and
April 1919 there was an actual decrease of 8 per cent, but
an increase of 3 per cent when correction is made for
seasonal variations. Between April 1919 and April 1920
these clearings rose by 50 per cent ; after which date they,
along with wholesale prices, began to decline. During the
war period itself, for successive years they rose as follows : [2]

Year	Per cent
1914–15	14
1915–16	19
1916–17	17
1917–18	22

Thus in the post-war Boom non-financial clearings expanded at a much higher rate per annum than they had
done during the war itself.

The statistics of income movements, if they were available, would have been of outstanding interest. During

---

[1] London and Cambridge Economic Service, Memorandum No. 46.
[2] Calculated from the Seventy-first Statistical Abstract of the United Kingdom, p. 189.

the second war direct estimates by the Treasury for 1938
and for the subsequent years have been published in the
Chancellor of the Exchequer's well-known White Papers.
But for the earlier war there are no such direct estimates,
and we have to depend on somewhat dubious inferences.
Annual figures, for financial years ending on 31st March,
were, indeed, published of income brought under review for
purposes of income tax. But these figures are very unsatisfactory for our purpose, both because the bulk of
wage-earners' incomes are not brought under review, and
because the incomes that are so brought relate, in large
part, to three-year averages. Between the year ending
5th April 1917 and that ending 5th April 1918, the rise
recorded was 19 per cent. It was 27 per cent between the
latter year and that ending 5th April 1919. Between that
and the financial year ending 5th April 1920 it was 23 per
cent.[1] This suggests a fair degree of continuity, which
allows of the month's income of April 1920 being some 23
per cent more than that of April 1919.

The above figures, as I have said, are very unsatisfactory
as indices of movements in total money income. Moreover,
they refer to annual flows, whereas our interest is in monthly
flows. There are, however, two indirect tests of change in
money income which it is possible to apply. The first has
to do with the statistics of non-financial clearings. There
is *a posteriori* evidence that money income in other periods
has moved nearly parallel to these clearings. Thus, for the
years 1924–33, Mr. Colin Clark made direct estimates of
national income.[2] In the following table these incomes,
as estimated by him, and non-financial clearings are
brought together in series form by dividing the income and
clearings respectively of year x by the income and clearings of year $(x - 1)$ and putting down the result against the
year x.

[1] *Ibid.* p. 144.   [2] *National Income and Outlay.*

Year	Income	Income of Year x divided by that of Year (x−1)	Non-financial Clearings of Year x divided by those of Year (x−1)
1924	4035		..
1925	4357	108	102
1926	4173	97	94
1927	4359	104	105
1928	4339	99	102
1929	4384	101	100
1930	4318	98	93
1931	3889	90	90
1932	3844	99	98
1933	3962	103	103

Between the two tables there is evidently a close parallelism. This suggests that income moved very nearly in proportion to non-financial clearings. It must be observed, however, that, since the recorded movements are small, the divergences could not in any case be large ; so that the appearance of parallelism may be deceptive. Moreover, even if the parallelism as between years is a true one, it does not follow that a similar parallelism holds between the same months in successive years. None the less, since Mr. Clark's income estimates were not in any degree based on the clearings figures, this table suggests *prima facie* that, for our period, April 1919–April 1920, changes in non-financial clearings probably constituted a good index of changes in total money income ; or, rather would suggest this if it were not for one fact. This fact is that the period witnessed the removal of a large number of Government controls and the re-entry into activity of many intermediary dealers who had been squeezed out during the war. This must have meant that the trans-action velocity of bank deposits expanded a good deal relatively to their income velocity ; which implies that money income grew in a substantially smaller proportion than non-financial clearings, *i.e.* substantially less than 50 per cent. Against this consideration is to be set our knowledge that in times of boom the proportionate part played by industries making capital goods tends to rise relatively to that played by those making consumption goods ; while a smaller number of transactions is probably carried on the back of a pound's worth of additions to capital than on that of a pound's worth of consumption goods. This factor, if working alone, would entail that, as a boom progresses, money income will grow *more* rapidly than non-financial clearings. It seems fairly certain, however, that in 1919–20 the weight of this factor is substantially less than that of the one working in the opposite sense.

The second test has to do with the product of average money wage rates and volume of employment. There is evidence that the proportion of aggregate money income to aggregate wages bill is usually very stable, even during the course of short-period boom and slump fluctuations. Thus Mr. Colin Clark gives the following table for the percentages of home-produced income, less Government income, per annum over the period 1924–35 — a period which, of course, includes the great 1930 slump — that were earned as wages.

1924	1925	1926	1927	1928	1929	1930	1931	1932	1933	1934	1935
42·1	40·0	40·9	42·1	42·3	41·8	40·5	42·8	42·5	42·0	41·5	40·5

There are, however, two peculiarities about the period April 1919–April 1920. The first is that there were many soldiers coming back into industry, who, in general, received there more than their army pay ; which implies that rates of pay per British man of the employee class must have risen in a larger proportion than the weekly rate of wages paid in industry. The second is that, after the removal of price controls, shortages of supply gave opportunities to a number of entrepreneurs to make, for a short time, profits even higher than are usual at the peak of a boom.

Both these considerations indicate that the proportionate rise in aggregate money income is likely in our period to have been larger than that in the product of quantity of labour at work multiplied by rate of money wages. This product between the Mays (which, as will be seen in the next chapter, give more reliable figures than the Aprils) of 1919 and 1920 rose by something over 23 per cent. Hence money income must have risen substantially more than 20 per cent.

On the joint evidence of these two tests I conclude that, between April 1919 and April 1920, aggregate money income in this country per month probably rose by something between 25 and 35 per cent. I do not think we can safely attempt a closer estimate than that ; and this estimate, or more strictly, this guess, may itself very well be wrong.

II. THE SLUMP

Since we have not in this period to make comparisons with what happened during the war years, and since such comment as was required on the character of the available data has already been made in the preceding pages, the facts to be set out now can be summarised very briefly.

Currency in the hands of the public fell from its maximum in July 1920 by some 22 per cent to a minimum in February 1923. In December 1922 it was 14 per cent less than in April 1920.

Deposits did not turn down seriously till the middle of 1922, when they were as high as in April 1920 and some 20 per cent higher than in April 1919. They never again fell nearly to the April 1919 level. In December 1922 they were 2 per cent less than in April 1920.

Non-financial clearings began to fall in April 1920 at the same time as wholesale prices, and thereafter fell, losing 40 per cent by July 1921. They then attained a wavering

stability. In July 1921 they were at about three-fifths
of their maximum and about 10 per cent below their level
in April 1919. In December 1922 they were, when seasonally corrected, very much the same as — some 3 per cent
higher than — in July 1921.

For the period of the Slump the reasons set out on
pp. 156-7 suggesting that money income was probably moving
less markedly than non-financial clearings are no longer
applicable. It is, therefore, *prima facie* to be expected
that the collapse of these clearings by July 1921 to 40 per
cent below their level in April 1920 corresponded to a more
or less parallel collapse in aggregate money income. This
suggestion is, however, very much out of line with the
facts about rates of money wages. These, in July 1921,
were actually higher by some 8 per cent than in April 1920,
and, though employment was some 16 per cent worse,
this only gives a reduction in employment multiplied by
money wage rates, between April 1920 and July 1921, of
about 10 per cent.[1] It is quite impossible, in spite of the
evidence in other periods of high stability in the proportionate share of total income accruing to labour, that
this proportionate share in July 1921 can have been as
large as in April 1920 ; but we have no means of knowing
how much smaller it was. Thus the extent to which
money income fell in this part of the Slump, like the extent
to which it grew during the Boom, cannot be estimated at
all accurately : the best we can do is to fix for it widely-
spread limits. If, however, we compare May 1920 with
the end of 1922, when the wage fall was over, we get
more coherent results. Non-financial clearings (seasonally

---

[1] Annual income assessed for income tax was 2 per cent more in the financial
year ending April 1921 than in the preceding year ; in that ending April 1922, 8 per
cent less than in 1920–21 ; in that ending April 1923, 4 per cent less than in 1921–2 ;
in that ending April 1924, 2 per cent less than in 1922–3. These figures being based
on three-year averages are practically useless as indices of the relation between
income immediately before and immediately after a down-turn.

corrected) had fallen by 36 per cent and employment multiplied by money wage rates by 30 per cent. This suggests
that money income, by the time stability was roughly
attained, had fallen to some two-thirds of what it was near
the peak of the post-war Boom.

III. THE DOLDRUMS

From the beginning of 1923 to the end of 1925 the Bank
of England's estimates for notes and coin in the hands of
the public in Great Britain and Ireland show no substantial
variation. Deposits, despite a slight wobbling, remained
sensibly constant till the end of 1924. Afterward, for the
next few months, they tended slightly downward. Non-
financial clearings also wobbled slightly, but, when seasonally
corrected, were only a little higher at the time the Gold
Standard was restored, in April 1925, than they had been
in January 1923. Thus, so far as monetary indices go,
in calling this period the Doldrums I have chosen an
appropriate name. It was a period of relative quiescence,
during which none of the indices of monetary change
made any large movement. None the less, the " wobbles "
in non-financial clearings ought not to be ignored. There
was no significant trend of movement during 1923, but
from January 1924 till the middle of that year there was
a rise, when corrections are made for seasonal fluctuations,
of some 7 per cent. After that till the end of our period
the figure was fairly stable.

CHAPTER III

PRICES OF COMMODITIES AND MONEY RATES OF WAGES

PRICES and money rates of wages — a particular kind of price which it is convenient to examine separately — constitute the link between the real and the money worlds, between real resources and their output of real income on the one hand and money income on the other. Rising prices mean that money income is running ahead of real income, falling prices that it is lagging behind. The changing relations in which the two sorts of income stand to one another react to modify the absolute magnitude of both. Thus prices and price movements are at once effect and cause, playing a central part in all short-period economic changes. The purpose of this chapter is to set out the broad facts concerning them over the course of our period.

During the Breathing Space between November 1918 and April 1919 the *Statist* index number of wholesale prices fell by 5 per cent, the *Economist*'s by 7 per cent. The Board of Trade Cost of Living index, if we take the middle of the two limiting figures given by Bowley for November 1918, fell by 7 per cent. Money wage rates were approximately unchanged.

This preliminary period was a prelude to the large upward price swing of the Boom year. Between April 1919 and April 1920 the *Statist* index number rose 44 per cent and the *Economist* number 43 per cent. Since the method of construction of the Board of Trade index number was altered in January 1920, it is not suitable for

use over this period.[1] During the war the corresponding
movements had been as follows. Wholesale prices, whether
measured by the *Statist* or the *Economist* index number,
rose fairly steadily by about 2 per cent (cumulative) per
month, *i.e.* 27 per cent per annum, till the middle of 1917.
After that, until the Armistice, they rose much less rapidly.
The total rise over the sixteen months from June 1917
till November 1918 was under 10 per cent. This check
was, no doubt, partly due to the fact that price control
was extended over a large number of commodities from
the middle of 1917 onwards. Thus the upward swing of
the wholesale price indices was substantially higher during
the year of post-war Boom than it had been during any
war year. British wholesale index numbers relate in the
main, it must be remembered further, to raw materials
and articles of food. According to the Federal Reserve
Board, the increase of these was substantially less in our
period than the increase in the general body of British
wholesale prices. The Board has constructed an index
number worked out for six groups of commodities, namely
Goods Produced (55 items), Goods Imported (42 items),
Goods Exported (40 items), Raw Materials (38 items),
Producers' Goods (35 items) and Consumers' Goods (24
items). Between April 1919 and April 1920 prices for the
Raw Materials group rose 41 per cent, a figure slightly
less than those of the *Statist* and *Economist*. But for the
group Goods Exported they rose enormously more, and
for the group Producers' Goods very much more ; with
the result that the Federal Reserve Board's final index for
all commodities (*i.e.* goods produced plus goods imported)
at wholesale in this country rose, not by 41 per cent, but
by 56 per cent.

---

[1] If we ignore the change of method and take the figures printed in the Abstract
of Labour Statistics at their face value, the April–April rise works out at 38 per
cent. Mr. Rothbarth has made for me an adjustment to cover the transition, and,
if this is used, the rise amounted to 42 per cent.

Turning to retail prices, we find that between the two Aprils the Ministry of Labour's Cost of Living index rose by 18 per cent, and its index for food alone by 19 per cent. This movement was of the same order as those experienced during the war. It should be noticed, however, that, while April 1920 marked the end of the up-swing in wholesale prices, the Cost of Living and the retail price of food continued to rise for several months longer. When they reached their maximum, in October 1920, they were respectively 35 and 41 per cent higher than in April 1919.

Between the same two Aprils Dr. Bowley's index of money wage rates in the United Kingdom, which is based on the payments stipulated for a normal week's work [1] in eleven broad groups of industries, rose by 14 per cent. But this is somewhat deceptive, since in May 1920 the index took a large jump above what it was in April. If we compare the two Mays, the rise works out at 21 per cent, which, no doubt, gives a truer picture. During the war period, indices of general wage movements should, in view of the wide dispersion of rates, be looked at somewhat distrustfully. Dr. Bowley has, however, offered estimates for the successive Julys of the war years.[2] If we use the upper figures of the ranges that he suggests — very little difference would be made by using the lower ones — we get a rise of 10 per cent between July 1914 and July 1915 ; 9 per cent between July 1915 and 1916 ; 15 per cent between July 1916 and 1917 ; and 28 per cent between July 1917 and 1918. Thus for the first three years of the war wages had lagged behind the Cost of Living, but

[1] London and Cambridge Economic Service, Introductory No., p. 14. It must be remembered that the normal week contained on the average one-tenth fewer hours in 1919 than in pre-war times. *Per contra* the efficiency of wage-earners in producing output was probably increasing, partly in consequence of improved equipment. Lord Keynes (*A Treatise on Money*, vol. ii, p. 178) suggests that 1 per cent per annum might be allowed for this.

[2] *Prices and Wages in the United Kingdom, 1914–20*, p. 106. The percentage rise between July 1918 and July 1919 was 19 ; between July 1919 and July 1920 21.

thereafter gained rapidly. On the background then of
war experience, the rise in money wage rates during the
year of post-war Boom was neither abnormally large nor
abnormally small. Like the Cost of Living and retail
food prices, money wage rates continued to rise after
wholesale prices had turned down ; but the rise was continued for three months longer — till nine months, instead
of six months, after this. In January 1921, at their highest
level, money wages were 18 per cent above what they were
in April 1920, notwithstanding that, by that date, the
Statist wholesale number was 26 per cent lower than in
that April. The wage rise was considerably more marked
among labourers than among skilled workers.[1]

This movement of wage rates, it should be observed in
passing, was accompanied by very serious labour unrest.
On 16th July 1919 a strike took place in the Yorkshire
coal mines, involving 140,000 men, which lasted nearly a
month. It affected adversely employment in the iron
and steel and in the woollen industries.[2] From 27th September till 5th October there was a general railway strike,
which, it is estimated, in one way or another rendered
375,000 work-people unemployed for varying periods.[3] In
October there was a strike of iron founders, with considerable reactions on employment in engineering and ship-
building. It was not settled till 12th January 1920, its
cessation then being partly responsible for the improvement
in employment that occurred in the following months.[4]
During 1919 as a whole no less than 2,600,000 work-people
were directly involved in disputes, and the working days
lost by them, apart altogether from unemployment induced
elsewhere, numbered 34,000,000 — a total that had only
been exceeded before in 1912.[5] During 1920 the total

---

[1] Cf. Bowley, *Prices and Wages in the United Kingdom, 1914–20*, p. 106.
[2] *Labour Gazette*, 1919, p. 389.   [3] *Ibid.* p. 415.
[4] *Ibid.* 1920, p. 57.   [5] *Economist*, 1919, p. 384.

number of work-people directly involved in disputes was 2,000,000 and the number of working days lost 27,000,000.[1]

In the Slump which followed the Boom, wholesale prices fell. The *Economist's* index number turned down in April 1920, the *Statist's* in May, the Federal Reserve Board's (for Great Britain) in June, and the Board of Trade's in August. Thereafter these prices fell even more rapidly than they had risen. The *Statist* and the *Economist* index numbers stood, in April 1921, at 8 and 14 per cent and the Federal Reserve Board aggregate index number for Great Britain at about 4 per cent, below their level when the Boom started in the April of two years before. From then onwards the decline became less rapid, but still continued. After another year, in April 1922, a fairly stable level was reached ; and by December 1922, when, on our reckoning, the Slump was over, the *Statist* index number had fallen to 30 per cent below its level in April 1919 and to some 49 per cent of its peak level. The Federal Reserve Board's general index for Great Britain once more stood in its old pre-war relation to the raw material index. It had fallen to some 22 per cent below its level in April 1919 and to half its peak level.

Cost of Living and retail prices, which had gone on rising till October 1920, six months after wholesale prices had turned, fell rapidly till September 1921. They then stood once more at about their level in April 1919. The Government subsidy on bread was, as stated in Part IV, Chapter II, withdrawn in November 1920, but the concurrent reduction in the import price of wheat enabled this to be done without bread prices being much affected. After September 1921 the Cost of Living and retail prices continued to fall slowly till May 1922, when a rough stability was attained. In December 1922 the Cost of Living stood at about two-thirds of what it had been at

[1] *Labour Gazette*, 1921, p. 6.

its maximum (in October 1920), and 13 per cent below its level in April 1919. The corresponding figures for the retail prices of food were three-fifths and 15 per cent. The fall from the peak, like the preceding rise, was in a substantially smaller proportion for these indices than for wholesale prices. But approximate stability was reached for the two sets at about the same date, April 1922. Thus the period of fall for the Cost of Living and the retail price of food was shorter, whereas the period of rise had been longer, than for wholesale prices.

Money wage rates did not turn till February 1921, and in the April of that year were still much above what they had been in April 1919. After that they fell rapidly, much more rapidly than the other price indices, till December 1922, when they were at two-thirds of their maximum and 14 per cent below their level in April 1919. Their swing-down since February 1921 had been some 9 per cent greater than that of the Cost of Living and some 6 per cent greater than that of retail food. In April 1922 they stood again in substantially the same relation to these prices as they had done three years before.

The end of 1922 marks, on my way of reckoning, the end of the Slump and our entry into the Doldrums. It is characteristic of this period that, by an early stage in it, the widely dispersed indices of various sorts of prices had gathered themselves together, so that their relative levels approached again fairly closely to what they were in pre-war times. This is very clearly brought out in the summary table on p. 167 prepared by Dr. Bowley,[1] to which I have added a final line for money wages, *i.e.* the price of labour. As Dr. Bowley points out, apart from exports, by the third quarter of 1923 all the indices of wholesale prices are within the limits, as against 1913, of 150 ±7. The export figures in 1923 show an appreciation of 22 per cent in terms

---

[1] London and Cambridge Economic Service, Special Memorandum No. 5, p. 1.

MOVEMENT OF PRICE INDICES

			1913, Average	1920, Maximum		1923, Third Quarter
				Date	No.	
Wholesale Prices	General	Board of Trade .	100	April	324*	157
		Statist . .	100	Feb.	309*	149
		Economist .	100	March	310	157
		Food —				
		Board of Trade .	100	Sept.	280	155
		Statist . .	100	June	323	156
		Materials, etc.—				
		Board of Trade .	100	March	356	157
		Statist . .	100	Feb.	314	143
		Imports —				
		All . .	100	2nd Qr.	297	153
		Food . .	100	4th Qr.	336	152
		Materials .	100	2nd Qr.	328	156
		Manufactures .	100	4th Qr.	293	154
		Exports —				
		All . .	100	3rd Qr.	376	192
		Materials .	100	3rd Qr.	497	192
		Manufactures .	100	3rd Qr.	376	192
Retail Prices		Food . .	100	Oct.	284	168
		Cost of Living .	100	Oct.	270	173
		Cost of Living excluding rent .	100	Oct.	301	178
Money wage rates (price of labour per week)			100	Jan. 1921	277	174

* Dr. Bowley's table appears to contain two slips. The Board of Trade maximum was 325 in April 1920, the *Statist* maximum was 313 in April 1920 (cf. *Statistical Journal*, 1921, p. 260).

of general prices. "Part of this excessive rise", Dr. Bowley writes, " is connected with the increase of wages both for manufacture and for transport."[1] The rise of retail prices and of money wages was on the average, as against 1913, some 13 per cent greater than that of wholesale prices

[1] *Ibid.* p. 2.

other than those of exports. All the retail indices and
the money wage index are within the limits 173 ± 5.

During the course of the Doldrums down to April 1925
the movements of our several series were as follows.
Between January 1923 and June 1924 the Board of Trade
wholesale index number moved up, with a slight wobbling,
by some 4 per cent ; the Cost of Living index moved down
by about 4 per cent ; the retail price of food moved down
by about 6 per cent ; the money rate of wages moved up
by 1 per cent. After June 1924 all of these indices, other
than money wage rates, rose a little till the end of 1924,
but thereafter relapsed again by April 1925 towards the
level of June 1924. The money rate of wages was 1 per
cent higher in April 1925 than it had been in that June.
Thus, not only relatively to the large movements of the preceding three years, but absolutely also, prices and money
wage rates during the portion of the Doldrums with which
we are concerned were not far from stable.

CHAPTER IV

CAUSES AND CONDITIONS OF THE MONETARY BOOM

EXPANSIONS of money income, which are the dominant characteristic of monetary booms, can only, except in very peculiar circumstances, be started and developed if the controllers of industry — in war principally the Government, in peace business leaders — have a keen desire to use — not to hold — purchasing power. In times of peace, with which alone we are here concerned, that desire is generated and developed by expectations of good money returns, no matter whether these expectations are well or ill founded. Unless such expectations exist, or can be created, mere readiness on the part of banks to provide money, even to provide it at very cheap rates, cannot, as our experience in the early 'thirties has shown, bring a boom to birth. Nobody wants to borrow money for use unless he can see ways of using it to get a good return ; and, if money is forced upon him, say, by the purchase from him of securities, he will simply hold it as an idle savings deposit in his bank : or, if we prefer other language, an increase in the quantity of bank money will be offset by a corresponding decrease in its income velocity.

After a brief period of hesitancy and uncertainty following the Armistice the business world came rapidly to the conclusion that prospects were bright. It might perhaps have been expected that a brake would be imposed by the existence of substantial Government stocks of certain commodities : for example, motors, scientific apparatus, machine-tools and chemicals. Both the Government and the business world were, however, concerned that the disposal of these stocks should be undertaken at an early date, the latter because their existence represented a significant element of uncertainty and hence a drag on the market. The Minister of National Service and Reconstruction assured the House of Commons that " the policy which the Government is following with regard to the disposal of the stocks of materials which it holds " was to " get down the price of raw material to a level not higher than the anticipated post-war prices of that material ". Generally disposal was undertaken through ordinary trade channels, so as to compete as little as possible with existing merchants and manufacturers. Glycerine manufacturers, for example, sold Government stocks *pari passu* with their own production. Non-ferrous metals were marketed through recognised merchants and brokers on a commission basis ; and mechanical transport was mostly sold through the ordinary dealers in the trade. In a few cases, indeed, a conflict of interest appeared between the Government and private producers ; the former being interested in slower disposal at a higher price, the latter (provided they were producers and sellers and not buyers of it) in a temporary lowering of price and rapid disposal. For example, as late as eighteen months after the Armistice the world's stocks of lead about equalled Europe's pre-war annual import. The Government showed a desire to maintain the existing price in order to unload its stocks without loss ; whereas Australian producers pressed for a lower price to stimulate consumption in the future, when they would have the market more nearly to themselves. In general, however, the Government's stocks were disposed of smoothly ; their existence did not in any serious degree damp down the optimism of the business world.

The development of this optimism is illustrated by the fact that the prices of speculative securities were rising from the beginning of 1919. The eight securities in this

group listed by the London and Cambridge Economic
Service rose by 12 per cent between January and April,
and by 20 per cent between January and May. In the
same period the yield on their four fixed-interest securities
had already begun to fall slightly. The general attitude of
the business world is well illustrated by the following
extracts from the usually sober columns of the *Economist*.
In the issue of 18th October we read : " With a comparatively small volume of American competition, which is
bound to get smaller, with Germany, Belgium, Russia and
other pre-war rivals practically out of the race, and with
the world's hunger for steel to satisfy, the trading opportunities for British steel are golden ".[1] On the same date
we read again : " The prospects of spinners and manufacturers in Lancashire were never brighter than at the
moment. Large profits continue to be made and big
dividends declared. Although since the beginning of the
year an extensive business had been done, there are no
indications of markets abroad being over-supplied. . . . It
is believed that all cloth made in Lancashire during the
next two or three years will be needed." [2] A week later a
Sheffield correspondent, in an article on the iron and steel
trade in the same paper, wrote : " When it becomes
possible to observe the economic effects of the recent war
in true perspective it will probably be found that the most
outstanding result is a new lease of life for British trade "
— largely because of the damage to German competition.[3]
By way of entertainment I cannot resist comparing these
paeans with the following extract from the same admirable
paper's issue of 25th December 1920 : " Seldom have the
outstanding features of our economic position been more
unfavourable at this season of goodwill and festivity than
they are this year. With unemployment rife, short time

[1] 18th October 1919, p. 609.
[2] *Economist*, p. 610.   [3] *Ibid*. 25th October 1919, p. 759.

general, demoralised stock markets, stocks of goods difficult to sell — or even unsaleable — when offered below cost of production, and a consequently uncomfortable feeling on the part of all who own them or have lent money against them, we have a most depressing setting for the festival, which in pagan times welcomed the turning of the sun towards longer days and a more genial warmth, and under the Christian era bids us think of peace and hope and friendliness." [1] Even journalists are not omniscient !

For this optimistic outlook there was, as the above quotations themselves show, some solid ground. Throughout the world, and here not less than elsewhere, there was a great banked-up desire for all sorts of goods and services, the supply of which during the war had been cut off or, at all events, greatly curtailed. Much equipment too had been allowed to run down and was in urgent need of renovation or repair. There was thus plenty of work needing to be done, and, with proper organisation, the various civilian industries, all expanding, might have been expected to provide markets for one another's output, thus converting desire into demand. There was every reason to anticipate good employment and production all round, unless some violently restrictive action was taken by the monetary authorities. Nothing of that sort was done and, by the summer of 1919, employment all round *was* good. Moreover, the expectation of high returns, in many industries at all events, was in fact realised. This was notoriously so in the textile industries and in the ship-building industry. Thus conditions leading to prosperity were in fact present, though, as after-events were to show, business optimism outran the facts.

The emergence of this optimistic attitude into action would have been greatly hampered if the Government's restrictions upon new company issues imposed during the

---

[1] *Economist*, 25th December 1920, p. 1121.

war had been continued far into the peace. In their report published in November 1918 the Committee on Financial Facilities wrote : " Commercial issues of new capital having been largely in abeyance since the commencement of the war, it is reasonable to expect a very large number of appeals for new capital ". Moreover, " the increased Cost of Living and high taxation will induce many people to seek a high return on their capital with less consideration for safety, and will consequently encourage the issue of enterprises of a speculative, or unessential, character ". Hence, " whilst we are in favour of an early removal of all measures of state control of finance and industry alike, at the same time we are of opinion that it will be advisable to maintain after the war some control over new issues, at any rate until such time as state borrowing in connection with the war is completed ".[1] Thus the risk of a strong post-war boom with serious after-effects was clearly forecast. None the less, the Government in March 1919 freed from control all new issues whose proceeds were to be applied inside the United Kingdom ; [2] and in November the Treasury granted a general licence for new issues whose proceeds were to be used abroad, thus freeing all kinds of new issues.

Subsequent happenings are described in the *Economist* of 3rd January 1920 as follows : " After the removal of the ban on domestic issues, company prospectuses began to appear more frequently, but the June issue of the funding loan called a halt, and, when the new issue campaign was again beginning to gather force, the holiday season intervened. Then came the railway strike (27th September–5th October), but, with that trouble safely out of the way,

---

[1] Par. 37 : printed in Kirkaldy, *British Finance, 1914–21*, p. 434.

[2] *Economist*, 29th March 1919, p. 514. This was a long step in advance of the preliminary and cautious policy adopted three months earlier, when it was officially announced that the Local Government Board in conjunction with the Treasury were ready to consider applications from local authorities to raise loans for urgent schemes of public utility, but could only in very special circumstances make advances from the local loans fund (*Ibid.* 7th December 1918, p. 771).

the prospectus rush began in earnest and continued un-
abated until Christmas week. In the last quarter of 1919
about £105 millions were raised by borrowers, other than
the British Government, as compared with about £106
millions in the whole preceding nine months."[1] Large new
issues continued to be made during the first quarter of
1920. They then fell off with the summer and the Yorkshire coal strike of 16th July–14th August, but were still
substantial at the end of 1920, when the Boom, in most of
its manifestations, had dwindled away.[2] Statistics for
new issues, " excluding Government loans, etc.", are reported by the Midland Bank and printed in the London
and Cambridge Economic Service Bulletins. From these
it appears that, while the monthly figures vary in a very
erratic way, the quarterly figures show a steady rise from
the first quarter of 1919 till the first quarter of 1920. In
the former of these two quarters they were some £35
millions, in the latter £127 millions ;[3] in both quarters
much the greater part of the money raised being for use in
this country. It may well be that the action of the Government in removing restrictions in this field was premature
and too sweeping, that it made feasible and encouraged a
number of mistaken speculative ventures, thus opening a
road for the spirit of optimism to emerge into action, and
so being in part responsible, when the crash came, for the
rapid retreat that followed.

It has been argued that, besides opening a road for it,
the Government also played a direct part in stimulating,
first, business optimism and, later, business pessimism, by
its tax policy. Thus Mr. Henry Clay writes : " The optimistic finance of Mr. Bonar Law and Mr. Chamberlain, or
perhaps it would be fairer to say of the Coalition Government, has a good deal to answer for. The country was

---

[1] *Economist*, 3rd January 1920, p. 10.   [2] *Ibid.* January 1921, p. 5.
[3] Special Quarterly Issue, July 1923, p. 15.

under-taxed when it was prosperous ; the Government
preferred to increase the floating debt and to remit taxation
in 1919, although it was realising hundreds of millions by
the sale of war stores. The result was, first, an undesirable
inflation of credit and prices ; second, the necessity of
raising the Excess Profits Duty a year later, at the moment
when its effect in assisting depression would be greatest ;
and third, the very heavy pressure of taxation during the
depression. The Government's financial policy served
first to exaggerate the Boom and then to intensify the
depression." [1] The facts are as follows.

In the 1919 Budget the Excess Profits Duty was, indeed,
reduced from 80 to 40 per cent ; but taxes were increased
on beer and spirits and estate duties on estates of over
£15,000 ; the net result of these changes being estimated
at an increase of £41 millions of revenue in the current year,
and £108·9 millions in a full year. In fact, during the fiscal
year, 1st April 1919 to 31st March 1920, tax revenue
amounted to £999 millions, as against £784 millions in
1918–19. In the Budget of 1920, introduced when industry
was still very active, further additions to taxation were
made, estimated to yield £76½ millions in the current year
and £198 millions in a full year ; the Excess Profits Duty
being raised again, this time to 60 per cent. The standard
rate of income tax was still left intact, but the super-tax
level was lowered from £2500 to £2000, while various
adjustments were made which were estimated to reduce
the net yield by £1 million in the current year and £16
millions in a full year. In fact, aggregate tax revenue in
1920–21 was £1031 millions. In the Budget introduced in
April 1921, when depression was in full swing, the Excess
Profits Duty was abolished and the duty on spirits and
sparkling wines was reduced.

This record does not support Mr. Clay's thesis. In the

---

[1] *The Post-War Unemployment Problem*, p. 21.

first years of peace, to increase taxation, instead of, as many people might have expected, substantially reducing it, was not the act of a financial profligate feeding fuel to a boom. Of course, it may still be argued that in April 1921, when the depression had become deep, the Government ought deliberately to have budgeted for a large deficit to be financed by the creation of bank money in the hope of helping industry towards recovery.

The emergence of optimism into action was also probably stimulated in some degree by the rapid removal of war controls. Had the Government kept its powers, and had it possessed the will and courage to exercise them in defiance of what would certainly have been powerful pressure, it might, by restricting the uses to which important materials could be put, have checked activity, and so also business optimism, the motive force behind the monetary expansion of the Boom period. Moreover, a less evident eagerness to get rid of rationing and all kinds of price restrictions might have helped to hold in check the psychological rebound of the whole community from war-time restrictions, and so have contributed to the same end. As it was, we may fairly say that the driver, by throwing loose the reins on a horse already restive, made it more restive still.

Business optimism, however generated and whether warranted or unwarranted, led to a much more rapid turnover of balances than usual. This is shown by the fact that Metropolitan, Country and Provincial Clearings increased substantially, relatively alike to the deposits and to the current accounts of the London clearing banks. Messrs. Phelps-Brown and Shackle have made careful calculations of what they call the velocity of the total cheque-paid non-financial circulation — roughly non-financial clearings divided by current accounts — for every month from January 1919 to 1937. According to them this velocity worked out at 10·63 in April 1919 (10·30 in March), at 13·60 in April 1920, and at 13·70 in June 1920 — its maximum level apart from a freak figure in March 1920. This represents an increase between the two Aprils of 28 per cent, implying that, had deposits or current accounts not increased at all, non-financial clearings would have increased by some such percentage, as against the 50 per cent by which they did in fact increase. As was explained in Chapter II, it is unlikely that in this period money income grew in as high a proportion as non-financial clearings ; so we must not say that the public's more active use of their balances was responsible for an increase in money income as large as 28 per cent. Still, it was undoubtedly responsible for a substantial increase. Mr. Henry Clay, when he speaks of " the inflated bank credits, which sent prices soaring in the Boom of those years " (1919–20),[1] as though what the banks did was responsible for everything, is leaving out of account this very important fact.

But, in order to carry out their desire for expanded activity, business men, besides turning over their existing balances more rapidly, needed also more balances in the form of accommodation advances from the banks. Such accommodation advances were specially needed in industries which during the war had contracted in scale. Some firms indeed, having made good profits out of their war activities, were strongly placed and in a position to finance themselves. But many others would not have been able, without assistance, to rebuild their stocks and make good the wartime depreciation of their equipment. For these purposes it was in accordance with common practice that they should apply to the banks. Moreover, since all prices were much higher than before the war, they naturally needed finance on a scale considerably higher than they

---

[1] *The Post-War Unemployment Problem*, p. 61.

did then. " Manufacturers and traders informed the banks, in particular after the Armistice, that, on account of the great rise in prices, they required considerably more credit to run their businesses. This was true." [1]

In normal circumstances, if one set of industrialists seeks to expand, while another set is contracting, the additional finance required by the first is offset by reduced requirements on the part of the other. The transfer of activity that took place after the war was, however, of a very peculiar character. It was not a question of advances so far made to firms that were contracting being repaid and handed over instead to others that were expanding. The contracting firms were represented by the war industries. Their working capital was not reduced by sales, the proceeds of which could be handed over in repayment of bank loans. Rather, in large part the value of their working and fixed capital alike was destroyed by the advent of peace. Moreover, the debtor was the Government, a Government whose Budget was not balanced, but which had, in part, still to finance its expenditure out of loans. This did not, of course, make it impossible for it to repay the banks, for it could do this out of loans raised from the public. None the less, the extent to which banks could get back credit from the Government to transfer to individuals was limited by factors outside their control. How much did they in fact get back ?

The Government's borrowing from the commercial banks was, in part, by way of Treasury bills, and, in part, by way of balances borrowed from the banks by the Bank of England at interest — a system started in 1917 and abandoned in July 1919 — and credited to the Government by the Bank of England in the form of Ways and Means Advances. Between our two Aprils the London clearing bankers' holdings of Treasury bills fell from £197 millions

---

[1] Memorandum by Mr. Gibson in Kirkaldy's *British Finance, 1914–21*, p. 399.

to £69 millions, *i.e.* by £128 millions. Money at call and short notice lent to the money market by the clearing banks, of which a part may have been indirectly lent to the Government, fell by £63 millions, while bankers' balances at the Bank of England were substantially unchanged. It would thus seem that the loans to the Government for which the clearing banks were directly, or indirectly, responsible fell by not less than £130 and not more than £190 millions. To this extent the clearing banks' loans to industry were in effect credit transferred to industry from the Government. These banks, as already noted, appear to have deposits equal to about three-quarters of those of all the commercial banks of the United Kingdom.[1] Multiplying, therefore, by four-thirds we get, for all the commercial banks together, a transfer of between £170 and £250 millions.

The total credits asked for by industry and provided by the banks amounted, however, to much more than this. Thus, for the London clearing banks, between April 1919 and April 1920, advances, *i.e.* loans and overdrafts, increased from £508 to £862 millions, *i.e.* by £354 millions, a large part of which presumably went directly or indirectly into industry, and commercial bills discounted from £91 to £148 millions, *i.e.* by £57 millions.[2] Again using our four-thirds multiplier, we may, therefore, guess that from £500 to £550 millions of bank credit altogether was provided for industry between our two Aprils.[3] Hence some £300 to £350 millions of credit was newly created by the banks for industry, over and above the transferred credit. This roughly corresponds with a £400 millions increase in the total deposits of the commercial banks — inferred from a recorded increase of £300 millions for the London clearing

---

[1] Cf. Kirkaldy, *British Finance, 1914–21*, p. 74.

[2] Macmillan Committee on Finance and Industry, Appendix I, p. 284.

[3] The corresponding figure from January 1919 to April 1920 works out at a little less than £600 millions.

banks. The extra deposits represented an increase between our two Aprils of about 19 per cent.[1]

It has sometimes been argued that the expansion of Bank deposits during the post-war Boom was made larger than it would otherwise have been by an after-working of the methods of finance adopted by the State during the war. These methods, it is claimed, since they left behind a great mass of floating debt in the form of short-dated Treasury bills — over £1000 millions in January 1919 — opened a road for post-war credit expansion which, had the war been financed without resort to these bills, would have been closed. Now, that large outstanding issues of Treasury bills *might have* served as a basis for the creation of large new bank credits is unquestioned. Banks holding these bills — and the same thing is true of private holders — could, by refusing to renew them, have forced the Government to apply to the Bank of England for Ways

---

[1] This increase, it will be noticed, was not based on a corresponding proportionate increase in " cash and balances at the Bank of England ". That item, on the contrary, decreased from £198 to £181 millions ; and the proportion fell from 13·9 to 10·6 per cent. In this context, Keynes' observation (*A Treatise on Money*, vol. ii, p. 58) may be cited : " The relatively low figures (for the proportion) for the first quarter of 1921 are probably to be explained by the fact that this was the beginning of the post-war publication of monthly figures, so that the conventional ratios of the different banks had not yet had time to settle down ". During the war itself, figures for the proportion obtained for all the joint-stock banks of the United Kingdom, for successive Decembers — December was, of course, the chief window-dressing month — are :

1913	16·7
1914	19·5
1915	18·0
1916	22·1
1917	18·7
1918	18·2
1919	17·9

In these figures, however, the base is not "cash and balances at the Bank of England ", but "cash and balances at the Bank of England, *etc*." The "etc." represents " balances with and cheques in the course of collection on other banks in the United Kingdom and cheques, drafts, etc. in transit " ; items that might be looked on as cash in the course of a few days (Kirkaldy, *British Finance, 1914–21*, p. 85). This accounts for the large proportions in the above table.

and Means Advances. The proceeds of these Advances, when expended, would normally appear in the balances of the commercial banks at the Bank of England. The banks would then be able greatly to expand their loans to the public, without reducing below its normal level their proportion of " cash and balances at the Bank of England " held against their deposit liabilities. It is not, however, a question here of what might have happened, but of what did happen. There is no evidence that refusals to renew Treasury bills did in fact force the Government on to the Bank of England.[1] On the contrary, the average monthly amount of Ways and Means Advances, which had been high during the latter part of the war and by July 1919 had risen to £514 millions, thereafter fell very rapidly to £32 millions in November, and never again rose above £63·1 millions (in December 1920).[2] Nor is there any apparent connection between the volume of Treasury bills, or of Treasury bills plus Ways and Means Advances, and the state of bank credit during the post-war monetary Boom. Between April 1919 and April 1920 Treasury bills did, indeed, rise from £983 to £1060 millions, but, meanwhile Ways and Means Advances fell from £232 to £45 millions ; while in April 1921, when depression was deep, Treasury bills and Ways and Means Advances together were slightly higher than they had been at the peak of the Boom. The Treasury bill position, and equally the state of the floating debt as a whole, cannot, therefore, claim any part in actually facilitating, though, no doubt, there was in it a power to facilitate, the credit expansion of the post-war period.[3]

[1] In June–July 1919, Ways and Means Advances were, indeed, abnormally high and Treasury bills abnormally low (71st Statistical Abstract, p. 184), in connection with the issue of the Victory loan, but in the following month this abnormality had disappeared.

[2] Cf. Kirkaldy, *British Finance, 1914–21*, p. 161.

[3] Statistical Abstract of the United Kingdom, 71st issue, p. 184. After the end of 1921 Ways and Means Advances were not, in general, resorted to by the

This, however, is a side issue. The fundamental fact is that business optimism about the prospects of industry stimulated an expansion in money income by leading to an increase in the stock of bank money in existence as well as by heightening the frequency of its turnover into income. But this does not exhaust our subject : there remains a further important factor affecting the scale of the Boom and the state of money income. This is monetary policy. Had the Bank of England decreed a very high Bank rate and, by open-market operations, made that rate effective, it could have restricted the amplitude of the Boom — the swing-up of money income — in two ways. First, even if this policy had left business men's expectations of returns from the use of money in industry unaltered — so to speak, left the demand schedule intact — nevertheless, by putting up the price for borrowing money, it would have lessened the amount of money that they chose to borrow and use. But secondly, and more important, the enforcement of a high rate, particularly if it were maintained for some time, would have created an opinion that prices must soon stop rising, or even fall, and so have worsened the prospect of returns from money used in industry and lessened the amount that business men wanted to have at the old price. At the same time it would have lessened their keenness to turn over rapidly such balances as they had ; in other language, would have made it less attractive for them to keep resources in the form of goods rather than of money ; in yet other language, would have heightened their desire for liquidity. Thus a policy of high Bank rate made effective in the market would have fought against and to some extent restrained the development of the Boom. Now, had the Gold Standard not been abandoned when the New York exchange was unpegged in March 1919, it

Government except to tide over monetary shortages of revenue, and that only to the extent of a few millions.

would have been very difficult for the Bank of England to keep the discount rate during the summer of 1919 down to the 5 per cent level at which it had stood since 15th April 1917. For British prices were rising a good deal more steeply than American prices, and the New York exchange was falling. Thus the Federal Reserve Board's comparative international price indices showed, between April and September, a rise of 17 per cent for England against 8 per cent for the United States, and the New York exchange fell from 4·65 to 4·18. As things were, however, the Bank rate was not raised till November and then only to 6 per cent, in spite of a continued relative rise in English prices and a continued fall in the exchange. It was the abandonment of the Gold Standard that, as was explained in Chapter I, gave the Treasury and the Bank of England freedom in this matter. That act of policy, coupled with the way in which the freedom conferred by it was used, was thus a very important, if an indirect, factor in promoting and accentuating the scale of the Boom.

CHAPTER V

CAUSES AND CONDITIONS OF THE
MONETARY SLUMP

BOOMS during the course of great wars can never break down into slumps, because, on the one hand, a warring government's demand for money to use is insatiable, irrespective of the cost, and, on the other, inconvertible paper currency can be issued without limit, so that the banks are enabled to create any desired amount of credit without running the risk of being left without means to meet valid cheques drawn upon them. Peace-time booms, however, may and do come to an end, either through a check to the expectations that have hitherto led business men to seek and use money, or through a check to the readiness of bankers to supply it, or through a combination of both these things.

The suggestion has sometimes been made that the post-war Boom was stopped by deflation, in the sense of an absolute reduction in the quantity of bank money in existence. But in truth bank deposits, as represented by the deposits of the London clearing banks, did not contract. On the contrary, till August 1922, in all except three separated months, they were higher than they were in April 1920 at the peak of the Boom. It is true, of course, that *the rate at which they were increasing* became much less rapid than it had been ; and this is an important fact. But the view that the Boom was broken and the Slump started by an absolute contraction in the supply of bank money is demonstrably incorrect.

It follows that the down-turn, and the subsequent rapid decline, which characterised the post-war Slump must have been the result of happenings on the demand side, or, more precisely, of movements in the attitude of business men towards the prospect of returns from using money in industry. In their minds, and not anywhere else, the immediate cause of the Slump, like the immediate cause of the preceding Boom, resided.

This attitude of mind operated through decisions to turn over balances less rapidly, or, if we prefer it, to transfer money from active deposit to savings deposits, decisions which imply reducing the income velocity of money. For, while, with a certain amount of wobbling, the volume of deposits trended gently upwards till the middle of 1922, non-financial clearings took a definite down-turn in April 1920 and, thereafter, fell continuously for more than a year. According to the statistics prepared by Messrs. Phelps-Brown and Shackle, the velocity of the total cheque-paid non-financial circulation, *i.e.* roughly, non-financial clearings divided by current accounts, after a wobble round March, definitely turned down in July 1920, and thereafter fell steadily with scarcely a break till July 1921. It stood at 13·60 in April 1920 and at 10·49 (23 per cent less) a year later; at 13·61 in July 1920 and at 8·98 (34 per cent less) a year later. This velocity is, of course, a transaction, not an income, velocity; but, as was explained in Chapter II, during the period covered by the Slump the two sorts are likely to have changed in much the same proportion. However that may be, with the stock of deposits sensibly constant, it is clearly only through shifts in their income velocity that movements in the minds of business men could, and in the post-war Slump did, act upon money income, money expenditure and effective demand — three names, all of which for our present purpose mean substantially the same thing.

What then was it that swung the attitude of business men downward? It is sometimes suggested that the

N

dominant factor was a contraction in the sale of British goods abroad. This, however, was certainly not so in the early stages of the Slump. When normal seasonal changes are removed, the value of British exports did, indeed, reach its maximum in July 1920 and subsequently decline. But the decline was not extensive for some months ; and in November we were still exporting a bigger value, and *a fortiori* a bigger quantity of goods, than in April. The *Economist* writes : [1] "Although trade depression developed seriously long before the end of the year, most branches of British industry engaged in the export trade were well occupied for almost the whole of 1920 in working off old orders. Thus the figures of overseas trade for the full year make a brave showing, and the effects of the depression, and of the long-continued fall in prices, were not very clearly reflected in the Board of Trade returns until January 1921. A summary of the value figures of imports, exports and re-exports in 1920, compared with 1919, reads as follows :

Class of Trade	Calendar Year		Increase or Decrease in 1920	
	1919	1920		
	£	£	£	%
Imports . .	1,626,156,212	1,936,742,120	+310,585,908	+19·1
British exports .	798,638,362	1,335,569,027	+536,930,665	+67·1
Re-exports .	164,746,315	222,405,957	+ 57,659,642	+34·9
Total exports .	963,384,677	1,557,974,984	+594,590,307	+61·8

These figures refer to merchandise only."

At a later stage no doubt, as the whole world became more and more impoverished, the failure of foreign markets played its part in accentuating our own depression. Thus we also read in the *Economist* : " Our old customers are not producing that surplus of commodities which they

[1] *Economist*, 1921, p. 346.

used to produce and to exchange for British goods. Apart altogether from difficulties of exchange, the sugar and wheat and flax and timber and oil, which we used to receive from Eastern and Central Europe in payment for our exported goods, are not being produced in the old pre-war quantities. We cannot sell, because our customers cannot buy. In the Far Eastern markets, to which for twelve months in 1919 and 1920 we sold great quantities of textile goods at almost any price, the fall in silver and other causes have restricted purchasing power. China and India can no longer pay the prices which they paid up to six months ago. In the markets of South America and the Dominions our customers have satisfied their immediate necessities and now will not buy from us if they can obtain what they want at lower prices elsewhere. Competition, which for six years had been suspended, is returning to the overseas markets, and British goods cannot command war prices any longer. They have to be sold on their merits, in competition with American goods, and with goods which are being turned out by the reviving European countries, Belgium and Germany. We have within the last few months suddenly discovered that our cost of production is too high for our customers' willingness or capacity to pay. We have fewer customers than we had, and those who remain are poorer than they were. In the United States the same discovery has been made, and in the same way. Costs have gone up, production per man employed has gone down, and the consumer — at home and overseas — has struck. The immediate result is widespread unemployment. Existing stocks are being sacrificed, there is a great apparent fall in prices, but new goods are not being made. They cannot be made, under present conditions of cost, at prices which the world is now disposed to pay." [1] But it was not misfortune abroad that first caused the

[1] *Ibid.* 1921, p. 159.

bright outlook upon which our business men had been
gazing to darken, thus breaking the post-war Boom and
ushering in the Slump.[1]

It was, I suggest, something much simpler. As we have
seen, after the war there was an enormous mass of what we
may call once-for-all work to be done. Huge losses of
shipping awaited replacement. The capital equipment of
railways and many industrial establishments had been
allowed to deteriorate, and an immense amount of delayed
work of maintenance and repair was called for. The stocks
of many things in the hands of dealers and shopkeepers
had perforce fallen very low and needed to be built up
again. When these various tasks had been carried so far
as it was found practicable to carry them, there was nothing
obvious to take their place. It was as though the public
had in a short once-for-all rush stocked itself with some
new kind of durable commodity, such as motor cars or
radio sets, and, thereafter, only called for the much smaller
rate of output needed for replacements and for the small
annual increment of new customers. In conditions such
as these, at all events with industry organised as it was at
that time, with no large scheme of public works to intervene
and take up the slack, entrepreneurs would find their
opportunity for using money to advantage cut down.
Openings of which they had been availing themselves were
no longer there to be exploited. This was the primary
force at work.

But there was also something else. It has been urged
strongly by Mr. Hawtrey that the down-turn in business
expectations which took place in the spring of 1920 was
directly due to monetary policy. As a prelude to a discussion of this thesis a brief reminder is needed of what that
policy was. Throughout the summer and autumn of 1919
the Bank rate was maintained at 5 per cent, as it had been

---

[1] Cf. *ante*, Part III, Chapter I, section II.

since 15th April 1917. On 7th November 1919 it was raised to 6 per cent, while concurrently the Treasury bill rate on three and six months bills was raised to 5½ per cent. This was the first overt step towards arresting in peace-time that general expansionist tendency which during the war itself the authorities had, from time to time, checked, but had failed to bring to an end. A second step soon followed. In accordance with a recommendation made by the Cunliffe Committee on Currency and Finance in their Second Report on 3rd December, the Treasury, twelve days later, fixed for 1920 a maximum of £320 millions for the fiduciary issue of currency notes, and announced that this maximum would be reduced to £248 millions by 1924.[1] It also accepted the Committee's recommendation that henceforward the actual maximum fiduciary circulation of these notes in any one year should become the legal maximum of the following year. These rules, of course, did not fix a limit for the total note issue, since the Bank of England was still free to purchase gold and to issue notes based upon it : but the total issue had never been limited. In spite of these measures, the expansionist movement, as manifested in the various indices whose movements were described in Chapters II and III, continued. In the early part of 1920 bankers endeavoured to exercise a restraining influence by rationing credit to some extent among their customers. According to the *Economist* of 17th April some dealers in credit " had hoped that efforts lately made by the banks to check the demand for advances and to discriminate between them might have sufficed ".[2] But, in the view of the Treasury and the Bank of England, it did not suffice. They were stimulated to action by the fact that so many Treasury bills had been allowed to mature that a gap of £63 millions had to be

---

[1] Dearle, *An Economic Chronicle of the Great War*, p. 298.
[2] *Loc. cit.* p. 809.

filled.[1] On 15th April the Treasury bill rate was raised from 5½ to 6½ per cent and on the following day the Bank rate from 6 to 7 per cent, the highest rate, except for July and August 1914, since the American crisis in the autumn of 1907.[2] It was this step, in Mr. Hawtrey's view, that changed the attitude of the business world, and so broke the Boom.

It will be understood from what has already been said that Mr. Hawtrey is not arguing — an argument which, as we have seen, is inconsistent with the facts — that high Bank rate did this by causing a contraction in bank loans and deposits. He is arguing that it did it by affecting, not, so to speak, the supply of money, but business men's psychology and, through that, the demand for it. Thus he writes : " The effect of a movement of the Bank rate is largely psychological. It is required to offset, not the profits that traders have been making, but the profits that they expect to make in the future. If they can be brought to moderate their expectations, a comparatively low rate will be deterrent. Conditions in the spring of 1920 were obviously unsound, and the Government and the Bank of England were so evidently determined to stop the inflation that 7 per cent turned out to be enough." [3] Moreover, in order that this sort of shock may be effectively administered it is not necessary, in a period of expanding prices, for business men to be made to think that the monetary authorities are about to force prices down. Their action has been geared to an expectation that prices will *continue to rise*. If they do not, money that has been expended in the expectation that they will is likely to yield, not a

---

[1] *Economist*, January 1920, p. 11.   [2] Dearle, p. 312.

[3] *Currency and Credit*, p. 414. Evidence of this determination had been provided by the fixing of a limit to the fiduciary issue of currency notes in December 1919. On 16th April banks were released from their undertaking not to sell holdings of 5% War Loan, 1929–47, or 5% Exchequer Bonds, 1921, below their issue prices. This was a necessary sequel to the rise in Treasury Bill rate and Bank rate to their new higher level.

profit, but a loss. It is as bad, when a manufacturer has adjusted himself to rising prices, to be faced with prices that have become steady, as it is, when he is adjusted to steady prices, to be faced with the prospect of a fall. This point was well made by the late Lord Stamp in a discussion before the Royal Statistical Society in 1922 : " It has always appeared to me — but I may be wrong — that what actually happened was that it was not so much an actual deflation as the refusal to mature of an anticipated inflation which the business world had been allowed by inference and experience to expect was forthcoming. It is just the same feeling you have when you go upstairs in the dark and tread on a top step which is not there. That is what the business world did ; they were led to expect that the steps went on indefinitely, and they suddenly stopped, and, although the steps were not drawn away or made any lower, it had exactly the same shock on the system." [1] This is part of the reason why so slight a thing as a small rise in Bank rate can sometimes produce momentous effects. In general, as Mr. Hawtrey writes elsewhere : " It is not the *past* rise in prices, but the *future* rise, that has to be counteracted. The problem is a psychological one. As soon as the rate is high enough to offset the traders' hopes of future profits it becomes deterrent. And a very relevant factor in the psychological problem is the traders' expectations as to the intentions of the authority which fixes rates. If that authority means business, and can be relied on to push up rates relentlessly till they become deterrent, the *mere expectation* that this will happen may make quite a moderate rate adequate. For the prospect of rising prices is dispelled and normal standards of profit and interest are re-established in the traders' minds." [2]

That this would be the sort of process by which the

---

[1] *Journal of the Royal Statistical Society*, 1922, p. 212 (discussion).

[2] *Ibid.* p. 236 : Hawtrey, " The Federal Reserve System of the United States ".

imposition of a high discount rate breaks down a boom, when it does break it down, and that in fact such a process was operating in 1920, we may readily agree. But to agree to this is by no means to agree with what seems to be Mr. Hawtrey's thesis, that the 7 per cent Bank rate bore the whole, or even the main, responsibility for the monetary transformation scene in the middle of 1920. Mr. Hawtrey, in the summary of his thesis quoted above, himself observes that " conditions in the spring of 1920 were obviously unsound ". If so, it is surely strange that this unsoundness should have had nothing to do with the breaking of the Boom. The suggestion that raising the Bank rate to 7 per cent broke the Boom and initiated the Slump, if it means, as presumably it does, that, had the rate been kept at 6 per cent, the Boom would not have broken and the Slump would not have occurred, is surely over-strained !

While, however, in my opinion, Bank rate manipulations did not play the dominant rôle which Mr. Hawtrey assigns to them in generating the 1919–20 Slump, I have no wish to deny that in the development of that, as of other slumps, when it had once got under way, monetary factors were very important. Once the ascent of a boom is stopped, it very seldom happens that finance and industry thereafter go forward on an even keel. It seems to be the fate of economic man, when he has made a steep climb, to find himself, not on a plateau, but on the summit of a peak, which has to be descended on the other side. This happened in 1920. The explanation, or at all events a great part of it, lies in what Mr. Hawtrey and others have called the " vicious circle " or " vicious spiral " of deflation. A check to rising prices, by frightening dealers, causes them to restrict their orders from manufacturers, and this in turn causes manufacturers to check their hiring of labour. Money income available for spending is thus reduced, but the flow of output of finished commodities is not yet appreciably checked. Hence, in some degree, stocks are piled up and, in some degree, prices are pulled down. In both these ways dealers are further discouraged from placing orders. Manufacturers themselves, moreover, finding the prices of materials falling, hesitate to make for stock, in the thought that perhaps soon not only will these materials fall further, but also money wage rates will begin to follow them down ; in which case competitors who held back for a time would be in a more favourable position than themselves. More generally, to quote Mr. Hawtrey again : " Prices once on the down grade, the holding of commodities in stock means an actual loss. The prospect of this loss has itself a deterrent effect upon traders, who make a practice of holding commodities with borrowed money, and reinforces the deterrent effect of the rate of discount. In the first instance the rise in discounts discourages dealers from buying and impels them to sell. But the result is so to depress markets that their efforts to sell are ineffectual. The unwillingness of the dealers to buy means fewer orders to producers ; profits are smaller, less wages are earned, and thus the consumers' demand shrinks. The rush to sell in an unfavourable market forces down prices, and the fall of prices reinforces the original process. Therefore, once a high discount rate has become deterrent at all, it tends to grow more and more deterrent." [1]

There remain to be considered three secondary ways in which the Slump of 1920–22 fed upon itself, accentuating still further the pessimistic attitude of business men, out of which it had been born. First, and probably most important, was the wage situation. During the earlier stages of the Slump, money wage rates not merely failed to fall in consonance with non-financial clearings and wholesale prices. They continued to rise for some six

---

[1] *Journal of the Royal Statistical Society*, 1922, p. 238 : Hawtrey, " The Federal Reserve System of the United States ".

months after these had turned down; for some three months after the Cost of Living and the retail price of food had turned down. As we have seen, in January 1921 money wage rates were 18 per cent higher than in April 1920, while the *Statist* Wholesale index number was 26 per cent lower,[1] — the movement of this later index being substantially the same as the raw material index for England prepared by the Federal Reserve Board. These relative movements imply a great increase of costs as compared with selling prices. Hence the behaviour of money wage rates must have greatly aggravated the check to industry, which the monetary Slump entailed, even had it left the state of mind of business men unchanged. But it did not do that. With prices falling rapidly and money wage rates still obstinately rising, business men were bound to reflect that money wage rates must come down soon. This expectation would make them restrict their activity more than they would have done had they thought that the high wage rates would last for ever.

A second reaction to be borne in mind is this. At the height of the 1920 Boom a number of people bought income-yielding instruments for enormous sums, apparently with the idea that the current prices of the goods these instruments helped to make would last for ever. Many cotton mills, for example, and many ships changed hands at astonishing figures. Moreover, many tenant farmers bought their holdings at inflated boom prices; landlords being the more willing that they should do so in that to raise rents in corresponding measure would have been difficult and unpopular. "Changes of the war and immediate post-war period probably raised the proportion of occupying owners from about 11 to about 35 per cent of the total."[2] When the Slump came, all these

---

[1] Cf. *ante*, p. 164.

[2] *Agriculture in the Nineteenth Century*, Essays in Honour of Sir Daniel Hall, p. 58.

people naturally found themselves in financial difficulties, particularly those of them who had raised their purchase money by loan or mortgage. These difficulties affected their ability to provide working capital or improved equipment for their business, generated among them and among their creditors gloom and despondency, and so pushed the Slump still further downhill. Moreover, the collapse of prices led, as it was bound to do, to an attack, among other wages, upon those of coal miners, and so was ultimately responsible for the disastrous coal strike of April–June 1921, which, of course, in turn inflicted heavy damage on industry.

A third reaction has to do with the cancelling of orders. As a downward movement of prices develops there is apt to appear, as part effect of what has happened already, and as part cause of what is to happen presently, a tendency on the part of purchasers to cancel orders. On 20th November the *Economist* wrote : " Traders throughout the country are feeling very severely the requests which are now being received on a large scale for the cancellation of contracts ".[1] The *Economist* mentions specially cancellations from America and Spain. In Professor Kirkaldy's book, too, stress is laid on the cancelling of orders and the chief responsibility for this is laid on foreigners, who — for monetary contraction was taking place over a large part of the world — were themselves confronted with falling prices in their own countries. " One of the main causes that accelerated the fall in prices since April 1920 was the cancellation by foreign buyers of orders already placed with the United Kingdom for high-priced goods — in particular textiles. Cancellations were also received from the Colonies. Many of these cancellations related to goods already shipped, but not taken up by the consignees. . . . Cancellations within the home market have been largely

[1] *Loc. cit.* p. 902.

the result of cancellations received from abroad. Merchants and traders have begged manufacturers to cancel orders previously placed with them, in some cases offering part compensation, on account of cancellations received from abroad. Manufacturers in their turn have attempted to cancel orders they had previously placed for raw material. And so the chain of cancellations has tended to grow." [1] This naturally reacted seriously on the psychological attitude of business men.

In the light of the history here sketched out, an important thesis, upon which Mr. Hawtrey, along with others, has laid great stress, is likely to win general assent. With the Boom obviously broken and prices falling rapidly, the maintenance of a 7 per cent Bank rate for nearly a year undoubtedly aggravated and intensified the Slump. If what was aimed at was simply to stop inflation, there was no need to keep discount high once the down-turn had been definitely brought about. Writing of the United States, in which for some time a similar policy prevailed, Mr. Hawtrey asks : " How did such a mistake ever come to be made ? The explanation is, I think, simply that the working of the ' vicious circle ' of deflation was not understood. It was not realised that a deterrent re-discount rate, once it has taken effect, can safely be reduced, and that the falling prices and shrinking purchasing power will then do their work without extraneous aid." [2]

For the United States this comment and explanation are just. For this country, however, we need not infer from the action which the monetary authorities took that they did not understand the working of the vicious circle. Their purpose was not simply to arrest an inflation. They were also deeply concerned to prevent the New York exchange from running away, as it must have done if

---

[1] *British Finance, 1914–21*, pp. 260-61.
[2] *Journal of the Royal Statistical Society*, 1922, p. 249 : Hawtrey, " The Federal Reserve System of the United States ".

prices here had only fallen gently while American prices were rushing downward. Even as things were, English prices fell less steeply than American prices, and the exchange sagged. The mistake of the British authorities, if it was a mistake, was not one of technical analysis but one of broad policy, namely the decision described in Chapter I to restore our currency to pre-war gold parity in the near future. Once that decision was taken, with American prices moving as they did, to allow the monetary Slump here to become profound, in spite of the damage thereby done to industry and employment, was a necessary means to an accepted end.

CHAPTER VI

THE RELATION BETWEEN MOVEMENTS IN MONEY INCOME AND IN EMPLOYMENT DURING THE BOOM, THE SLUMP AND THE DOLDRUMS

THE question how far monetary movements entailing large upward and downward swings of money demand, and so money income, were *responsible* for the changes in the volume of employment with which they were associated, in the sense that, had banking policy been directed successfully to keeping money incomes stable, these changes would have been smaller than they were, is not one to which any complete answer can be given. Nevertheless, some light may be thrown on it.

Looking back to Chapter III of Part II, we find that, whereas between the Armistice and April 1919 employment in all occupations, including both the Forces and domestic service, contracted, according to my calculation, by round about 1½ million persons, the recovery during the Boom year from April 1919 to April 1920 amounted only to some half a million, *i.e.* 3 per cent of all persons attached to gainful occupations, or, at all events, to not very much more. This is a surprisingly small accompaniment to the tremendous monetary Boom. There was, of course, during the same period, a very large transfer from war work to peace work. None the less, in the light of what happened in other industrial fluctuations, there can be little doubt that the increase in employment which actually took place could have been " carried " by a much smaller monetary change ; which implies that the monetary Boom could have been held greatly in check without important injury to industrial recovery.

The relation of the monetary Slump to the associated industrial *débâcle* was more intimate. It is evident, indeed, that, provided the proportionate share of total income going to wage-earners remains constant, if money income falls in the proportion $\dfrac{100 - x}{100}$ and money wage rates fall in the proportion $\dfrac{100 - y}{100}$, the volume of employment must fall in the proportion $\dfrac{100 - x}{100 - y}$. *Prima facie*, therefore, a fall in aggregate money demand, *i.e.* money income, need not affect employment should money wage rates fall in the same proportion, but is likely to affect it adversely should they fall in a smaller proportion. In fact, however, as we saw in the last chapter, money wage rates continued to rise for some time after income and prices had begun to fall. This, as we also saw, inevitably discouraged and restricted the activity of business men. They would turn over their balances less quickly and borrow less from the banks ; so that the monetary Slump was accentuated and, therewith, the Slump in employment also. At a later stage, from the middle of 1921 onwards, when money rates of wages were tumbling faster than prices, this movement of theirs must, we may reasonably assume, have alleviated the situation and contributed towards bringing the Slump to an end.[1]

Between April 1920, when the Boom broke, and January 1923, when the Slump may be said to have ended, employment fell by over 10 per cent and non-financial

---

[1] Even those economists who maintain that, in a closed community, general reductions in money rates of wages would not help employment, because they would entail corresponding reductions in prices and money income, do not maintain this for an open community whose prices are determined, as ours were during this period, by a monetary policy based in the main on foreign exchange considerations.

clearings, corrected for seasonal changes, our rough index of money income, by 34 per cent. There can be little doubt, in view of what has been said, that the monetary movement, while itself partly an effect of the real situation, exercised also a very important causal influence ; so that a more liberal bank policy, had our preoccupation with exchange parity allowed of it, would have mitigated substantially the collapse of employment. It should be added that, had the monetary Boom been checked, with its associated up-swing in money wage rates, then, even though in the Slump period money demand for the services of productive resources, and so money income, had stood no higher than it actually did, a substantially higher level of employment could have been maintained.

The Doldrums, or, rather, that part of them in which we are interested, falls as regards employment into two divisions : first, a recovery from the Slump, then a relapse.[1] The former covered the whole of 1923 and the first half of 1924, the latter the remainder of our period. From January 1923 till June 1924, according to the Trade Union figures, the percentage of employment (employment minus unemployment) rose from 86·4 to 92·8 ; and in the same period the index of money wage rates rose from 177 to $178\frac{1}{2}$; so that employment multiplied by money wage rates rose by about 9 per cent. If we use the insurance figures instead of the Trade Union figures, the rise works out at about 5 per cent. Non-financial clearings corrected for seasonal variations stood in June 1924 at 531, as against 527, practically the same figure, in January 1923. But both June 1924 and January 1923 appear to have been abnormal months. If we compare either May 1924 with December 1922, or July 1924 with February 1923, we find a rise of about 4 per cent, practically the whole of which occurred in the first six months of 1924, to set against the

[1] Cf. *ante*, p. 40.

rise in the wages bill. Between June 1924 and March 1925 employment, according to the Trade Union returns, fell from 92·8 to 91·0, while money wage rates rose from 178½ to 181 ; which gives a negligible change, a rise of less than ½ per cent, in the money wages bill. Insurance figures also give a negligible change. Meanwhile non-financial clearings had risen, allowing for the abnormality of June 1924, between 1 and 2 per cent. It thus seems that during 1923 and the first half of 1924 money income expanded sufficiently to allow employment to improve alongside of a small increase in money wage rates ; the upward movement in non-financial clearings being associated, as was shown in Part V, Chapter II, with a period of cheap money. After the middle of 1924 the upward movement of non-financial clearings was checked by a stiffer bank policy — again as was shown in the chapter cited ; but money wage rates, under the impetus they had received, continued to rise. In these conditions it was to be expected that employment would again fall off ; as in fact it did.

THE UPSHOT FOR REAL INCOME
AND REAL WAGES

THE national income, whether in terms of money or of goods and services, is an ambiguous concept. In particular it is necessary to distinguish between the income of the Income Tax Commissioners, which includes important transfer elements, such as interest on War Loan and Pensions, and social income, from which these elements are excluded. In this chapter income means social income ; and real income means, not the money value, but the actual content of social income as represented in services and goods and reckoned in such a way that nothing is counted twice over. The warning given in Part III, Chapter I, about the difficulty of measuring changes in the size of inventories in which the proportionate amounts of the several items vary from time to time, is also relevant here.

In his study of the *Changes in Distribution of the National Income, 1881–1913*, Dr. Bowley concluded as follows : " The national dividend (*i.e.* real income of the country) increased more rapidly than the population in the generation before the war, so that average (real) income was quite one-third greater in 1913 than in 1881 ; the increase was gained principally before 1900, since when it had barely kept pace with the diminishing value of money ".[1] Thus, on the eve of the war real income per head did not show, and had not for some years shown, any tendency towards either expansion or decline ; and a continuation of movement along these lines might have been expected to yield substantially the same level of real income per head in 1924.

---

[1] *Loc. cit.* p. 26.

In setting out the actual position for that year, Bowley and Stamp, in their study of *The National Income, 1924,* convert figures for money income into real terms on the basis of an estimated price rise, as against 1911, of $88\frac{1}{2}$ per cent for all incomes. This percentage, which corresponds to 76 per cent as against 1914, is somewhat higher than the official wholesale price figure because manufactured goods and services are included — along with houses whose assessed value, of course, rose much less than the average. From calculations based on these figures and modified in the light of the evidence of the Census of Production, Bowley and Stamp concluded that, as against 1911, in spite of increased unemployment and the reduced working week, home-produced real income in Great Britain and Northern Ireland was some 7 per cent greater in 1924 than in 1911. Since population had increased by about 7 per cent, this means that home-produced real income per head in 1924 was about the same as in 1911. *Aggregate* real income, however, was not larger in 1924, but about the same then as it had been in 1911. For our receipts of real income from abroad had fallen off — the Board of Trade puts the money value of our overseas investment income at £220 millions in 1924 against £210 millions in 1913, which implies, of course, a large fall in real value — in consequence of war-time sales of foreign securities and because our interest payments to the United States exceeded reparations payments received here. Aggregate real income per head was some 5 or 10 per cent less than in 1911.[1]

Readers who recollect the discussion of physical productivity in Part III, Chapter I, will observe that there is a *prima facie* discordance between what was there said and the conclusions about real income reached by Bowley and Stamp. Whereas according to these authorities home-

[1] *The National Income, 1924,* p. 58.

produced real income was some 7 per cent greater in 1924 than in 1913, Hoffmann's index makes physical production 11·6 and Rowe's annual index 9·3 per cent less in 1924 than in 1913.　Accepting Rowe's index as probably more authoritative than Hoffmann's, we have to examine the relation between its findings and those of Bowley and Stamp.　First, the starting date used by the latter has to be transferred from 1911 to 1913.　From a table given by Bowley in his *Wages and Income* it can be inferred that aggregate real income was some 2 per cent higher in 1913 than in 1911.[1]　Thus his aggregate home-produced income will be some 5 per cent higher in 1924 than in 1913. Secondly, Bowley and Stamp's home-produced income, when expressed in real terms, presumably allows for the low prices at which imports interchanged against our exports were sold here.　Rowe's index of physical production does not, of course, do this.　Hence, to get a figure comparable with Bowley and Stamp's, we ought to take account of the fact that, as between 1913 and 1924, the portion of our physical output sold abroad " produced " per unit more goods entering into real income than they did in 1913.　In 1924 the general price level of British exports stood 90 per cent above the 1913 level, while the prices of British imports stood only 50 per cent above that level.　The Balfour Committee [2] suggest that the export figure should be reduced from 90 to 80 per cent in view of quality changes, but, even so, we have the result that a unit volume of British goods of the same consistency as a unit volume in 1913 was buying in 1924 $\frac{180}{150}$ times as large a bale of foreign imports of 1913 consistency as it did in 1913.　That is to say, a representative unit of British exports unchanged from 1913 was able to purchase 20 per cent more imports in 1924.　A main reason for this marked

---

[1] *Loc. cit.* p. 94.　　　　[2] Cf. *loc. cit.*, *Survey of Overseas Markets*, p. 4.

shift in our favour of the terms of trade was, no doubt, the fact that our imports consist principally of raw materials and food. For, as against pre-war times, these commodities throughout the world (apart from special taxation) fell greatly in value relatively to manufactured goods, of which we are large exporters. The expansion of agricultural production in the New World under the stimulus of the war, the resistance there to subsequent contraction, and the determination of many European countries to re-establish, or even expand, the pre-war level of their agriculture were responsible for that.[1] If, then, the proportion of our output sold abroad be put at about one-fourth [2] with an improvement of the terms of trade of 20 per cent, Rowe's figure, for comparison with Bowley and Stamp's, should be raised 5 per cent, say to 4 per cent below the 1913 standard. Thirdly, as we saw in Part III, Chapter I, physical production only engages a little more than half, some 54 per cent, of the labour power of the country ; so that the real income contributed by it is probably only a little more than half of aggregate home-produced real income. It may be taken as certain that unemployment in the occupations concerned with physical production was much more marked in 1924, as against 1913, than in other occupations as a whole. A 4 per cent fall in physical productivity does not, therefore, imply as much as a 4 per cent fall in real home-produced income as a whole ; it is consistent even with a rise in that income. These considerations taken together enable us to conclude that

---

[1] The latter part of the above paragraph so far is taken from *The Economic Position of Great Britain*, April 1936, by A. C. Pigou and Colin Clark, p. 27. It is *prima facie* something of a paradox that the terms of trade should have turned in our favour during a period in which the volume of our *imports* as well as of our exports declined. As Professor D. H. Robertson has pointed out, however, a substantial part of our imports consist in raw materials to be subsequently embodied in exports ; and that part will naturally fall off when exports fall off (*Economic Essays and Addresses*, pp. 166-7).

[2] Cf. *ante*, Part III, Chapter I.

Rowe's physical production figures are not incompatible with some small rise in home-produced real income in 1924 as against 1913 ; though it is difficult, I think, to reconcile them with a rise as large as Bowley and Stamp's 5 per cent. It must be remembered, however, that even apart from the theoretical ambiguities discussed in Part III, Chapter I, estimates of this character are subject to substantial error ; Bowley and Stamp being careful to express their results, not in an absolute index figure, but in an index figure ± 5%. We may be fairly sure, in any event, that aggregate home-produced real income was, at the worst, not appreciably less in 1924 than in 1913 and may well have been better ; while aggregate real income, including income from property abroad, was, at the worst, not much less than, and may have been as large as, it was in 1913.

From a general social point of view the most important part of the national real income is that which accrues to wage-earners ; for these in the aggregate constitute the bulk of the population and, as individuals, enjoy incomes so small that slight percentage changes in their amounts are, nevertheless, very significant.

Let us consider, first, *rates* of real wages. Attempts to estimate changes in these are subject to the same difficulty about making indices of measurement as were described in Part III, Chapter I, in connection with real income ; though here, since the range of commodities affected is smaller, the practical importance of the difficulty is somewhat less. At all events there is a well-recognised customary procedure. This is to combine statistics of money wage rates with the Ministry of Labour's figures for "The Cost of Living", *i.e.* the price of the collection of things (including house room) on which the money income of a representative working-class family was found, by an investigation of the Board of Trade conducted in 1904, to be spent. On this basis the Colwyn Committee [1] (1927) print the following table :

Year	Weekly Rate of Money Wages for Adults (Annual Average)	Cost of Living Index Annual Average	Real Rate of Wages
1914 (end of July)	100	100	100
1920	256	249	103
1921	240	226	106
1922	185	183	101
1923	169	174	97
1924	171	175	98
1925	175	176	99

The Balfour Committee, proceeding along the same general lines, wrote in 1926 : " It is a legitimate inference from the available data that, in industries in which time rates of wages prevail, skilled workers employed in industries directly exposed to foreign competition were in 1924 on the average less well off than before the war, while, on the other hand, unskilled workers generally and workers, both skilled and unskilled, in the so-called ' sheltered ' industries have, generally speaking, if with some exceptions, improved their average position as regards purchasing power ".[2] The Committee concluded that, on the average, the real level of *weekly* full-time wages at the end of 1925 was about the same as before the war.[3]

Stamp and Bowley's conclusions on this matter are more optimistic. They are set out in *The National Income, 1924*, as follows : " The average man at full work in 1924 obtained about 60s. a week. The corresponding figure for 1914 is 32s. ; the working week has been reduced about 10 per cent in the period and the average hourly earnings of men have increased from about 7½d. to

---

[1] Report of the Committee on National Debt and Taxation, p. 7.
[2] *Survey of Industrial Relations*, p. 10.   [3] *Ibid.* p. 98.

15½d." [1] They estimated that the average earnings of all wage-earners for a full working week had increased 94 per cent between 1914 and 1924. They explained the difference between their figure and that of the Ministry of Labour, which was 71 per cent, as follows. First, " there is definite evidence that, in some of the greater industries, earnings have increased much more rapidly than piece or time rates " ; for example, with improved appliances a piece-worker will make more product, and so will get higher weekly pay at the same piece wage. Secondly, " there has been some change-over from time to piece rates " — which, in general, yield higher earnings. Thirdly, there has been some shifting of numbers in favour of the better-paid occupations and industries, which must tend to raise the average.[2] On this basis they proceed as follows : "Average earnings of all wage-earners for a full working week are estimated to have increased 94 per cent between 1914 and 1924, while the Cost of Living index rose 75 per cent. Real *weekly* earnings measured on this basis therefore rose about 11 per cent." This, of course, refers to persons in full employment.

To ascertain the movement of annual earnings of wage-earners between 1914 and 1924 we have to take into account the fact that the proportion of persons unemployed was substantially larger at the later date. Bowley and Stamp continue as follows : "Average *annual* real earnings, however, were reduced by increased unemployment, so that the rise in them was only 5 per cent, and, if the estimate errs by excess, working-class households in 1924 were on the average hardly better off than in 1914. But, since wages of unskilled men have increased more than those of skilled, at least in the towns, the households least well off in 1914 have improved their position." [3] In their final

---

[1] *The National Income, 1924*, pp. 30-31.
[2] *Ibid.* p. 31.   [3] *Ibid.* p. 31.

survey Bowley and Stamp sum up the situation thus : " The distribution of income between wage-earners, other earners, and unearned income, was changed slightly in favour of the earning classes. Manual workers on the average made slightly increased real earnings, and there have also been transfers for their benefit in insurance schemes and other public expenditure. In addition they have the advantage of a reduction of about one-tenth of the working week. This change can be connected with the reduction in the real income derived from house property and investments bearing fixed rates of interest. The indications are that profits as a whole, reckoned before tax is paid, form nearly the same proportion to total income at the two dates. Within the wage-earning classes women and unskilled workers have received a substantial real advance in wages ; the great majority of skilled workers made at least as much (after allowing for the rise of prices) in 1924 as in 1911." [1]

To many minds the fact that a few years after the most tremendous war experienced up to then the people in this country were very nearly as well off, in some respects better off, than they had been before must seem an astonishing paradox. How was this possible ? Monsieur Theunis, presiding over the Geneva Economic Conference of 1927, put the essential point in a clear light : " The eight years of post-war experience has demonstrated the outstanding fact that, except in the actual fields of conflict, the *dislocation* caused by the war was immensely more serious than the actual destruction. The main trouble now is neither any material shortage in the resources of Nature nor any inadequacy in man's power to exploit them. It is all, in one form or another, a maladjustment — not an insufficient productive capacity, but a series of impediments to the full utilisation of that capacity." The dislocation

[1] *Ibid.* pp. 58-9.

of which Monsieur Theunis speaks manifested itself for this country in the failure, described in Part II, Chapter IV, to adjust the supply of labour in a number of important industries, particularly export industries, to the greatly altered demand for it, with resultant heavy unemployment. Had we somehow succeeded in avoiding that, our post-war position would, of course, have been by that much better. But the damage we suffered through these dislocations, regrettable as it was, did not, as the employment statistics show, affect a large proportion of our economy. To the main fabric of that economy no serious damage had been done. The war was not in the main waged by eating up existing capital equipment, nor was any large amount of capital equipment destroyed. In the main it was waged by current effort and current abstinence. Of course, in a certain degree capital equipment was allowed to run down ; renewals and repairs on the railways, for example, were not carried out as thoroughly as usual ; and so on. Of course, too, the additions to capital equipment, which, had peace continued, would have been made out of new savings, were not made, the savings being used instead to finance the war. Our holdings of capital abroad, too, were depleted by sales of foreign securities and the accumulation of foreign debt, so that, as shown above, our real income from property abroad, which in 1911 was equivalent to about one-tenth of the home-produced income of that year, had by 1924 fallen by a half. Our stock of capital was thus substantially less after the war than it would have been at that time if there had been no war. But, when account is taken of the new factories and other installations which had been erected to serve war needs and some of which were also useful for peace, it was certainly not much, and may well have been not at all, less than it was in 1914. Moreover, there were on the credit side improvements in organisation and technique in a number of industries, which, without making any claim to special knowledge, we may reasonably assume the strenuous effort of war-time to have helped forward.

That things worked out so would not have surprised Mill. " The possibility ", he wrote, " of a rapid repair of disasters mainly depends on whether the country has been depopulated. If its effective population have not been extirpated at the time and not starved afterwards, then, with the same skill and knowledge which they had before, with their land and its permanent improvements un-destroyed, and the more durable buildings probably unimpaired, or only partially injured, they have nearly all the requisites of their former amount of production." So Mill wrote.[1] Marshall, following a similar line of thought, delves deeper : " Ideas, whether those of art and science or those embodied in practical appliances, are the most ' real ' of the gifts that each generation receives from its predecessors. The world's material wealth would quickly be replaced, if it were destroyed but the ideas by which it was made were retained. If, however, the ideas were lost, but not the material wealth, then that would dwindle and the world would go back to poverty. And most of our knowledge of mere facts could quickly be recovered if it were lost but the constructive ideas of thought remained ; while, if the ideas perished, the world would enter again on the Dark Ages." [2]

The war recently ended has inflicted on this country damage through air bombardment incomparably more severe than anything suffered in 1914–18. Our loss of foreign assets and accumulation of external debt have been much greater : while our post-war commitments in military preparedness are also practically certain to be on a much higher scale. None the less, our experience of

[1] *Principles of Political Economy*, Book I, Chapter 5, Section 7.
[2] Marshall, *Principles of Economics*, Fifth Edition, p. 780.

what happened " last time " *plus* the reflection cited
above, *plus* the fact that the number of our young men's
lives sacrificed has been substantially smaller, warrant
a hope that the foundations of our economic strength
have not been irretrievably impaired.

STATISTICAL APPENDIX

SECTION I

EMPLOYMENT AND UNEMPLOYMENT

TABLE I

THE Z8 RETURNS

(Supplied by the Statistics Branch of the Ministry of Labour)

ESTIMATED NUMBERS EMPLOYED IN INDUSTRIES AND SERVICES IN GREAT BRITAIN AND IRELAND* IN JULY 1914 AND AT VARIOUS DATES FROM NOVEMBER 1918 TO NOVEMBER 1920, AS SHOWN BY THE Z8 REPORTS

Thousands

Note.—The figures shown in some reports were occasionally revised in later reports. In the table below the latest available figure for each date has been taken, not necessarily the figure given in the Report for that date.

Occupational Group	Mid-July 1914†	11th Nov. 1918	31st Jan. 1919	End April 1919	End July 1919	Week ending 25th Oct. 1919‡	End Jan. 1920§	Pay Week ending 24th April 1920	End July 1920	Pay Week ending 24th Nov. 1920
Industries:										
Males	6,302	5,263	5,256	5,844	6,039	6,187	6,403	6,634	6,626	6,502
Females	2,179	2,976	2,523	2,398	2,442	2,466	2,499	2,511	2,465	2,330
Total	8,481	8,239	7,779	8,242	8,481	8,653	8,902	9,145	9,091	8,832
Transport and Services, etc.:										
Males	3,507	2,322	2,461	2,896	3,120	3,226	3,339	3,402	3,460	3,445
Females	1,018	1,869	1,860	1,739	1,703	1,628	1,571	1,555	1,557	1,541
Total	4,525	4,191	4,321	4,635	4,823	4,854	4,910	4,957	5,017	4,986
Total of above:										
Males	9,809	7,585	7,717	8,740	9,159	9,413	9,742	10,036	10,086	9,947
Females	3,197	4,845	4,383	4,137	4,145	4,094	4,070	4,066	4,022	3,871
Total	13,006	12,430	12,100	12,877	13,304	13,507	13,812	14,102	14,108	13,818
Agriculture (G.B.): permanent labour only:										
Males	800	578	578	634	659	654	649	700‖	—	—
Females	80	95	81	90	96	81	67	74‖	—	—
Total	880	673	659	724	755	735	716	774‖	—	—
Total of all above:										
Males	10,609	8,163	8,295	9,374	9,818	10,067	10,391	10,736	—	—
Females	3,277	4,940	4,464	4,227	4,241	4,175	4,137	4,140	—	—
Total	13,886	13,103	12,759	13,601	14,059	14,242	14,528	14,876	—	—

* The Z8 enquiries covered most industries and services. The classes of males not included, with a revised estimate of the numbers engaged in July 1914, were given on page 4 of the Report for July 1918. For females the enquiries did not cover domestic service or very small dressmaking workshops or workrooms. For agriculture the enquiries related to Great Britain only.

† For agriculture the figures relate to the end of July.

‡ For agriculture the figures relate to 8th November (England and Wales) and 15th November (Scotland).

§ For agriculture the figures for Scotland included relate to 15th November 1919.

‖ No enquiries were made in the case of Agriculture in April, July or November 1920. The figures for April 1920 given in the table were stated to be "very rough estimates included for the sake of completeness only".

TABLE II

DEMOBILISATION RETURNS

(This table has been confirmed by the War Office)

The number demobilised since 11th November 1918 to noon on the 20th February 1920 was :

Officers—173,955.   Other ranks—3,754,079.

The monthly totals (so far as details are available) were as under :

Period	Officers	Other Ranks
11.11.1918 to 3. 1.1919	2,159	314,672
4. 1.1919 to 29. 1.1919	18,952	610,307
30. 1.1919 to 1. 3.1919	23,770	810,994
2. 3.1919 to 29. 3.1919	18,449	426,370
30. 3.1919 to 3. 5.1919	25,357	352,591
4. 5.1919 to 29. 5.1919	13,665	181,512
30. 5.1919 to 28. 6.1919	11,945	139,911
29. 6.1919 to 6. 8.1919	13,193	121,741
7. 8.1919 to 27. 8.1919	5,782	75,473
28. 8.1919 to 27. 9.1919	7,177	189,431
28. 9.1919 to 31.10.1919	10,426	204,338
1.11.1919 to 28.11.1919	10,488	172,380
29.11.1919 to 12. 1.1920	7,412	95,480
13. 1.1920 to 30. 1.1920	2,650	26,524
31. 1.1920 to 20. 2.1920	2,530	32,355
11.11.1918 to 20. 2.1920	173,955	3,754,079

These figures include :
Royal Naval Division :

540 officers   11,874 other ranks.

Royal Air Force :

16,708 officers   230,387 other ranks.

Notes

(i) The total of other ranks includes 143,603 discharged from Class W and W(T) and P and P(T) of the Reserve, *i.e.* men who had been released from the Army prior to the Armistice.

(ii) The total number demobilised to 30th April 1920 (final figures available) was 186,050 officers and 3,843,065 other ranks.

TABLE III

RECRUITS AND RE-ENLISTMENTS OF EX-SOLDIERS SINCE THE
ARMISTICE *

(This table has been confirmed by the War Office)

Period	Numbers (in thousands)
Up to January 25, 1919	1
April 26, ,,	18
July 26, ,,	86
October 25, ,,	134
January 31, 1920	155
April 24, ,,	178
May 15, ,,	182

* Re-enlistments of serving soldiers are excluded.

TABLE IV

NET OUTFLOW FROM THE ROYAL NAVY EACH MONTH DURING
THE PERIOD NOVEMBER 1918 TO NOVEMBER 1920

(Supplied by the Naval Branch of the Admiralty)

1918		1920	
November.	2,950	January .	3,450
December .	24,700	February .	4,000
		March .	5,450
1919		April .	1,500
January .	61,850	May .	1,700
February .	43,200	June .	1,100
March .	28,400	July .	100
April .	22,050	August .	—*
May .	18,050	September	850
June .	12,700	October .	250
July .	6,550	November.	...
August .	4,950		
September	10,400		
October .	4,800		
November.	8,450		
December .	3,400		

The above figures exclude the Royal Naval *Division*.

* Net increase of 250 recorded in respect of this month.

P

TABLE V

NUMBERS OF PERSONS HOLDING OUT-OF-WORK DONATION POLICIES, REGISTERED AS UNEMPLOYED

Date (End of Month)	Ex-Service			Civilians			Grand Total
	Males	Females	Total	Males	Females	Total	
1919							
January .	53,316	238	53,554	199,923	425,226	625,149	678,703
February .	165,429	828	166,257	255,855	526,508	782,363	948,620
March .	305,251	1,012	306,263	235,947	518,035	753,982	1,060,245
April .	379,799	1,258	381,057	239,366	472,905	712,271	1,093,328
May .	384,919	2,002	386,921	163,162	221,128	384,290	771,211
June .	370,696	2,147	372,843	113,276	120,006	233,282	606,125
July .	361,457	2,206	363,663	99,054	78,167	177,221	540,884
August .	334,925	2,027	336,952	88,041	53,091	141,132	478,084
September	300,251	2,021	302,272	65,586	35,145	100,731	403,003
October .	340,244	3,998	344,242	101,407	33,778	135,185	479,427
November	353,668	5,155	358,823	Civilian donation ceased in November 1919			...
December .	365,695	4,915	370,610				...

Ex-Service donation continued until 31st March 1921. The numbers of ex-Service men and women, holding out-of-work donation policies, registered as unemployed in 1920 and in the first three months of 1921 were as follows :

End of Month	Number	End of Month	Number
1920		**1920** (*contd.*)	
January . .	377,116	October . .	267,316 *
February . .	293,144	November . .	192,144
March . .	240,508	December . .	264,598
April . . .	219,226		
May . . .	196,508		
June . . .	174,224	**1921**	
July . . .	139,866	January . .	322,419
August . .	143,186	February . .	338,449
September .	158,759	March . .	279,236

* The increase was due to a stoppage of work, resulting from a trade dispute in the coal-mining industry.

From the 18th Abstract of Labour Statistics.

TABLE VI

PERCENTAGE UNEMPLOYED AT THE END OF EACH MONTH
AMONG MEMBERS OF TRADE UNIONS MAKING RETURNS,
1918–25

Year	All Trade Unions Making Returns												Yearly Mean
	Jan.	Feb.	Mar.	Apr.	May	June	July	Aug.	Sept.	Oct.	Nov.	Dec.	
1918	1·0	0·9	1·2	0·9	0·9	0·7	0·6	0·5	0·5	0·4	0·5	1·2	0·8
1919	2·4	2·8	2·8	2·7	2·1	1·7	2·0	2·2	1·6	2·6	2·9	3·2	2·4
1920	2·9	1·6	1·1	0·9	1·1	1·2	1·4	1·6	2·2	5·3*	3·7	6·0	2·4
1921†	7·1	8·7	10·2	15·1*	19·9*	20·6*	16·9*	16·6*	15·0	15·7	16·1	16·2	14·8*
1922†	16·5	16·2	16·2	16·8	16·2	15·5	14·5	14·1	14·4	14·0	14·2	13·8	15·2
1923†	13·6	12·9	12·2	11·2	11·2	11·0	10·9	11·1	10·9	10·5	10·2	9·3	11·3
1924†	8·5	8·2	7·8	7·5	7·0	7·2	7·4	7·9	8·6	8·7	8·6	9·2	8·1
1925†	9·0	9·4	9·0	9·4	10·1	12·3	11·2	11·4	11·4	11·3	11·0	11·0	10·5

* Affected by the general coal-mining stoppage.
† The figures from 1921 onwards exclude pottery trade operatives. From July 1924 onwards
building trade operatives are also excluded.

From the 18th Abstract of Labour Statistics.

Table VII

ADJUSTED TRADE UNION UNEMPLOYMENT PERCENTAGES

The table below is extracted from one printed by Professor Hilton in the *Journal of the Royal Statistical Society* for March 1923. The "crude" figures are those actually returned. The adjusted figures were obtained by weighting the Trade Union percentages for each of the various groups of Unions making returns roughly in proportion to the estimated numbers of work-people in those groups, instead of in the proportions in which Trade Union membership is represented in the returns. This has the effect of reducing the influence of variations in engineering and ship-building. Since the publication of Professor Hilton's paper some of the crude figures have been revised; consequently those here printed do not always coincide with the final figures copied from the 18th Abstract of Labour Statistics in my Table VI.

| Month | 1918 | | 1919 | | 1920 | | 1921 | | 1922 | |
| | Trade Union Percentages | | Trade Union Percentages | | Trade Union Percentages | | Trade Union Percentages | | Trade Union Percentages | |
	Crude	Adjusted	Crude	Adjusted	Crude	Adjusted	Crude	Adjusted	Crude	Adjusted
January	1·0	1·0	2·4	2·3	2·9	2·0	6·9	6·4	16·8	14·2
February	0·9	0·9	2·8	2·7	1·6	1·2	8·5	8·0	16·3	13·7
March	1·2	1·3	2·8	2·7	1·1	0·9	10·0	9·4	16·3	14·0
April	0·9	1·0	2·7	2·5	0·9	0·8	17·6*	14·8*	17·0	14·4
May	0·9	0·9	2·1	1·8	1·1	0·9	22·2*	19·3*	16·4	13·6
June	0·7	0·8	1·7	1·5	1·2	1·0	23·1*	19·9*	15·7	13·0
July	0·6	0·6	2·0	1·9	1·4	1·2	16·7	15·5	14·6	12·6
August	0·5	0·5	2·2	2·2	1·6	1·3	16·3	15·0	14·4	11·9
September	0·5	0·5	1·6	1·5	2·2	1·9	14·8	13·1	14·6	11·8
October	0·4	0·5	2·6	1·9	5·3	4·1	15·6	13·8	14·0	11·6
November	0·5	0·5	2·9	2·0	3·7	3·3	15·9	13·7	14·2	11·5
December	1·2	1·1	3·2	2·2	6·0	5·6	16·5	13·5	14·0	11·2

* General coal-mining stoppage in progress.

TABLE VIII

PERCENTAGES OF UNEMPLOYMENT AMONG INSURED WORK-PEOPLE IN THE UNITED KINGDOM

PERCENTAGE NUMBER OF INSURED WORK-PEOPLE UNEMPLOYED IN THE UNITED KINGDOM* AT THE END OF EACH MONTH FROM SEPTEMBER 1919 TO DECEMBER 1925, DISTINGUISHING MALES AND FEMALES

Month	1919 M.	1919 F.	1919 Total	1920 M.	1920 F.	1920 Total	1921 M.	1921 F.	1921 Total	1922 M.	1922 F.	1922 Total	1923 M.	1923 F.	1923 Total	1924 M.	1924 F.	1924 Total	1925 M.	1925 F.	1925 Total
January	...	...	...	6·3	4·8	6·1	9·8	14·8	11·2	19·4	13·8	17·8	14·8	9·1	13·3	12·5	10·0	11·9	11·9	9·3	11·2
February	...	...	...	4·4	4·8	4·4	11·6	17·0	13·1	18·7	13·2	17·2	13·8	8·6	12·4	11·1	9·3	10·6	12·1	9·2	11·3
March	...	...	...	3·5	4·5	3·6	13·8	19·4	15·4	17·8	11·6	16·1	12·8	8·6	11·7	10·3	8·6	9·8	11·9	8·9	11·1
April	...	...	...	2·6	3·6	2·8	18·9	23·6	20·2	17·8*	10·7*	15·9*	12·4	8·8	11·5	10·2	8·2	9·7	11·7	8·8	10·9
May	...	...	...	2·5	3·4	2·7	22·4	25·9	23·4	16·7	8·9	14·6	12·1	9·0	11·2	9·9	7·9	9·4	11·8	8·5	10·9
June	...	...	...	2·5	3·2	2·6	22·5	22·0	22·4	16·1	7·3	13·7	12·2	8·9	11·3	10·0	7·6	9·3	13·0	8·6	11·9
July	...	...	...	2·6	3·6	2·7	18·9	15·5	17·9	15·4	7·0	13·1	12·3	9·5	11·8	10·4	7·8	9·8	11·8	9·5	11·2
August	...	...	...	2·7	4·2	2·9	16·6	13·0	15·6	14·9	7·1	12·8	12·4	10·0	11·8	11·2	8·5	10·5	13·1	9·5	12·1
September	...	...†	...†	3·5	5·6	3·8	15·4	11·1	14·2	14·8	6·9	12·7	12·3	10·0	11·7	11·3	8·6	10·6	13·3	8·5	12·0
October	...†	...†	...†	Coal Dispute			16·1	10·5	14·5	14·7	6·9	12·6	12·4	9·7	11·7	11·7	8·8	10·9	12·7	7·7	11·4
November	5·3	5·6	5·4	4·1‡	2·1‡	3·5‡	18·9	12·9	17·2	14·9	7·6	13·0	12·2	9·6	11·5	11·6	8·7	10·8	12·2	7·8	11·0
December	7·0	4·6	6·6	7·1§	9·9§	7·9§	19·5	14·1	18·0	14·5	8·1	12·8	11·2	8·9	10·6	11·5	8·7	10·7	11·6	7·3	10·5

* From April 1922 inclusive, the figures relate to Great Britain and Northern Ireland only.
† No figures available from December 1918 to October 1919.
‡ In November 1920 the Unemployment Insurance Act of 1920 came into operation.
§ From December 1920 inclusive, the figures include a due proportion of persons working systematic short-time in such a way as to qualify for Unemployment Benefit.

(From the 18th Abstract of Labour Statistics.)

Table IX

ABSOLUTE NUMBERS UNEMPLOYED * AND PERCENTAGES OF UN-
EMPLOYMENT AMONG INSURED WORK-PEOPLE MONTH BY
MONTH FROM DECEMBER 1920 TO DECEMBER 1925 IN GREAT
BRITAIN

Date†	Males		Females		Total	
	No.	%	No.	%	No.	%
1920						
December .	559,185	7·1	298,655	9·4	857,840	7·8
1921						
January .	768,452	9·8	444,934	14·1	1,213,386	11·0
February .	911,896	11·6	508,291	16·1	1,420,187	12·9
March .	1,078,654	13·6	583,198	18·5	1,661,852	15·0
April .	1,482,647	18·7	714,296	22·8	2,196,943	19·9
May .	1,764,711	22·2	784.684	25·1	2,549,395	23·0
June .	1,774,458	22·3	654,778	21·0	2,429,236	21·9
July .	1,477,151	18·5	450,548	14·5	1,927,699	17·4
August .	1,298,953	16·3	376,618	12·2	1,675,571	15·1
September.	1,215,353	15·2	323,813	10·5	1,539,166	13·9
October .	1,275,156	15·9	307,937	10·0	1,583,093	14·3
November .	1,498,402	18·6	379,159	12·4	1,877,561	16·9
December .	1,552,449	19·3	414,482	13·6	1,966,931	17·7
1922						
January .	1,544,938	19·1	403,175	13·2	1,948,113	17·5
February .	1,496,308	18·5	387,053	12·7	1,883,361	16·9
March .	1,424,982	17·6	338,749	11·2	1,763,731	15·8
April .	1,436,852	17·7	307,751	10·2	1,744,603	15·6
May .	1,351,358	16·6	254,464	8·5	1,605,822	14·4
June .	1,298,789	15·9	205,305	6·8	1,504,094	13·5
July .	1,247,722	15·2	196,267	6·6	1,443,989	12·9
August .	1,213,126	14·8	199,720	6·7	1,412,846	12·6
September.	1,204,294	14·7	192,595	6·5	1,396,899	12·5
October .	1,194,963	14·5	193,701	6·5	1,388,664	12·4
November .	1,217,500	14·8	212,271	7·2	1,429,771	12·8
December .	1,183,148	14·3	225,865	7·7	1,409,013	12·6
1923						
January .	1,212,076	14·7	256,745	8·7	1,468,821	13·1
February .	1,126,804	13·6	240,559	8·2	1,367,363	12·2
March .	1,045,517	12·6	240,704	8·2	1,286,221	11·5
April .	1,019,622	12·3	249,334	8·5	1,268,956	11·3
May .	992,330	11·9	255,970	8·8	1,248,300	11·1
June .	1,003,563	12·0	252,119	8·7	1,255,682	11·2
July .	1,014,256	12·2	267,528	9·2	1,281,784	11·4
August .	1,026,574	12·3	286,656	9·9	1,313,230	11·7
September.	1,018,997	12·2	283,435	9·7	1,302,432	11·6
October .	1,028,812	12·3	276,209	9·5	1,305,021	11·6
November .	1,007,339	12·0	276,647	9·5	1,283,986	11·4
December .	930,420	11·1	257,773	8·8	1,188,193	10·5

* Including a due proportion of persons working systematic short-time in such a way as to qualify for Unemployment Benefit.
† At or near end of month.

From the 18th Abstract of Labour Statistics.

TABLE IX—*continued*

Date *	Males		Females		Total	
	No.	%	No.	%	No.	%
1924						
January .	1,041,125	12·4	292,764	10·0	1,333,889	11·8
February .	916,899	10·9	273,359	9·3	1,190,258	10·5
March .	848,514	10·1	253,778	8·6	1,102,292	9·7
April .	838,098	10·0	241,664	8·2	1,079,762	9·5
May .	814,521	9·7	231,723	7·8	1,046,244	9·2
June .	820,284	9·7	224,256	7·5	1,044,540	9·2
July .	862,126	10·2	231,603	7·8	1,093,729	9·6
August .	927,074	11·0	251,019	8·4	1,178,093	10·3
September .	940,281	11·1	256,129	8·6	1,196,410	10·5
October .	973,799	11·5	260,980	8·7	1,234,779	10·8
November .	968,509	11·4	261,137	8·7	1,229,646	10·7
December .	956,032	11·3	260,813	8·6	1,216,845	10·6
1925						
January .	995,232	11·7	277,819	9·2	1,273,051	11·1
February .	1,007,877	11·9	271,532	9·0	1,279,409	11·1
March .	993,098	11·7	259,354	8·5	1,252,452	10·8
April .	976,052	11·5	251,392	8·3	1,227,444	10·6
May .	988,020	11·6	239,413	7·8	1,227,433	10·6
June .	1,097,037	12·8	244,042	8·0	1,341,079	11·6
July .	990,078	11·6	270,886	8·8	1,260,964	10·8
August .	1,104,602	12·9	274,390	8·9	1,378,992	11·9
September .	1,116,375	13·1	243,770	7·9	1,360,145	11·7
October .	1,070,067	12·5	217,666	7·1	1,287,733	11·1
November .	1,024,270	12·0	220,276	7·2	1,244,546	10·7
December .	970,997	11·4	203,764	6·6	1,174,761	10·1

* At or near end of month.

SECTION II

PRODUCTION

I

NOTE BY MR. ROTHBARTH ON HOFFMANN'S AND ROWE'S INDICES OF PRODUCTION

Hoffmann's and Rowe's indices of production are printed in the text (Part III, Chapter I). Rowe's *annual* index takes account of building but assigns it a low weight ; Hoffmann does not take account of building. In the new series of the London and Cambridge Economic Service timber and timber products are not represented with the exception of furniture. The textile industry has a smaller weight in Hoffmann than in Rowe. This is due to the fact that Rowe uses the textile figures to represent the clothing industry, for which there is no separate information (excepting in the case of shoes), and accordingly assigns to them a large weight. The chemical industry is better represented in Rowe, who uses confidential information. By far the most important difference, however, is the inclusion of agriculture in Rowe's index with a weight of 17 per cent. Hoffmann's index purports to be an index of manufacturing production.

Rowe's *quarterly* index excludes agriculture and relies actually more heavily on import statistics. A source of error in timing is introduced by the possibility of variations in commodity stocks. Altogether this index is less reliable than the annual index.

The satisfactory agreement of Hoffmann's and Rowe's index need not be taken as evidence of the soundness of the two indices. It is at least in part due to the fact that, in the nature of things, both authors are forced to use the same material on which to base their estimates. Highly manufactured products are heterogeneous, and we very rarely possess output statistics. We are, therefore, obliged to rely on raw material consumption statistics and employment statistics and on the Census of Production.

TABLE II

VOLUME OF PRODUCTION AND VOLUME OF EXPORTS
(Annual)

Mr. Rothbarth has called my attention to a table of estimates of the volume of British exports published by Dr. W. Schlote in his *Entwicklung und Strukturwandlung des englisches Aussenhandels von 1700 bis zum Gegenwart* (Statistical Appendix). When this table is set beside Hoffmann's Index of Production it appears that exports in the period 1907–13 were relatively much larger than they had been in 1900 — perhaps because exports of capital were high. The comparative figures are set out in the following table :

Year	Schlote's Index of Volume of Exports	Hoffmann's Index of Industrial Production
1900	72·5	89
1907	100	100
1908	91	94
1909	95	96
1910	103	99
1911	107	103
1912	112	104
1913	115	115
1919	61	98
1920	80	104
1921	57	66
1922	80	83
1923	90	102
1924	93	108

TABLE III

TIMING OF THE UP-SWING AND DOWN-SWING OF THE 1919–20 BOOM

INDUSTRIES MAINLY CONCERNED WITH INVESTMENT AND
MIXED INVESTMENT AND CONSUMPTION GOODS

Industry Group	Date of Up-swing		Date of Down-swing	
Building	March	1919	September	1920
Works of construction . .	March	1919	June	1920
Ship-building . . .	March	1919	June	1920
Engineering	March	1919	August	1920
Construction of vehicles . .	April or May	1919	July	1920
Iron and steel manufactures .	February	1919	September	1920
Tinplate manufacture . .	June	1919	August	1920
Wire manufacture . . .	March	1919	July	1920
Anchors, chains, nails .	February	1919	July	1920
Copper, tin, lead, zinc . .	March	1919	July	1920
Chemicals	March	1919	June	1920
Brick, tile and building material .	March	1919	July	1920
Electrical apparatus . .	March	1919	July	1920
Coal	December	1918	August	1920
			or January	1921

INDUSTRIES CONCERNED WITH CONSUMPTION GOODS

Industry Group	Date of Up-swing		Date of Down-swing	
Textiles				
Cotton	March	1919	June	1920
Woollen	December	1918	October	1920
Worsted	December	1918	May	1920
Linen	December	1918	April	1920
	or June	1919		
Jute	April	1919	June	1920
Hosiery	November	1918	October	1920
	or March	1919		
	or August	1919		
Lace	December	1918	May	1920
Other textiles . . .	December	1918	July	1920
Other Consumption Goods				
Boots and shoes . . .	December	1918	May	1920
Shirts and collars . .	December	1918	June	1920
Readymade tailoring . .	April	1919	November	1920
Printing and bookbinding . .	December	1918	July	1920
Pottery	September	1918	February	1921
Food preparation . . .	October	1918	March	1920
Rubber and rubber manufactures	February	1919	June	1920
Hardware and hollow-ware .	February	1919	April	1920
Leather and Leather goods .	April or May	1919	June	1920
Clocks, plate, jewellery . .	April or May	1919	June	1920

Table prepared by Mr. Rothbarth.   Source : *Ministry of Labour Gazette* ;
Employers' Returns and Returns under the 1911 and 1916 Insurance Acts.

TABLE IV

MERCHANT SHIP-BUILDING IN THE UNITED KINGDOM

(Extracted from the Quarterly Ship-building Returns of Lloyd's
Register of Shipping)

(In thousand gross tons)

Quarter ended	Under Construction at Beginning of Quarter		Commenced during Quarter	Launched	Approximate Tonnage completed, estimated from foregoing Figures
	Under Construction	Suspended			
	(1)	(2)	(3)	(4)	(5)
31 March 1920	2994	...	708	454	308
30 June 1920	3394	...	589	523	405
30 Sept. 1920	3578	...	594	483	441
31 Dec. 1920	3731	...	506	580	528
31 March 1921	3709	...	393	434	303
30 June 1921	3799	497	69	322	338
30 Sept. 1921	3530	735	51	308	298
31 Dec. 1921	3283	731	55	467	698
31 March 1922	2640	722	51	334	455
30 June 1922	2236	617	39	149	355
30 Sept. 1922	1920	481	82	307	385
31 Dec. 1922	1617	419	231	261	379
31 March 1923	1469	348	355	228	332
30 June 1923	1492	181	241	239	395
30 Sept. 1923	1338	130	112	66	179
31 Dec. 1923	1271	242	245	115	121
31 March 1924	1395	164	228	362	149
30 June 1924	1474	101	375	365	332
30 Sept. 1924	1517	52	253	360	302
31 Dec. 1924	1468	37	195	353	366

SECTION III

PRICES AND MONEY WAGES

COST OF LIVING, RETAIL FOOD PRICES AND MONEY WAGE
RATES : INDICES

(JULY 1914 = 100)

Year and Month	RETAIL		WAGES
	Ministry of Labour		Average of 11 Weekly Wage Rates
	Cost of Living	Food	
	% of	Pre-war	%
1918			
October	220–25	223	
November . . .	220	229	⎫ 179 (July 1918)
December . . .	220	230	⎭
1919			
January	220	230	206
February . . .	215	220	207
March	210	213	207
April	205	207	207
May	205	204	209
June	207	209	210
July	215	217	216
August	215	216	216
September . . .	220	222	218
October	225	231	218
November . . .	225	234	220
December . . .	225	236	226
1920			
January	230	235	229
February . . .	230	233	229
March	232	235	234
April	241	246	235
May	250	255	253
June	252	258	261
July	255	262	264
August	261	267	266
September . . .	264	270	270
October	276	291	270
November . . .	269	282	274
December . . .	265	278	276
1921			
January	251	263	277
February . . .	241	249	276
March	233	238	275
April	228	232	⎧ 271 ⎫
May	219	218	⎨ 269 ⎬
June	219	220	⎩ 264 ⎭
July	222	226	253
August	220	225	243
September . . .	210	210	237
October	203	200	233
November . . .	199	195	227
December . . .	192	185	223
1922			
January	188	179	217
February . . .	186	177	214
March	182	173	214
April	181	172	206
May	180	170	202
June	184	180	197
July	181	175	194
August	179	172	191
September . . .	178	172	181

TABLE I—(*contd.*) 231

| Year and Month | RETAIL | | WAGES |
| | Ministry of Labour | | Average of 11 Weekly Wage Rates |
	Cost of Living	Food	
	% of	Pre-war	%
1922			
October	180	176	180
November . . .	180	178	179
December . . .	178	175	178
1923			
January	177	173	177
February . . .	176	171	177
March	174	168	177
April	170	162	177
May	169	160	177
June	169	162	176
July	171	165	174
August	173	168	174
September . . .	175	172	174
October	175	173	174
November . . .	177	176	173
December . . .	177	175	173
1924			
January	179	177	173
February . . .	178	176	174
March	173	167	176
April	171	163	176
May	169	160	177
June	170	162	178½
July	171	164	179
August	172	166	179
September . . .	176	172	179
October	180	179	178½
November . . .	181	180	179
December . . .	180	178	179
1925			
January	179	176	180
February . . .	179	176	181
March	175	170	181
April	173	167	181
May	172	166	181
June	173	167	181
July	173	168	180
August	174	170	180
September . . .	176	172	180
October	176	172	180
November . . .	177	174	180
December . . .	175	171	180

From the London and Cambridge Economic Service.

Cost of Living Index.—Ministry of Labour's index showing movements and cost of maintaining unchanged the standard of living prevalent in working-class households before the war. For 1st of month, but placed against previous month— *e.g.* reading for 1st March is shown against February,— to facilitate comparison with *Statist* index.

Retail Food Prices.—As above, for food only.

Wages Index.—Average of index numbers (as percentage of July 1914) of rates of wages for normal week of (*a*) bricklayers and labourers, (*b*) engineering fitters and labourers, (*c*) compositors, (*d*) dock labourers, (*e*) railwaymen, (*f*) woollen workers, (*g*) cotton workers, (*h*) miners, (*i*) agricultural labourers. In general it includes changes reported up to end of month. From March 1922 it includes those reported by the middle of the month.—Prepared by Dr. Bowley.

TABLE II

PRECEDING TABLE READJUSTED BY MR. ROTHBARTH SO THAT
1913 AVERAGE=100

RETAIL PRICES * AND WAGE † RATES

(1913 ‡=100)

	Jan.	Feb.	Mar.	Apr.	May	June	July	Aug.	Sept.	Oct.	Nov.	Dec.
1918 §												
Cost of Living	...	...	...	...	...	...	...	...	...	216–221	...	...
											216	216
Food . .	...	...	...	...	...	...	...	...	...	227	223	224
Wage rates .	...	...	...	...	...	...	181	...	...	...	...	...
1919												
Cost of Living	216	211	206	201	201	203	211	211	216	221	221	221
Food . .	224	214	207·5	202	199	203·5	211	210	216	225	228	230
Wage rates .	208	209	209	209	211	212	218	218	220	220	222	228
1920												
Cost of Living	226	226	227	236	245	247	250	256	259	271	264	260
Food . .	229	227	229	240	248	251	255	260	263	283	275	271
Wage rates .	231	231	236	237	255·5	264	267	269	273	273	277	279
1921												
Cost of Living	246	236	228	224	215	215	218	216	206	199	195	188
Food . .	256	242·5	232	226	212	214	220	219	204·5	195	190	180
Wage rates .	280	279	278	(274)	(272)	(267)	255·5	245·5	239	235	229	226
1922												
Cost of Living	184·5	182·5	178·5	177·5	176·5	180·5	177·5	175·5	174·5	176·5	176·5	174·5
Food . .	174·5	172·5	168·5	167·5	165·5	175·5	170·5	167·5	167·5	171·5	173·5	170·5
Wage rates .	219	216	216	208	204	199	196	193	183	182	181	180
1923												
Cost of Living	173·5	172·5	170·5	166·5	165·5	165·5	167·5	169·5	171·5	171·5	173·5	173·5
Food . .	168·5	166·5	164	158	156	158	161	164	167·5	168·5	171·5	170·5
Wage rates .	179	179	179	179	179	178	176	176	176	176	175	175
1924												
Cost of Living	175·5	174·5	169·5	167·5	165·5	166·5	167·5	168·5	172·5	176·5	177·5	176·5
Food . .	172·5	171·5	163	159	156	158	160	162	167·5	174·5	175·5	173·5
Wage rates .	175	176	178	178	179	180·5	181	181	181	180·5	181	181
1925												
Cost of Living	175·5	175·5	171·5	169·5	168·5	169·5	169·5	170·5	172·5	172·5	173·5	171·5
Food . .	171·5	171·5	166	163	162	163	164	166	167·5	167·5	169·5	166·5
Wage rates .	182	183	183	183	183	183	182	182	182	182	182	182

* Ministry of Labour index. The figures as published in the *Ministry of Labour Gazette* up to the
1st of each month. They are placed against the previous month.
† Average of 11 weekly wage rates. London and Cambridge Economic Service.
‡ The 1913 figures are taken from Bowley, *Wages and Income since 1860*, p. 30 and p. 12.
§ The 1918 figures are taken from Bowley, *Prices and Wages in the United Kingdom, 1914–20*.

TABLE III

CHANGES IN WEEKLY WAGE RATES

Trade	4 Aug. 1914	30 April 1919	29 Feb. 1920	31 Dec. 1920	28 Feb. 1922	30 Sept. 1922	31 March 1923
Building							
Bricklayers .	100	188	223	249	214	176	176
Labourers . .	100	229	284	325	254	198	198
Ship-building							
Riveters . .	100	198	213	231	189	146	120
Labourers . .	100	254	278	308	248	175	169
Engineering							
Fitters and Turners	100	198	212	230	189	148	145
Labourers . .	100	256	280	310	250	177	177
Iron and Steel							
Labourers . .	100	250	250	350	220	200	200
Railways							
Porters . .	100	283	310	365	300	260	260
Foremen . .	100	183	200	237	207	185	185
Coal-miners . .	100	215	223	285	150	130	130
Wool and Worsted Spinners and Weavers (Time workers) . .	100	207	225	301	214	185	185
Cotton . .	100	205	205	260	205	169	161

From the *Manchester Guardian Commercial*, European Reconstruction, Section 16, p. 867.

WHOLESALE PRICE INDEX NUMBERS AND NEW YORK EXCHANGE

Year and Month	Board of Trade *	Statist	Econo-mist	International Wholesale Price Index Federal Reserve for England		Federal Reserve Board for U.S.A.	New York Exchange, dollars to £ †
				Raw material	General Index		
1913 (average)	100	100	100	100	100	100	4·86
1918 October .	243	230	231				
November	242	228	231				
December	241	228	226				
1919 January .	239	224	217	210	227	201	4·76
February	234	220	215	208	222	194	4·76
March .	229	217	212	206	210	195	4·70
April .	228	217	214	207	214	200	4·65
May .	234	229	222	211	224	206	4·66
June .	242	235	230	216	234	207	4·60
July .	240	243	239	222	242	216	4·43
August .	258	250	241	234	249	223	4·27
September	262	252	245	239	251	217	4·18
October .	270	264	252	250	261	218	4·17
November	280	271	259	255	272	225	4·10
December	287	276	273	261	287	233	3·75
1920 January .	297	288	288	270	305	248	3·65
February	310	306	303	281	320	248	3·40
March .	319	307	310	287	329	253	3·75
April .	325	313	306	292	334	267	3·91
May .	325	305	304	306	340	269	3·85
June .	322	300	291	308	339	262	3·95
July .	317	299	292	307	326	254	3·85
August .	313	298	287	307	322	240	3·62
September	311	292	284	301	315	232	3·51
October .	302	282	266	290	297	214	3·47
November	287	263	245	282	280	196	3·41
December	264	243	220	265	260	179	3·49
1921 January .	246	232	209	233	244	168	3·74
February	225	215	192	213	226	157	3·88
March .	211	208	289	202	213	152	3·91
April .	205	199	183	201	206	146	3·93
May .	202	191	182	198	201	145	3·98
June .	298	183	179	196	197	142	3·78
July .	194	186	178	192	196	145	3·63
August .	190	181	179	193	195	146	3·65
September	187	175	183	195	194	146	3·72
October .	181	163	170	187	187	145	3·87
November	173	161	165	177	177	145	3·97
December	168	157	162	173	172	142	4·16
1922 January .	164	156	159	171	170	142	4·22
February	162	155	158	168	167	146	4·36
March .	160	157	160	170	168	147	4·38
April .	160	158	159	167	167	149	4·41
May .	160	159	162	169	171	158	4·45
June .	160	159	163	167	169	161	4·45
July .	160	157	163	168	171	165	4·45
August .	156	152	158	170	168	165	4·46
September	154	150	156	166	165	164	4·43
October .	155	153	158	165	163	165	4·44
November	157	153	159	166	165	164	4·48
December	156	152	158	166	166	164	4·61

* † [For notes see next page.]

TABLE IV—(contd.)

Year and Month	Board of Trade *	Statist	Economist	International Wholesale Price Index Federal Reserve for England		Federal Reserve Board for U.S.A.	New York Exchange, dollars to £ †
				Raw material	General Index		
1923 January .	157	153	161	167	165	166	4·65
February	158	155	163	171	168	166	4·69
March .	160	156	163	178	173	169	4·70
April .	162	158	164	180	175	170	4·66
May .	160	156	164	179	173	167	4·63
June .	159	151	160	177	171	164	4·61
July .	157	147	156	171	168	159	4·58
August .	155	147	156	165	164	159	4·56
September	158	150	160	164	165	163	4·54
October .	158	150	161	165	166	163	4·52
November	161	156	169	171	171	163	4·38
December	163	157	170	179	177	163	4·36
1924 January .	165	161	174	178	178	163	4·26
February	167	163	174	182	180	163	4·31
March .	165	162	173	183	180	160	4·29
April .	165	161	173	186	181	158	4·35
May .	164	161	169	178	177	156	4·36
June .	163	160	169	173	174	154	4·32
July .	163	163	173	171	174	156	4·37
August .	165	162	172	171	173	158	4·50
September	167	166	176	168	172	156	4·46
October .	170	172	180	171	175	159	4·49
November	170	171	180	174	176	160	4·61
December	170	174	180	175	177	165	4·70
1925 January .	171	171	177	176	178	168	4·78
February	169	169	177	175	178	167	4·77
March .	166	165	174	172	175	168	4·78
April .	163	162	169	169	171	163	4·80
May .	159	160	166	164	166	162	4·85
June .	158	155	162	161	164	163	4·86
July .	158	158	165	161	163	165	4·86
August .	157	158	165	160	161	164	4·86
September	156	157	164	158	158	165	4·85
October .	155	153	161	155	157	164	4·84
November	154	157	160	154	156	166	4·85
December	153	154	158	155	155	164	4·85

* For the Board of Trade index number, the figures for 1919 have been interpolated by Mr. Rothbarth by means of the *Statist* index number of wholesale prices. It was impossible to use the old Board of Trade index, as it behaves very differently from the new. On the other hand, the *Statist* index fluctuates very much like the Board of Trade index, if account is taken of the fact that the *Statist* figures refer to the end of each given month, whereas the Board of Trade figure refers to the mean of the month. Accordingly, the arithmetic mean of two end-of-the-month *Statist* figures is used to approximate the mean. When this procedure is applied to 1920, the fluctuations of the monthly mean of the *Statist* figures are seen to be very similar to the monthly mean of the new Board of Trade index.

† Cable rate : New York on London. Sources : Bowley's figures in the *Review of Economic Statistics, 1922*, p. 153, for the first half of each month up to December 1920 ; for the second half of each month, *Economist* data for one day each week ; from January 1921 to December 1925, Federal Reserve Bulletin.

The *Statist* and *Economist* figures refer to the end of the month ; the Board of Trade index is an average for the month.

Prepared by Mr. Rothbarth.

DETAILED FEDERAL RESERVE BOARD INDICES OF WHOLESALE PRICES IN ENGLAND

(1913 = 100)

Year and Month	Goods produced (55)	Goods Imported (42)	Goods Exported (40)	Raw Materials (38)	Producers' Goods (35)	Consumers' Goods (24)	All Commodities (97)
1919 (average).	238	247	275	226	261	241	241
1920 ,, .	315	294	438	291	355	292	314
1921 ,, .	207	171	183	197	178	219	201
1922 ,, .	169	155	155	168	145	181	167
1919							
January . .	221	244	242	210	238	241	227
February .	215	240	231	208	229	234	222
March . .	202	233	222	206	200	226	210
April . .	208	230	219	207	213	225	214
May . .	220	234	232	211	237	229	224
June . .	231	241	233	216	257	236	234
July . .	240	247	265	222	269	244	242
August . .	250	246	278	234	277	243	249
September .	253	246	302	239	277	241	251
October . .	262	259	332	250	288	249	261
November .	273	269	345	255	310	260	272
December .	283	280	399	261	331	267	287
1920							
January . .	302	298	452	270	358	289	305
February .	316	314	478	281	392	291	320
March . .	327	319	483	287	406	300	329
April . .	332	324	486	292	409	306	334
May . .	341	322	484	306	406	310	340
June . .	344	306	469	308	396	311	339
July . .	330	299	452	307	363	302	326
August . .	322	304	439	307	352	297	322
September .	319	288	421	301	341	296	315
October . .	301	272	392	290	309	282	297
November .	285	253	369	282	278	267	280
December .	266	230	328	265	244	255	260
1921							
January . .	252	207	246	233	231	261	244
February .	234	190	201	213	213	246	226
March . .	219	182	189	202	198	231	213
April . .	211	180	185	201	184	225	206
May . .	209	167	182	198	179	216	201
June . .	206	161	179	196	173	213	197
July . .	204	164	174	192	165	222	196
August . .	202	165	168	193	161	223	195
September .	199	170	171	195	165	212	194
October . .	192	163	175	187	166	200	187
November .	182	154	164	177	153	191	177
December .	176	152	158	173	147	186	172
1922							
January . .	174	149	158	171	147	181	170
February .	171	148	151	168	144	181	167
March . .	172	147	153	170	142	183	168
April . .	171	148	152	167	143	183	167
May . .	175	153	155	169	146	191	171
June . .	172	154	158	167	148	186	169
July . .	172	158	158	168	147	190	171
August . .	170	155	159	170	143	183	168
September .	165	157	154	166	143	177	165
October . .	160	161	149	165	144	170	163
November .	161	165	154	166	146	172	165
December .	164	163	157	166	146	177	166

TABLE VI

WHOLESALE PRICES OF BUILDING MATERIALS AND OF MATERIALS IN GENERAL

(June 1924=100)

Date	Unweighted Average of 12 Building Material Prices	Sauerbeck *Statist* Index of All Materials	
		Annual	2nd and 3rd Quarter respectively
July 1914 . .	55	60	...
December 1914 .	57		...
July 1915 . .	66	74	...
December 1915 .	71		...
July 1916 . .	85	96	...
December 1916 .	87		...
July 1917 . .	98	123	...
December 1917 .	103		
July 1918 . .	112	141	140
December 1918 .	134		139
July 1919 . .	128	152	141
December 1919 .	138		173
July 1920 . .	167	181	185
December 1920 .	163		156
July 1921 . .	138	105	110
December 1921 .	119		97
July 1922 . .	106	90	90
December 1922 .	101		91
June 1923 . .	99	92	...
December 1923 .	99		
June 1924 . .	100	100	...
December 1924 .	101		
June 1925 . .	99	98	...
December 1925 .	98		

Table prepared by Mr. Rothbarth.

TABLE VII

(a) CHAMBER OF SHIPPING FREIGHTS INDEX

Year	Jan.	Feb.	Mar.	Apr.	May	June	July	Aug.	Sept.	Oct.	Nov.	Dec.	Yearly Average
1920	123	138	141	127	121	112	95	84	84	93	80	58	100
1921	46	38	37	39	39	43	43	40	34	31	30	33	38
1922	33	34	33	31	33	30	28	28	27	28	30	31	30
1923	29	29	29	32	31	29	28	25	26	27	27	28	28
1924	31	32	32	31	30	29	27	28	28	30	29	28	30

(b) CHAMBER OF SHIPPING TIME CHARTER INDEX

Year	Jan.	Feb.	Mar.	Apr.	May	June	July	Aug.	Sept.	Oct.	Nov.	Dec.	Yearly Average
1920	149	149	134	120	105	112	94	81	78	84	81	60	100
1921	60	42	40	36	37	37	35	35	34	30	30	30	36
1922	30	30	30	28	27	26	25	25	25	24	25	24	27
1923	24	24	24	24	24	22	21	20	19	19	19	20	22
1924	22	24	24	24	24	24	22	21	22	25	25	24	23

These tables have the base chosen to make the geometrical average of 1920 equal to 100. All the yearly averages given are geometrical averages.

From a Memorandum prepared by Mr. Corlett.

TABLE VIII

IRON AND STEEL PRICES

Date	Price of Steel Plates	Wages per Hour or Piece	Price of Coal	Railway Rates	General Wholesale Prices
1913 (average) .	51	65	49	100	46
1919 1st quarter .	100	100	100	100	100
,, 2nd ,, .	114	130	100	100	109
,, 3rd ,, .	132	140	125	100	116
,, 4th ,, .	136	155	125	100	130
1920 1st quarter .	152	160	125	125	147
,, 2nd ,, .	170	175	125	125	138
,, 3rd ,, .	176	192	144	200	135
,, 4th ,, .	176	200	144	200	104
1921 1st quarter .	160	200	144	200	89
,, 2nd ,, .	140	183	144	200	85
,, 3rd ,, .	106	164	125	200	86
,, 4th ,, .	82	130	100	200	77
1922 1st quarter .	72	109	92	175	76

From a Memorandum prepared by Mr. D. Burn.

TABLE IX

THE TERMS OF TRADE (*i.e.* EXPORT PRICES ÷ IMPORT PRICES)

The following table gives the average values of imports, exports and re-exports as given by the Board of Trade and the average value of exports in terms of imports obtained by dividing the second column by the first and multiplying by 100. The figures for 1924 have been modified (by the Board of Trade) to exclude the effect of the exclusion of the Irish Free State from the statistics. The figures given refer to the average for the quarter and to the average for the year from 1920. For 1919 only the average for the year is available. In all the series 1913 is taken as base ($=100$).

Date	Imports		Exports		Re-exports	$\dfrac{\text{Export Price}}{\text{Import Price}} \times 100$	
Average 1919 .		240		277	191		115
1920 I . .	284		326		220	115	
,, II . .	285		358		229	125	
,, III . .	289		276		240	130	
,, IV . .	283		373		213	132	
Average 1920 .		285		358	225		125
1921 I . .	220		334		156	151	
,, II . .	192		283		129	147	
,, III . .	182		241		108	132	
,, IV . .	170		226		116	133	
Average 1921 .		190		269	124		141
1922 I . .	149		218		101	147	
,, II . .	152		196		123	128	
,, III . .	155		196		118	127	
,, IV . .	153		189		129	123	
Average 1922 .		152		199	116		132
1923 I . .	146		196		106	134	
,, II . .	148		188		136	127	
,, III . .	151		192		129	127	
,, IV . .	152		184		131	120	
Average 1923 .		149		190	126		127
1924 I . .	150		193		112	128	
,, II . .	154		185		146	120	
,, III . .	155		190		134	123	
,, IV . .	160		188		145	118	
Average 1924 .		155		189	132		122

Table prepared by Mr. Corlett.

SECTION IV

CURRENCY, BANK NOTES, BANK DEPOSITS AND CLEARINGS

TABLE I

CURRENCY OF GREAT BRITAIN AND IRELAND
(Bank of England)
£ millions

	(1)	(2)	(3)	(4)	(5)	(6)	(7)	(8)	(9)	(10)	(11)
Month	Bank of England Notes	Scottish Bank Notes	Irish Bank Notes	Total Notes Issued	Estimated Coin	Total Notes and Coin	Bank of England Reserve	Held by London Clearing Banks	Held by Scottish and Irish Banks	Estimated Circulation	Estimated Circulation 1935 = 100 after Seasonal Adjustment
1919											
Jan.	411·9	24·8	30·8	467·5	108	576	29·2	107·8	50·9	388	...
Feb.	410·9	24·6	30·4	465·8	109	575	30·1	104·4	49·3	391	...
Mar.	422·8	25·6	30·6	479·0	109	588	29·2	105·4	50·3	403	...
Apr.	444·4	26·6	31·5	502·5	110	612	27·7	113·1	52·0	419	...
May	448·4	27·7	32·2	508·2	110	618	27·5	110·5	54·5	426	...
June	449·1	28·0	31·5	508·6	110	619	27·8	117·2	54·3	420	...
July	446·4	27·6	29·5	503·6	111	614	27·6	113·1	51·9	422	...
Aug.	440·5	26·7	28·8	496·0	111	607	26·9	112·1	50·1	418	...
Sept.	435·1	27·0	29·0	491·1	111	602	25·6	111·9	50·2	414	...
Oct.	440·3	27·4	30·2	497·9	111	609	22·5	115·0	51·7	420	...
Nov.	441·6	28·3	30·6	500·5	111	612	20·3	114·0	53·4	424	...
Dec.	454·5	28·7	30·5	513·7	111	625	19·9	124·7	54·0	427	...
1920											
Jan.	446·3	27·2	28·4	501·9	106	608	25·3	113·6	50·8	418	...
Feb.	447·7	27·0	27·2	501·9	95	597	33·1	105·0	49·1	410	...
Mar.	456·8	27·4	27·1	511·2	85	597	31·3	95·8	49·0	420	...
Apr.	462·7	28·4	27·7	518·7	80	599	24·2	98·4	50·5	425	...
May	468·6	29·7	27·9	526·2	79	605	19·7	100·9	51·9	432	...
June	477·8	30·7	26·6	535·1	76	611	19·8	105·9	51·7	434	...
July	486·4	29·9	25·9	542·1	73	615	16·8	103·5	50·4	444	...
Aug.	482·5	28·6	25·9	537·0	71	608	16·1	107·7	49·2	435	...
Sept.	475·7	28·9	26·1	530·7	71	602	15·4	108·8	49·4	428	...
Oct.	477·5	29·2	26·5	533·2	71	605	14·2	110·9	50·3	429	...
Nov.	474·1	29·7	26·2	530·0	72	602	14·1	110·9	50·7	426	...
Dec.	484·5	30·2	25·8	540·5	73	614	13·3	107·6	50·6	442	...
1921											
Jan.	476·3	28·7	23·8	528·8	73	602	17·1	112·2	47·9	425	114·0
Feb.	464·8	27·8	22·4	515·0	72	587	18·2	108·7	45·1	415	112·4
Mar.	465·4	27·7	22·1	515·2	72	587	17·7	109·6	44·3	415	110·8
Apr.	466·4	28·1	21·8	516·3	72	588	18·2	113·2	44·8	412	109·5
May	462·3	27·9	20·2	510·4	71	581	18·2	113·8	43·3	406	107·5
June	453·1	27·4	19·2	499·7	71	571	18·5	110·6	41·5	400	104·8
July	450·5	27·2	18·6	496·3	71	567	18·6	111·9	40·4	396	103·8
Aug.	449·4	25·7	18·7	493·8	71	565	19·8	112·7	39·2	393	103·2
Sept.	442·4	25·4	19·2	487·0	71	558	21·6	112·4	39·2	385	103·3
Oct.	438·3	25·4	19·5	483·2	70	553	22·4	108·7	39·4	383	102·3
Nov.	438·6	25·8	19·8	484·2	70	554	22·6	109·0	40·1	382	102·3
Dec.	446·7	25·7	19·9	492·3	70	562	21·2	106·2	39·9	395	102·1
1922											
Jan.	437·3	24·7	18·8	480·8	70	551	23·4	111·7	38·1	378	101·5
Feb.	428·2	23·8	18·3	470·3	70	540	24·8	108·5	36·6	370	100·5
Mar.	425·9	23·7	18·3	467·9	69	537	24·9	107·6	36·3	368	99·0
Apr.	431·0	24·1	18·6	473·7	69	543	25·3	112·6	36·7	368	97·1
May	425·2	24·7	18·2	468·1	68	536	25·7	108·6	37·1	365	97·0
June	423·8	24·6	17·7	466·1	68	534	25·1	99·9	36·5	373	97·0

TABLE I—(contd.)

£ millions

	(1)	(2)	(3)	(4)	(5)	(6)	(7)	(8)	(9)	(10)	(11)
Month	Bank of England Notes	Scottish Bank Notes	Irish Bank Notes	Total Notes Issued	Estimated Coin	Total Notes and Coin	Bank of England Reserve	Held by London Clearing Banks	Held by Scottish and Irish Banks	Estimated Circulation	Estimated Circulation 1935=100 after Seasonal Adjustment
1922											
July	421·3	24·4	17·4	463·1	68	531	21·8	108·3	36·5	364	95·2
Aug.	420·7	23·3	17·4	461·4	67	528	21·3	110·6	34·9	361	95·0
Sept.	413·7	23·1	17·4	454·2	66	520	23·6	108·3	34·9	353	94·4
Oct.	412·5	23·1	17·7	453·3	66	519	23·5	106·4	35·2	354	94·6
Nov.	410·8	23·7	17·9	452·4	66	518	23·5	104·8	36·0	354	94·6
Dec.	418·6	23·9	17·9	460·4	66	526	21·9	102·4	35·9	366	94·4
1923											
Jan.	409·1	22·8	17·2	449·1	66	515	23·8	106·8	34·7	350	94·4
Feb.	402·8	22·1	17·0	441·9	65	507	24·6	104·5	33·3	345	93·7
Mar.	405·1	22·2	17·0	444·3	65	509	23·7	104·3	33·2	348	93·3
Apr.	409·2	23·4	17·5	450·1	65	515	24·2	103·4	34·7	353	93·7
May	410·0	23·8	17·5	451·3	65	516	23·4	105·5	35·2	352	93·2
June	410·2	23·9	17·1	451·2	65	516	23·0	94·4	34·8	364	95·1
July	412·6	23·6	16·7	452·9	65	518	21·2	103·8	34·3	359	93·6
Aug.	412·9	22·5	16·6	452·0	65	517	22·1	105·0	33·3	357	93·5
Sept.	407·4	22·3	16·6	446·3	65	511	23·3	105·3	33·1	349	93·2
Oct.	405·3	22·1	16·9	444·3	65	509	23·4	103·6	33·0	349	93·1
Nov.	405·1	22·6	17·2	444·9	65	510	23·0	103·6	33·9	350	93·6
Dec.	415·4	22·9	17·3	455·6	65	521	20·6	105·4	34·0	361	92·9
1924											
Jan.	407·7	21·8	16·5	446·0	65	511	21·7	106·5	32·8	350	94·6
Feb.	401·8	21·2	16·2	439·2	65	504	22·5	103·0	31·5	347	94·5
Mar.	404·3	21·3	16·4	442·0	65	507	22·5	102·0	31·5	351	94·4
Apr.	413·1	22·6	16·8	452·5	65	518	22·3	104·9	33·3	358	94·6
May	411·2	23·1	16·6	450·9	65	516	22·9	103·0	33·4	357	95·0
June	415·1	23·2	16·4	454·7	65	520	21·8	100·0	33·2	365	94·7
July	417·0	23·2	16·3	456·5	65	522	21·1	102·9	33·2	365	95·0
Aug.	417·3	22·0	16·3	455·6	65	521	22·2	105·1	32·3	361	95·0
Sept.	411·6	21·7	16·3	449·6	65	515	23·6	103·5	32·1	356	94·9
Oct.	410·6	21·9	16·6	449·1	65	514	24·9	102·5	32·3	354	94·7
Nov.	410·4	22·5	16·9	449·8	66	516	25·2	103·6	33·3	354	94·6
Dec.	416·8	22·9	17·1	456·8	66	523	21·9	108·1	33·8	359	92·5
1925											
Jan.	405·8	21·8	16·3	443·9	66	510	22·6	106·8	32·6	348	93·8
Feb.	401·8	21·1	15·8	438·7	66	505	23·5	105·3	30·8	345	93·8
Mar.	403·7	21·5	16·3	441·5	66	508	24·0	103·8	31·4	349	93·9
Apr.	412·4	22·1	16·4	450·9	66	517	27·1	102·5	32·3	355	94·0
May	411·1	22·6	16·1	449·8	66	516	27·1	104·2	32·5	352	93·4
June	414·5	22·3	15·7	452·5	66	519	29·8	102·3	31·8	355	92·4
July	422·4	22·4	15·3	460·1	66	526	36·2	103·8	31·7	354	92·6
Aug.	425·3	21·1	15·1	461·5	66	528	38·7	105·4	30·5	353	92·4
Sept.	416·8	20·9	15·2	452·9	66	519	36·9	105·4	30·0	347	92·5
Oct.	408·7	21·1	15·7	445·5	67	513	30·8	105·5	30·7	346	92·2
Nov.	401·5	21·7	16·0	439·2	67	506	26·1	101·9	31·7	346	92·8
Dec.	401·3	21·9	16·0	439·2	67	506	20·4	97·1	31·8	357	92·6

Column (1).—Includes Currency notes and excludes Bank of England notes set aside as cover for them.

Columns (1) and (7).—Averages of Wednesday figures.

Columns (2), (3) and (9).—Averages for the period of four weeks most nearly corresponding to the calendar month (London, Dublin and Belfast Gazettes).

Column (5).—Excludes coin in the Currency Note Redemption Account or in the Bank of England Issue Department. In 1919 and 1920 the estimates of coin are affected by heavy payments of Gold Coin by the banks into the Bank of England. The resulting monthly figures of circulation during these years may in consequence be rather less representative than those for later years.

Column (8).—From the Report of the Committee on Finance and Industry.

TABLE II

DEPOSITS, 1913–19

(a) END OF YEAR DEPOSITS (EXCLUDING BANK OF ENGLAND AND SAVINGS BANKS) OF JOINT-STOCK BANKS OF ENGLAND, WALES, SCOTLAND AND IRELAND, TOGETHER WITH PRIVATE BANKS

(Extracted from the *Economist* in Kirkaldy, *British Finance, 1914–21*, p. **74**.)

End of	£ millions	Each Year divided by the One Before
1913	1033	...
1914	1135	110
1915	1244	109
1916	1444	116
1917	1706	118
1918	1988	116
1919	2356	118

(b) JUNE DEPOSITS OF JOINT-STOCK BANKS COMPARABLE (AS FAR AS POSSIBLE) WITH THE DEPOSIT FIGURES OF THE MACMILLAN REPORT

(Prepared by Mr. Rothbarth.)

June	Deposits (£ millions)	Each Year divided by the One Before
1913	640	...
1914	692	108
1915	876	126
1916	916	105
1917	990	108
1918	1250	126
1919	1627	130

The two sets of figures are not inconsistent; for, as Mr. Rothbarth has pointed out to me, big financial changes took place in the second half of each year. He suggests that this was probably due to the financing of imports of agricultural output in the autumn. The fact that in each June–June year there was only one big disturbance, whereas in each December–December year there were two, which were likely in parts to cancel one another, explains the greater variability of the June–June figures.

Table III

ADVANCES AND TOTAL DEPOSITS OF THE
LONDON CLEARING BANKS

The statistics are the aggregates of the ten London clearing banks, but, in the case of the National Bank, figures relating to offices in England only have been included. For some items in the table in the early years estimated figures have been taken.

(£ thousands)

Date	Advances (*i.e.* Loans and Overdrafts)	Total Deposits
1919		
January	475,828	1,426,653
February	482,813	1,382,874
March	506,873	1,408,675
April	508,436	1,434,575
May	510,751	1,454,360
June	527,597	1,627,063
July	593,248	1,504,806
August	614,983	1,509,042
September	652,020	1,535,832
October	659,381	1,569,761
November	692,749	1,598,457
December	730,957	1,676,816
Monthly average	579,636	1,510,743
Monthly average (excluding June and December)	569,708	1,482,503
1920		
January	777,630	1,708,034
February	815,761	1,683,859
March	861,719	1,693,942
April	861,661	1,707,296
May	860,622	1,672,381
June	844,438	1,718,858
July	838,289	1,715,187
August	834,014	1,720,306
September	831,172	1,720,040
October	822,807	1,755,080
November	815,843	1,743,543
December	815,128	1,797,818
Monthly average	831,590	1,719,695
Monthly average (excluding June and December)	831,952	1,711,967
1921		
January	810,027	1,794,289
February	822,805	1,741,816
March	844,458	1,694,730
April	823,170	1,697,977
May	807,637	1,715,124
June	795,743	1,764,847
July	789,977	1,768,898
August	776,514	1,743,907
September	767,683	1,754,556
October	759,649	1,793,772
November	748,807	1,765,468
December	735,518	1,808,055
Monthly average	790,166	1,753,620
Monthly average (excluding June and December)	795,073	1,747,054

TABLE III—*(contd.)*

(£ thousands)

Date	Advances (*i.e.* Loans and Overdrafts)	Total Deposits
1922		
January	735,762	1,801,754
February	725,135	1,778,232
March	725,786	1,716,941
April	720,183	1,721,450
May	699,169	1,723,586
June	701,719	1,743,052
July	699,509	1,710,895
August	698,020	1,666,119
September	695,805	1,638,518
October	705,891	1,666,329
November	717,720	1,651,568
December	717,288	1,671,042
Monthly average	711,832	1,707,457
Monthly average (excluding June and December)	712,298	1,707,539
1923		
January	717,458	1,670,884
February	729,311	1,622,684
March	732,999	1,579,801
April	729,180	1,594,691
May	730,064	1,589,393
June	733,832	1,628,246
July	728,990	1,618,179
August	724,611	1,589,388
September	722,574	1,591,883
October	730,138	1,610,954
November	731,954	1,608,339
December	742,937	1,664,813
Monthly average	729,504	1,614,105
Monthly average (excluding June and December)	727,728	1,607,620
1924		
January	743,718	1,652,065
February	754,545	1,607,110
March	771,585	1,589,746
April	771,812	1,600,165
May	772,320	1,602,127
June	778,156	1,647,449
July	775,394	1,621,846
August	772,765	1,593,792
September	777,954	1,604,276
October	786,891	1,609,202
November	790,426	1,606,457
December	794,807	1,654,728
Monthly average	774,198	1,615,747
Monthly average (excluding June and December)	771,741	1,608,679

TABLE III—(contd.)

(£ thousands)

Date	Advances (i.e. Loans and Overdrafts)	Total Deposits
1925		
January	798,529	1,624,224
February	806,186	1,612,098
March	827,876	1,584,688
April	829,923	1,588,026
May	828,785	1,572,862
June	835,616	1,623,083
July	833,141	1,607,704
August	819,496	1,587,198
September	814,844	1,595,814
October	815,981	1,601,222
November	814,916	1,597,173
December	834,507	1,638,297
Monthly average	821,650	1,602,699
Monthly average (excluding June and December)	818,968	1,597,101

From Appendix I (Table I) to the Macmillan Report on Finance and Industry.

TABLE IV

NON-FINANCIAL CLEARINGS (ANNUAL), 1913–19

METROPOLITAN PLUS COUNTRY PLUS PROVINCIAL CLEARINGS

Year	£ millions	Index Numbers	Each Year divided by the Year Before
1913	31,450	100	...
1914	30,620	97	97
1915	34,870	111	114
1916	41,580	132	119
1917	48,590	155	117
1918	59,430	189	122
1919	74,850	238	126

Calculated from tables in the 71st Statistical Abstract, p. 189.

Table V   247

NON-FINANCIAL CLEARINGS (MONTHLY): ENGLAND AND WALES
1919–25

Year and Month	Sum of Metropolitan, Country and Provincial Clearings		Year and Month	Sum of Metropolitan, Country and Provincial Clearings	
	£ millions	£ millions (seasonally corrected)		£ millions	£ millions (seasonally corrected)
1919			**1923**		
Jan.	570	520	Jan.	555	527
Feb.	498	522	Feb.	486	507 ⎫ 510
Mar.	530	514	Mar.	529	496 ⎬
April	525	536	April	504	513 ⎫ 513
May	601	580	May	526	509 ⎬
June	572	609	June	500	517 ⎭
July	702	650	July	527	497
Aug.	610	657	Aug.	477	499 ⎬ 497
Sept.	612	689	Sept.	441	496 ⎭
Oct.	701	655	Oct.	540	515
Nov.	712	713	Nov.	498	505 ⎬ 509
Dec.	738	741	Dec.	494	508 ⎭
1920			**1924**		
Jan.	849	778	Jan.	547	494
Feb.	786	809	Feb.	503	523 ⎬ 509
Mar.	873	859	Mar.	523	509 ⎭
April	787	798	April	510	519
May	778	771	May	545	518 ⎬ 529
June	745	771	June	486	531 ⎭
July	803	770	July	567	528
Aug.	714	742	Aug.	483	521 ⎬ 531
Sept.	713	746	Sept.	491	545 ⎭
Oct.	746	713	Oct.	564	530
Nov.	694	696	Nov.	523	525 ⎬ 532
Dec.	639	642	Dec.	540	542 ⎭
1921			**1925**		
Jan.	659	628	Jan.	594	538
Feb.	563	575	Feb.	510	531 ⎬ 535
Mar.	585	586	Mar.	551	536 ⎭
April	566	563	April	527	538
May	499	494	May	548	541
June	475	489	June	510	537
July	505	483	July	582	542
Aug.	494	512	Aug.	495	532
Sept.	482	512	Sept.	493	542
Oct.	537	519	Oct.	574	542
Nov.	507	509	Nov.	528	529
Dec.	508	509	Dec.	550	551
1922					
Jan.	520	497			
Feb.	480	502			
Mar.	543	514			
April	484	490			
May	543	514			
June	485	507			
July	543	516			
Aug.	498	519			
Sept.	458	514			
Oct.	527	502			
Nov.	507	514			
Dec.	485	499			

From London and Cambridge Economic Service, Special Memorandum No. 74, by E. H. Phelps-Brown and G. L. S. Shackle.

TABLE VI

ESTIMATED VELOCITY OF TOTAL CHEQUE-PAID NON-FINANCIAL
CIRCULATION, 1919-25

Messrs. Phelps-Brown and Shackle * describe their method of estimating this (transaction) velocity as follows : " We assume that total cheque-paid non-financial circulation (including encashments) will change proportionally to Metropolitan, Country and Provincial Clearings ; our estimate of the former in 1930 is 2·00 times the total of the latter for that year, and we assume this ratio to hold throughout. We assume further that that part of the whole cheque-paid non-financial circulation which is handled by the clearing banks in England and Wales is at all times what we have estimated it to be in 1930, namely 0·795 of the whole. For any given month, then, we take the total cheque-paid non-financial circulation handled by the Clearing Banks in England and Wales, expressed as an annual rate, to be given by twelve times the seasonally corrected total of Metropolitan, Country and Provincial Clearings for that month, multiplied by 2·00, multiplied again by 0·795. The result is then divided by the total current accounts of the Clearing Banks in England and Wales, as reported for that month in the Report of the Macmillan Committee."

TABLE

Month	1919	1920	1921	1922	1923	1924	1925
Jan. .	10·09	13·08	10·89	9·13	9·91	9·67	10·75
Feb. .	10·70	13·86	10·52	9·37	9·93	10·65	10·84
Mar. .	10·30	14·64	11·15	9·94	9·97	10·39	11·09
April .	10·63	13·60	10·49	9·46	10·22	10·54	11·34
May .	11·40	13·66	9·37	9·87	10·20	10·50	11·66
June .	10·45	13·70	9·07	9·55	10·01	10·33	10·96
July .	12·25	13·61	8·98	9·33	9·74	10·56	11·27
Aug. .	12·43	13·21	9·71	10·13	10·07	10·67	11·22
Sept. .	12·74	13·25	9·64	10·18	10·05	11·01	11·35
Oct. .	12·02	12·50	9·54	9·66	10·33	10·72	11·24
Nov. .	12·80	12·39	9·64	9·97	10·24	10·70	10·98
Dec. .	12·60	10·99	9·30	9·41	9·73	10·53	10·93

* London and Cambridge Economic Service, Special Memorandum No. 46, p. 33.

INDEX

THE END

PRINTED BY R. & R. CLARK, LIMITED, EDINBURGH